World View

CHANDLER & SHARP PUBLICATIONS IN ANTHROPOLOGY AND RELATED FIELDS

General Editors: L. L. Langness and Robert B. Edgerton

World View

MICHAEL KEARNEY

University of California, Riverside

Chandler & Sharp Publishers, Inc.

Novato, California

Library of Congress Cataloging in Publication Data

Kearney, Michael.
  World view.

  (Chandler & Sharp publications in anthropology and related fields)
  Bibliography: p.
  Includes index.
    1. Ethnophilosophy. 2. Cognition and culture. 3. Philosophy, Comparative.
  4. Social structure. 5. Methodology. I. Title. II. Series.
GN468.K42   1984   306   83-20945
ISBN 0-88316-550-3

International Standard Book Number: 0-88316-550-3
Library of Congress Catalog Card Number: 83-20945
Printed in the United States of America.

Book design by Joe Roter.
Cover design and art by Jackie Gallagher.
Edited by W. L. Parker.
Composition by Publications Services of Marin.

Contents

Preface   ix

Introduction   1

1. Issues and Approaches   9

Historical Materialism and Cultural Idealism   10
The Epistemology of Materialism and Idealism   10
   Historical Materialism   12
   Cultural Idealism   15
The Political Economy of Idealism and Materialism   16
   Why Idealism Is Conservative and Materialism is Not   17
Idealist Approaches to World View   23
   The Boas Tradition   25
     World View and Ethnosemantics   31
   The Redfield Tradition   37

2. Basic Concepts   41

World View   41
Perception and World View   42
Images, Assumptions, and Propositions   47
   Presupposition   48
Logico-structural Integration   52
   External Inconsistency   54
     World View and Truth   56
   Internal Inconsistency   58

3. World-View Universals   65

The Self and the Other   68
Relationship   72
  Ecological Relationship   74
  Individualism   75
Classification   78
  The Origins of Classification   78
  World-View Categories   80
Causality   84
  Psychological Sources of Idealism   88
Space and Time   89
  Perception of Space   92
  Perception of Time   94
   Past, Present, or Future   95
   Images of Time   98
Integration of Universals   106

4. A Cross-Cultural Model of World Views   109

Why There Are Different World Views   109
  External Causes   110
  Internal Causes   114
  Projection and Reification   117
The Model   119

5. Logico-structural Aspects of World View   123

Classic Greek Cosmology   124
Scientific and Biblical World Views   130
World View and Society   134
  Self, Time, and Society in Bali   135
   Definition of Self   135
   Calendars   141
   Ceremony and Absence of Climax   143

6. California Indian World View   147

Causality   148
Self and Other   150
Relationship with the Other   153

Classification   155
Time   158
Space   161
Power and Social Control   164
Conclusion   168

7. Mexican Peasant World View   171

Historic Determinants of Mexican Peasant World View   173
   Precolumbian Mexico   173
   Conquest and Colony   173
   After the Revolution   176
   The Present as History   177
Local Social and Geographic Environment   181
World View and Action   183
   Other   184
   Self, Relationship   187
   Time   192
   Causality   196
Projective Systems   197
Peasant Rationality   202

8. Conclusions, Criticisms, and Suggestions   207

Notes   213
References   226
Index   240

Preface

I was moved to write this book when, in the course of my previous work on world view, I struggled to discern exactly what a world view might be and how it was formed. World view has occupied an important place in anthropology, but surprisingly no comprehensive model of it has been formulated prior to this effort, which I regard as a preliminary attempt that I hope will engender further work.

The concept of world view is distinctly American in that it is a variant of the concept of culture which is the fundamental notion of American anthropology. Therefore, when I refer to "American" anthropology, or "American" anthropology's concern with world view, culture and so forth, I am referring for the most part to North American anthropology. In this general sense, the European counterparts of American cultural anthropology are British structural-functionalism and French structuralism. There are within these intellectual traditions concern with what is in effect world view, although not as great as in American anthropology. A critique, similar to the one developed here of American anthropology, could also be leveled against them. But that must be the subject of another study. The present one is therefore distinctly part of a dialog within American anthropology.

My prior involvement with world view has been marked by ambivalent feelings. On the positive side there is no doubt that it is a potentially powerful tool for exploring the recesses of socially constructed human consciousness, and thus has a potential—as yet largely unrealized—for liberation in all senses of the word. The negative side of world view as a social-science concept is that as it has been constituted in American anthropology it has, I argue, often functioned not to illuminate the social construction of consciousness but to the contrary to obfuscate such an advance. This conservative aspect of world view is not a result of anyone's intentional design. Rather, it is inherent in the constitution of the idea of world view itself, and the fundamental assumptions of culturology in general as they have evolved within American anthropology. This condition itself thus becomes an historical anthropological problem and necessitates a reflexive anthropological world view—one that can examine these adjacent paradigms as well as its own assumptions.

The basic argument that I develop is that the concept of world view, as a variant of American anthropology, is best regarded as embedded within American liberal bourgeois culture in general. If this position be substantiated, then it follows that the construction of a progressive, truly liberating model of world view must first roll back the hegemonic influence of the liberal model which hithertofore has preempted most theoretical space within this arena. Once this task is completed, it may then be possible to self-consciously develop a model of world view that is not encumbered by the tacit assumptions of liberal anthropology.

Carole Nagengast has labored through several earlier versions of my manuscript and John Comaroff also scrutinized and commented in detail on the next-to-final version. I have incorporated their suggestions in a number of places and thank them heartily. I am also indebted to other colleagues and friends who have read parts of or complete earlier versions of my manuscript, and offered their reactions. I take this opportunity to thank Gene Anderson, Pat Barker, Lowell Bean, Tom Blackburn, Bob Edgerton, Lew Langness, Harry Lawton, David Kronenfeld, Sandra Maryanski-Turner, Rick Mines, Rick Nihlen, Emiko Ohnuki-Tierney, Bob Randall, Clay Robarchek, Lynn Thomas, Ron Tobey, and Dave Warren.

In earlier phases of writing I benefited from the research and bibliographic assistance of Tekla Morgan, and in the latter phase from that of Michelle Butler. Their help was made possible by Intramural Grants from the Academic Senate of the University of California at Riverside. I also owe a special debt—as does the reader—to Bill Parker for his masterly editing of the manuscript.

World View

For my Father,
Francis Kearney

We are tending more and more
today to regard knowledge as
a process more than as a state.

—Jean Piaget

Introduction

Anthropological literature abounds with descriptions and analyses of the ways in which different peoples think about themselves, about their environments, space, time, and so forth. The investigation of such things is referred to as the study of *world view*. Although world view is one of the central subjects of American cultural anthropology, there is surprisingly little theoretical literature concerning it (see Kearney 1975). This lack of conceptual framework has been one of the main obstacles to the study of particular world views and their cross-cultural assessment. Therefore, as a contribution to the theory and study of world view, and also as a means of organizing this book, I am presenting a model of human world view. Though by no means comprehensive, this model does address the major issues having to do with the nature and role of culturally organized macro-thought: those dynamically interrelated basic cognitive assumptions of a people that determine much of their behavior and decision making, as well as organizing much of their body of symbolic creations — myth, religion, cosmology — and ethnophilosophy in general.

The first chapter of this book discusses the history of world-view studies and theories, and their place in contemporary anthropology. The main argument here is that there are two distinct traditions, two distinct ways of thinking and analyzing world views. One of these, and the one pre-eminent in anthropology, we can refer to as cultural idealism. The other, which has had little impact on anthropology, is the historical materialism that derives from Karl Marx. This present book is aligned with the second of these two schools of thought, and as such is in part a critique of the cultural idealist treatment of world view. The discussion of these two general theories is reflexive anthropology in that these two concepts of world view

1

are examined within their own social and historic contexts. The assumption here is that a world-view theory as well as any general world view is more often than not an outlook of a group or class, defined as such in opposition to others, hence it tends to be ideological in nature. That is, it serves to advance or perpetuate the social position of those who held the view, depending on how they sit in relation to their antagonists. In a classless society we would expect its world view to be affected by this different social condition. Because of this sociological relativity of world-view theory, the following order of priorities must be established: before we can deal with world view in general, we must examine not only the philosophical and scientific but also the ideological nature of world-view theory itself. Not to do this is to be unaware of the source and nature of the basic ideas informing our project. Another implication of this relativity is that there can be no neutral "value-free" starting point of analysis. The positivistic notion that there can and should be is, aside from being poor philosophy and poor science, an ideological prejudice, as is discussed in my first and fifth chapters. Here I am in agreement with Joan Robinson, who says the following about value judgments in the social sciences. She points out that every human being has ideological, moral, and political views. To deny these views, pretending not to have them and claiming to be purely objective, she says,

> must necessarily be either self-deception or a device to deceive others. A candid writer will make his preconceptions clear and allow the reader to discount them if he does not accept them. This concerns the professional honour of the scientist. But to eliminate value judgments from the subject-matter of social science is to eliminate the subject itself, for since it concerns human behavior it must be concerned with the value judgments that people make. The social scientist (whatever he may privately believe) has no right to pretend to know any better than his neighbours what ends society should serve. His business is to show them why they believe what they purport to believe (as far as he can make it out) and what influence beliefs have on behaviour. (Robinson 1970:122)[1]

One of the basic axioms of historical materialism is that the ideas in a society are to a great extent a result of their social origin within that society, especially the class in which they originate. Building on this principle, we examine the idealist and materialist models of world view in terms of their class origins, and in doing so consider the degree to which their basic assumptions serve the special interests of the respective classes with which they are associated. Here we see that cultural idealism as an intellectual tradition comes primarily out of the upper strata of class societies in the same way that theology and other idealist ideologies do. Historical materialism, on the other hand, arising in opposition to idealism, is a world view which comes from the lower socioeconomic classes of complex societies and serves their class interests in that it demystifies the false consciousness created by idealist world views. In criticizing the cultural idealist tradition I do not mean to imply that there is nothing that can be salvaged from it. Chapter 2 thus concludes with a review of some orthodox concepts that are of use in building an alternative model of world view.

Chapter 3 introduces some basic concepts used in later chapters and also explores a set of *world-view universals* (Self, Other, Relationship, Classification, Causality, Space, Time) which I argue are necessary aspects of any human world view. Because they are world-view universals, they thus afford a means of comparing world views cross-culturally. There are two aspects of a world view. There is first of all its *content*, the description of which is the basic empirical, ethnographic task. But apart from the content of a world view is the *structure*—the basic categories of thought—which it has in common with all human world views. This problem of the origin and structure of world view is the heart of Chapter 3. Here there are two perennial antagonistic positions: either, as the empiricists argue, the categories of knowledge are given to us by reality; or, as the rationalists hold, they are inherent features of the human mind and do not necessarily exist in the outer world. Any discussion of world-view universals must ultimately come to terms with this opposition. This short essay does not, however, afford an opportunity to do so at length. And I therefore take this opportunity to alert the reader that the basic philosophic stance of my treatment of universals is a rationalism modified with a strong dose of what might be called dialectical constructionism or interactionism, which proceeds, as in the psychology and epistemology of Marx and Piaget, by the interaction between subject (Self) and the object (Other).

While Chapter 3 shows how the structures of the world-view universals are to a great extent systematically integrated, one of the main points of Chapter 4 is that the contents of these universals are also in various ways interdependent. This chapter discusses the forces that shape this organization of world views and considers the complementary question of the role of world view in shaping behavior and society. One intent of this chapter is to further dispel the likely expectation that this world-view theory is yet another example of idealist anthropology. Such a misconception is understandable. Although this world-view theory does not posit idealist or nominalist assumptions about the relationships between thought and environment (environment taken broadly to include both geography and social institutions and relationships), it does have a mentalist bias in its pragmatic insistence that the best immediate understanding of behavior is offered by understanding the thoughts that underlie the behavior. Furthermore, it assumes that, other things being equal, the economy of human thought and the nature of culture are such that cognitive assumptions at work in one area of life, say economic production, will also organize thinking in others, say religion or ideas about human nature. World-view theory thus addresses the problem of the integration of cultures, both synchronically and diachronically. Here I have attempted to go beyond the general paradigm of cultural integration in American anthropology with its attention to "themes," "patterning," and "configurations," by adding the consideration of logical as well as structural integration. Hence the barbarism *logico-structural integration*, which is discussed mainly in Chapter 5.

Part of the defense against the inevitable charge that this world-view theory is anthropological idealism proceeds by demonstrating that the debate over whether or not thought and superstructures in general are determined by material conditions and existing social arrangements is a spurious question. The debate between materialism and idealism is itself but a projection of a distinction in Western enthnophilosophy onto the anthropological data. The proper question is not whether mind or reality determines the structure of thought, but how do reality and thought shape each other. Chapter 4 thus discusses the influences of environment and history on world view as forces that are often contrary to internal logical and structural imperatives seeking their own formal equilibria.

It is inevitable, I suppose, that casual readers, and perhaps even more critical ones who are so predisposed by their dualistic Western world view, will assume that I am attempting to steer a middle course between materialism and idealism. My intent, however, is to bypass that entire tedious debate by giving ideas *nearly* equal importance as material and social conditions, much as a biologist examining either the present functioning or the evolution of an organism would grant comparable status to the digestive and nervous systems. In biology the issue is not whether one system determines the other, but how they evolve and work together. I think that this analogy of stomach and brain with reality and mind is not overdrawn (it is actually somewhat of an homology) and that such a stance will lead to a more realistic anthropology.

In the short run people's actions are best explained by the ideas they have in their heads. This is the main strategy of cultural anthropology. But in the long run the problem is to explain these ideas, and to do this we must examine the social, economic, political, technological, demographic, and geographic conditions in which they developed. In a word, we must examine their environment and history. And here the balance tips in favor of social and material conditions. We can say that this world-view theory is tactically mentalistic, but that strategically it is founded on historical materialism. To pursue the biological analogy, history is comparable to evolution. And just as the physical environment selects certain morphologies and behaviors, so historic forces shape world views, which of course then become historic forces themselves.

The view taken here is that humans, working with the conditions given to them by history — technology, environment, social structure, world view, and their social relations with other peoples — create their own society. As Marx (1969a:398) put it, "Men make their own history, but they do not make it just as they please; they do not make it under circumstances chosen by themselves, but under circumstances directly encountered, given and transmitted from the past. The tradition of all the dead generations weighs like a nightmare on the brain of the living." A people live and work within such constraints and fashion their world through praxis that is guided by images and assumptions, by ideas about reality. The elaboration of culture proceeds by this dialectic relation between individual and collectivity, and between collectivity and history. The truly unique thing about humans is that images and assumptions intervene between needs and actions to such a great extent. Images and assumptions differ greatly from one society to another, and, having a certain autonomy of their own, become forces in history. But the more fundamental issue is, how do these ideas come to be formed?

An exclusive concern with culture seen as a set of rules, structures, or ideas of whatever form is doomed to incompleteness, to never getting to the motive force of human society. Cultures and societies exist in history, through time, and are constantly self-creating by responding to historically given conditions. Idea systems and culture in general, while having a certain autonomy, are primarily responses — continuities — of that which has gone before. Intellectual creativity does occur; new ideas do pop up rather like mutant genes. (To pursue the biological analogy we can say that it is the environment which selects "mutant" ideas.) But the primary forces shaping ideas are the nonmental external social and environmental realities that the perceiving mind responds to. Ideas do influence ideas, they do combine and recombine, but it is primarily ideas from the past that shape those of the present, and when this historicity of ideas is recognized, the practical conditions that originally shaped them are seen as being indirectly the main influence on the present.

A world view is linked to reality in two ways: first by regarding it, by forming more or less accurate images of it, images that mirror the world; and second, by testing these images through using them to guide action. By being put into action faulty images are corrected and brought more into line with the external world. And of course in the process of acting, of getting on with making a living, the actors modify the world they perceive. This dialectic relation operates not only at this level of macrothought and macrobehavior, but at the most primary levels of perception. This is the main

point of the discussion of perception in Chapter 2. It is at the level of sensory awareness and perception that the validity of historical materialism is
most apparent. Although the thinking, perceiving, mobile organism constantly interacts with its environment, altering it and its relationship with it
(feedback), still, in final analysis the environment is primary: heat is perceived as heat, and food as food.

Sahlins (1976) has recently argued that culture is autonomous and leads
a life of its own largely undetermined by material or economic conditions.
What Sahlins does not realize in criticizing historical materialism is that
more often than not history and economic infrastructure are indeed primary
because they are given to a local society by virtue of its relationships vis-à-
vis other societies. Few peoples make their own history and create their own
culture entirely by themselves. Much of it is made for them by their neighbors. Culture is to a large extent a response to such external conditions. This
case is easiest to make for state societies and peoples who have been dominated by states. In such cases, and we are now talking about almost all
known contemporary human societies, their infrastructures are but one link
in the world system. Local cultures are not free to evolve like some island
isolate with no ecological interaction with other species. Inevitably these
relationships are hierarchical. Some of the interacting societies have more
power and wealth than others. And within each local society there are
similar asymmetries between strata. Inevitably the more wealthy and
powerful are most able to shape society in their interest and in response to
the resistance offered by the less wealthy and powerful. In both cases each
stratum—each subsociety and subculture—responds to externally given
conditions. In the tradition of historical materialism such relationships are
summed up as class conflict. But Sahlins and other culturologists do not
deal with the dynamics of class. This is like writing a natural history of
malaria and failing to mention mosquitoes.

The situation with pristine aboriginal tribal and band societies is more
ambiguous. For here history-making of the kind we have been talking about
just above is less pronounced. And local societies are under less external re-
straint in organizing their own modes of living and elaborating a cognitive
construction of their reality. But if history has less power to shape the
economic and social relationships in such societies, the natural environment
has more. As local autonomy is greater, so is technological sophistication
less. And the less sophisticated a people's technology which mediates
between their physical environment and their social and cultural forms, the
greater determining power the former has on the latter. Here, where class
relationships are absent, the more purely material aspects of historical
materialism exert the most force in shaping world view and culture in
general. Thus, it is not simply because of some spontaneous unconscious

processes that hunting and gathering nonagricultural peoples such as aboriginal California Indians (Chapter 6) have a world view markedly different from that of middle-class New York apartment dwellers, and that Mexican peasants (Chapter 7) have yet another.[2] This primacy of history and of environment taken broadly is represented graphically in the world-view model by the wider arrows in Figures 2 and 7.

Each of the basic ideas presented in the first five chapters is illustrated with ethnographic examples, but to demonstrate more fully the integration of one entire world view, Chapter 6 presents an analysis of California Indian world view, employing the concepts presented in the preceding chapters.

Chapter 7, "Mexican Peasant World View," is somewhat more ambitious. In addition to showing how some of the universals of a world view are integrated among themselves, it demonstrates how the contents of the universals have been formed through history. The argument here is that peasant world view—its origin, nature, and the conditions which perpetuate it—can be understood only in an historic perspective that includes economic, political, and demographic relationships with the greater world of which any peasant community is a part. This is the reason for the long section on *historic determinants* in this chapter. Implicit in this historic treatment is a critique of contemporary non-Marxist anthropology's neglect of history, which seriously limits its ability to understand the workings of complex societies. The main structural differences between the California Indian societies of Chapter 6 and the Mexican peasantry is that the former have no social classes while the latter exists within a class society. Furthermore, I take the position that peasants, as I define them in terms of relationships of production, themselves constitute a class within the capitalist economy and state. Being a class within a class society correlates with a type of world view different from that of California Indians. Much of this difference results from the large role ideology (Chapter 1) plays in world-view formation in class societies and its relative absence in classless societies.

Chapter 1

ISSUES AND APPROACHES

Although world view is a subject of immense importance in the social sciences and philosophy, a coherent theory of world view is nonexistent. Since a purpose of this essay is to advance the study of world view, a reasonable way of beginning is to look at the present state of the art. Having done this we will be able to stand on the shoulders of those who have gone before—not that we will necessarily want to stand on all of them since, as I see it, some stand taller than others. As the Introduction notes, this book takes a definite point of view on several fundamental issues in world-view theory. Because these ideas are at odds with many anthropologists and philosophers who have written about world view, it seems appropriate to begin by jumping into the middle of these controversies. This is not to imply there is intense debate on these issues in American anthropology, for there is not. Rather, the majority of my colleagues are either unaware of them or simply choose to ignore them for whatever reason.

As I see it, the best way to begin this overview is by contrasting the two main approaches to world view: historical materialism and cultural idealism. Since this book is within the first tradition, this order of presentation will serve to alert the reader to some of the basic assumptions of the author.

HISTORICAL MATERIALISM AND CULTURAL IDEALISM

Idealist and materialist philosophies, which are the foundations of anthropological theories, are both fundamental world-view assumptions, and are therefore susceptible to analysis in the same way that we might analyze the world view of any other "natives." This section thus turns world-view theory back onto itself and does so by contrasting the model presented here with the prevalent general concept of world view in contemporary cultural idealist anthropology. Such reflexive anthropology of course does not in any way free us from the necessity of choosing a theoretical vantage point. In such an analysis, as in *all* anthropological endeavors, we must take a partisan position. Therefore, I shall of necessity choose my weapon. The following pages are thus a first approximation and application of it, and the main target is cultural idealism. Included here is a discussion of why cultural idealism has dominated American anthropology while historical materialism has been relatively ignored. We begin with a discussion of the philosophical foundations of each tradition and their ideological implications.

THE EPISTEMOLOGY OF MATERIALISM AND IDEALISM

A world view is a set of images and assumptions about the world. There are three basic problems in the study of world views. One is: What are the necessary and therefore universal types of images and assumptions which are part of any world view, and what are the specific contents of these universals in any particular world view? The second problem with which an adequate theory of world view must deal is the formation of these images and assumptions; that is, What relationship do they have with the world which they represent? Finally, and most important, is the question of a world view's influence on behavior, on practical affairs. The first of these problems is the subject of Chapter 3, while Chapter 4 deals with the second and third. Here it is worthwhile to anticipate these issues and examine the major ways in which anthropologists and philosophers have dealt with the nature of world views and their relation to reality. Since a world view is knowledge about the world, what we are talking about here is epistemology, the theory of knowledge.

Broadly speaking, there are in pre-Marxist philosophy and psychology two conflicting notions about the nature of ideas (images and assumptions) and their relationship to the world; these are referred to as empiricism and rationalism. The empiricist tradition argues that all ideas arise from experience, that is, from sensation of the environment, and from perception of the resultant ideas within the mind. Since we think only by forming and perceiving ideas in our mind, and since all ideas arise originally from sensation, there can be no knowledge of the world prior to experience. In other words, there are no innate ideas in the mind. John Locke most clearly states the empiricist position. He speaks of the human mind at birth as a clean sheet of paper without any writing on it, without any ideas. This no doubt seems reasonable to most educated people today. But when Locke was writing in the 1600s, the opposite or rationalist view was more in favor. Locke's *An Essay Concerning Human Understanding* was a refutation of Plato, Descartes, and the Scholastics who all in their own way maintained that certain basic features of knowledge were inherent in the mind.

Varieties of rationalism seek to analyze human knowledge by focusing on the structure and content of the mind. Implicit in this position is a concept of "mind" which is assumed to exist more or less as an organ separate from the brain, perhaps comparable to the "soul." The rationalist approach to human knowledge thus turns attention away from experience and therefore from the world to the structure and working of the mind. In devaluing the power of experience to shape knowledge, rationalism is aligned with philosophical idealism.

In its most extreme form idealism argues that ideas are the primary features of reality. They may possibly have some manifestation in material form, and when this occurs, the material entities or conditions emanate from the ideas. In less extreme forms, idealism accepts the independent existence of matter, but gives priority to immaterial forces as determining the material world. In different idealist traditions these range from the will of God or other incorporeal spirit beings, to presumed eternal metaphysical truths, to human ideas. All idealist philosophies assume that material conditions are shaped by some immaterial force that operates essentially independent of matter and is responsible for material phenomena. Thus, at one extreme there are the beliefs in ethereal creator gods who will the world into existence and Plato's ideal images that are the prototypes of material objects. In less religious and metaphysical variations of idealism, primary importance is given to the power and independence of human thought. In this humanistic idealism, human behavior and history in general are explained as a result of the appearance and interaction of ideas. Most of cultural anthropology is a variant of this tradition: personality, themes, patterns, structures, and the like are assumed to shape behavior. Attention is focused on these mental constructs and not on how they appear and evolve as a result of changing environmental and social conditions.

Opposed to idealism is another long intellectual tradition in philosophy that argues for just the opposite relationship between ideas and material conditions, i.e., ideas in the mind are determined by the external conditions in which they appear. In terms of epistemology this is the empiricist position. But when this view becomes the basis for a theory of human behavior and of human history in general it is more appropriate to speak of materialism. Here, in contrast to idealism, ideas, rather than being primary, are seen as epiphenomena of matter: rather than ideas shaping the world, just the opposite is held to be true; ideas are seen as arising in the human brain as more or less accurate reflections of the external world.

Historical Materialism

As was mentioned in the Introduction, the extreme forms of idealist and materialist positions are both terribly simplistic. For it is certainly the case that both material and social conditions for one and ideas themselves for another affect human knowledge and action. The critical issues are, which is primary and how do they interact?

The most comprehensive analysis of this issue was made by Karl Marx, who began by fighting his way out the intellectual morass of philosophical idealism that dominated German academic life in the mid nineteenth century. This period resulted in several of the most powerful criticisms of idealism ever written (Marx 1975; Marx and Engels 1975, 1976). This personal odyssey from the lofty and illusory heavens of idealism to a practical theory of knowledge and history still serves as a model for anthropology students seeking to escape the fetters of cultural idealism. Marx's new outlook, which came to be known as historical materialism, is at one level a model of human knowledge and at the other of the process whereby human history was unfolded.

The core of this analysis is the recognition that before people can engage in such "higher" activities of the mind as philosophy, religion, and art they must feed and shelter themselves. Material needs are primary and if they are not fulfilled there can be no human society and culture. In this view, social organization and culture to a great extent serve in any particular instance to meet these material needs. Thus, as a first approximation in the analysis of a social formation it is useful to identify what in Marxist terms are called the *base* (mode of production) and the *superstructure*. The base in classical Marxist theory consists of *forces of production* and *relations of production*. The forces of production include the so-called means of production, i.e., natural resources and the technology for converting them into things that are of value to humans. These means of production, when coupled with human labor power, comprise the forces of production. The relations of production have to do with the division of labor whereby the forces of production are utilized, with the ownership of the production forces, and with the distribution of the values that are created by work or that otherwise exist in the society. The superstructure consists of such institutions as law, education, churches, and the family, beliefs, world view, and social-science theory. What anthropologists refer to as culture is a major part of the superstructure. The distinction between base and superstructure is relatively clear-cut in capitalist society. In other social formations aspects of superstructure are often embedded in the base. This is especially true in classless societies, but even here it is usually possible to analytically isolate the superstructural functions of different parts of the social formation (see Godelier 1978).

In historical materialism priority is given to the base in shaping the superstructure. Marx himself has expressed this as well as anyone.

> In the social production of their life, men enter into definite relations that are indispensable and independent of their will, relations of production which correspond to a definite stage of development of their material productive forces. The sum total of these relations of production constitutes the economic structure of society, the real foundation, on which rises a legal and political superstructure and to which correspond definite forms of social consciousness. The mode of production of material life conditions the social, political, and intellectual life process in general. It is not the consciousness of men that determines their being, but, on the contrary, their social being that determines their consciousness. (Marx 1969b:503)

Marx's materialist theory of history is often misunderstood to mean that economic conditions and relationships are the sole determinant of what he identified as the superstructure and of history in general. The following quotation from Engels set the record straight on this issue.

> According to the materialist conception of history, the *ultimately* determining element in history is the production and reproduction of real life. More than that neither Marx nor I have ever asserted. Hence if somebody twists this into saying that the economic element is the *only* determining one, he transforms that proposition into a meaningless, abstract, senseless phrase. The economic situation is the basis, but the various elements of the superstructure —political forms of the class struggle and its results, to-wit: constitutions established by the victorious class after a successful battle, etc., juridical forms, and even the reflexes of all these actual struggles in the brains of the participants, political, juristic, philosophical theories, religious views and their further development into systems of dogmas—also exercise their influence upon the course of the historical struggles and in many cases preponderate in determining their *form*. There is an interaction of all these elements in which, amid all the endless host of accidents . . . the economic movement finally assets itself as necessary.

Otherwise the application of the theory to any period of history would be easier than the solution of a simple equation of the first degree. (Engels 1970b:487)

Critics of historical materialism often impute a narrow economism to it, that is, allege that it sees individuals acting only out of material self-interest. This concept is absent from Marx's and Engels's work. Nor should their ideas on human nature and history be confused with the utilitarian concepts of Jeremy Bentham and his followers.

Historical materialism, while being neither an empiricist nor rationalist theory of knowledge, does give prime importance to material and social conditions as the origin of any particular self-consciousness and of knowledge in general. But this is only a starting point in the analysis, for the question immediately arises: to what does the environment in which ideas arise owe its nature? In the case of human beings, the answer is that to a very great extent this shaping environment is formed by previous human activity which was informed by the ideas about the world that those people held. In this view the issue of human knowledge is inseparable from human practical affairs and human history. Also, aside from ideas being shaped mainly by perception of the world, ideas are totally dependent on matter in that there can be no ideas without a material basis, namely the brain and the material conditions which maintain it. Matter can, of course, exist in the absence of ideas. Because of the primacy of environment in this interaction of subject and object, and because of this interaction by which knowledge arises through time and is relative to different conditions, this model is referred to as historical materialism.

The historic part of historical materialism (as opposed to the psychological) also has definite implications for the future of history. But the principles of historical materialism are best thought of not as predictions of things to come, but instead as a practical methodology for bringing them about—in other words, for political, economic, and intellectual struggle. The most important part of this methodology is analysis, which begins with asking questions about the past and the present. If the workings of the past and the present can be unlocked, then such analysis can possibly serve as a plan for consciously intervening in history to bring about a future in which more human potential is realized.

Closely aligned with the historical materialist tradition is the "research strategy" known as cultural materialism, most associated with Marvin Harris. Harris acknowledges the tremendous intellectual debt which he owes to Marx for the principle of infrastructural determinism (1979:xi, 55–56), but seeks "to improve Marx's original strategy by dropping the Hegelian notion that all systems evolve through a dialectic of contradictory negations and by adding reproductive pressures and ecological variables

to the conjuncture of material conditions studied by Marxist-Leninists"
(ibid.:ix). In attempting to distance himself from Marxist tradition Harris
attacks—and for the most part in my opinion, correctly—some of the more
arcane principles of dialectical materialism, which often as not have served
more of a left ideological than a scientific function. Dialectical materialism,
an attempt to build a comprehensive model for the natural sciences consistent with the historical methodology of Marx, is an intellectual program
developed mainly by Engels in his later life and by Lenin. Marx himself was
not significantly involved in this project, devoting himself instead to his
social, economic, and historical research, and to political activism. Harris,
however, consistently confounds the dialectical materialism of Lenin and
Engels with the historical materialism of Engels and Marx. One may dis-
agree with specific analyses that Harris has made in applying the theory and
method of cultural materialism. But it should be recognized that as a theory
of infrastructural determinism and as a research strategy, cultural materialism in its current state of development is not incompatible with the
fundamentals of historical materialism as outlined above. Harris is to be
applauded for insisting that a greater concern be given to population and
ecological "variables" as aspects of the mode of production. But, although
it may be politically expedient to distinguish one's work from Marxist
scholarship, the coining of a new label for an old research strategy is intel-
lectually unwarranted.[1]

What substantive differences do exist between cultural materialism and
Marxists center on the importance that class conflict is assumed to have in
influencing superstructure and history in complex societies. Insofar as individual cultural materialists might deny the importance of class conflict it is
best to set them apart, for in this regard they are definitely not aligned with
the historical materialist tradition. Harris is ambiguous on this issue. Class
relations do figure in some of Harris's studies, and in this regard too his
work is more or less theoretically consistent with a Marxist anthropology. It
is easy for Harris and other cultural materialists to avoid having to come to
grips with the dialectics of contradiction when they are working with classless societies, and therefore for them to argue that they can do good anthropology without the "Hegelian monkey" on their backs. But even in classless
societies the intricate relations of "positive and negative feedback" between
base and superstructure that so fascinate Harris are in the Marxist tradition
also referred to as dialectical relations. And in this regard Harris should
definitely stand up and be counted as a dialectician.

Cultural Idealism

The perennial debate between idealism and materialism is of extreme
importance to any theory of world view, since to study world view is of

necessity to take a stand on this issue. To date the prevalent approach to world view and to concepts like world view has been overwhelmingly idealist, and as such is consistent with the basic idealist nature of American cultural anthropology in general. The main component of this tradition is the concept of culture. Culture in this sense is the shared knowledge, most of which is tacit, that people acquire by growing up in their community. The main task that American anthropology has set itself is the study of this culture, which exists within the minds of the members of the community. Historical materialism locates culture in the superstructure. Thus the main criticism of cultural idealism from the perspective of historical materialism is that cultural anthropologists for the most part wander in the superstructures of societies without grounding their analyses in the base that is a major —usually the main—condition which shapes the social or cultural phenomena they are interested in. From the historical materialist point of view the base is the dog, which wags the tail of superstructure (which of course has thereby some effect on the dog's body). Cultural idealists mistakenly assume they have a hold on the dog when in effect they have only part of the tail. One of the main objectives of this essay is to rescue world view from the idealist camp and take it to its proper home—which is, as I argue, historical materialism.

One apparent reason for the overwhelming concern with idealist approaches in cultural anthropology, i.e., lack of a healthy materialist antidote, is that most influential anthropologists have been relatively affluent. Historically, cultural anthropology is an intellectual discipline that grew out of the upper classes in Europe and the Americas. And even today most anthropologists have not personally experienced hunger and poverty associated with life lived at a survival level. Consequently, living in a world of ideas, they tend to let this preoccupation with mental phenomena shape their anthropological theory and assume that ideas have the same importance in the lives of the people they study. But perhaps an even greater reason for the prevalence of idealism in anthropology and the social sciences in general is that idealism tends to be compatible with conservative political orientations.

THE POLITICAL ECONOMY OF IDEALISM AND MATERIALISM

The most innovative aspect of Marx's rethinking of the origin of human knowledge was the realization that it is greatly influenced by social conditions. Aside from the general knowledge available to individuals by virtue of the historic period they happen to live in, another major force in influencing their world view is their position in society, especially their class

membership. The Marxist concern with class analysis comes from the existence of an unequal distribution of wealth, power, and general well-being
among the various higher and lower strata of class societies. Throughout
human history this distribution has been such that the "upper" or ruling
class has tended to be numerically the smallest. This situation is inherently
unstable, for the members of the lower classes, outnumbering those of the
upper, are structurally disposed to seek a redistribution of the possessions
and prerogatives of the wealthy and powerful. To prevent such revolutions
the upper class relies ultimately on force, which is consolidated in the
apparatus of the state. But sheer repression alone is ineffective in the long
run. Some degree of passive acceptance of the status quo by the less
endowed is also necessary. In other words, the less endowed must view the
status quo as inevitable and bearable. Such attitudes, inimical as they are to
the class interests of the less fortunate but supporting as they are to those of
the ruling class, suggest their social origin. They tend to be developed and
propagated at the top of society for consumption by the bottom. When
ideas have this social function, it is appropriate to speak of them as
ideology. Now one of the most notable features of ruling-class ideology is
that it tends to be idealist in nature.

Why Idealism Is Conservative and Materialism Is Not

Idealist ideologies have their social origin in the most fundamental division of labor in class societies, which is that between mental and manual
work.[2] Mental work tends to be more desired, esteemed, and rewarded than
manual labor, and tends also to be concentrated in the upper strata of
society. Liberated from "real" work, those in the intellectual elite of society
are thus predisposed to solidify their position. They do this not only by
giving the results of their labor—ideas—higher value than the products of
manual workers, but also·by creating ideas which serve to mystify and legitimize the the existing social arrangement. I am not arguing that ruling-class
ideology is always or inevitably idealist, but that it is so more often than
not, and that as such it serves the conservative class interests of elites.

The interweaving of ideology within the structures of interlocking
social institutions in a society is a fundamental form of cultural hegemony
(Femia 1981; Gramsci 1971; Williams 1977). In Chapter 7 we will examine
the power of such hegemonic forces, replicated in religion, social structures,
and the family, to shape social consciousness to the benefit of privileged
classes in Mexican society. There we will see the predominant role of idealist
ideology in those particular instances of cultural domination. Irrespective of
their explicit content, idealist world view and idealist social science fulfill a

conservative ideological function by virtue of an implicit assumption within them. This assumption is that idealist truths are absolutely and eternally true. Since they are not anchored in the changing realities of the material world these truths have a timelessness; once established they are presumed to be true for all times and places. The first and most common variant of ruling-class idealist ideology is religion. Religion is a form of idealist thinking because of its belief that incorporeal beings or forces can influence human affairs and other worldly events. Establishment religions in state societies inevitably have a theory of creation that provides a charter, as Malinowski calls it, for society. According to creation myths in most religions, the present world of human social relationships has been established by some suprahuman power; social relations are made not by humans, but by a god, with the implication that only he can change them.

In complex societies, the ruling class inevitably has a monopoly of political and police power which it wields via the state. The state thus functions to maintain the status quo. But it can be effective for any long period only if the disinherited and disfranchised do not seriously question the inequities of the situation and entertain images of other realities more to their liking. The propagation of religious or other idealist concepts is thus an integral part of the state's function. At each stage in the evolution of state society there is a priesthood, or the intellectual counterpart of a priesthood, that elaborates and modifies these allegedly timeless verities so that they serve the needs of the ruling elite. Not only does the priesthood create eternal truths, it creates an eternal all-powerful god who pronounces them. Because he is all powerful and eternal, his will must be done. This supreme god is nothing more than the self-legitimizing power of the state, which has become reified in the consciousness of the believers. Because of this mystification most people do not realize that the source of these ideas is human, not divine. Inevitably, in state societies with establishment religions, the god's will most benefits the elite classes of that society. Religion is the prototype of all ruling-class idealist philosophies and it is for this reason that Marx said, the "criticism of religion is the premise of all criticism." All other idealist philosophies also convince believers that they are eternal truths rather than human creations and in doing so convince the believers that they are not capable of creating their own realities.

The first great challenge to religion in state societies is philosophy. But most of what philosophy does in challenging the supernaturalism of religion is to substitute the search for metaphysical truths, truths less mystified than religious truths but assumed to be equally absolute and unchanging. Insofar as these truths define the world and human affairs in terms of eternal verities, they also serve as conservative forces. For this reason nonreligious idealist philosophies and social theories both emanate primarily from the top of society. By their inherent nature they both legitimize the status quo.

The contemporary social and natural sciences represent a stage in the evolution of general human world view that is considerably less mystified than, say, medieval religious idealism. Yet it is ironic that modern empiricism, which starts from materialist assumptions, commonly tends to serve the needs of a conservative idealist ideology. How does this come about? It is made possible first of all by the epistemological assumption of empiricism that knowledge arises in human consciousness passively from experience. As a basis for scientific methodology this becomes positivism, which holds that theory is the end point of observation and experimentation. The creation of theory, abstract knowledge, is thus defined as the main goal of science. And what is theory but an approximation of some eternal truths? From the Marxist perspective, what is left out of this program is the realization that knowledge can be acquired only actively by interacting with the world. This means that just as knowledge in daily life arises out of practical affairs, so any science worth the name is an applied science that is constantly validated by being put into use. A theoretical science in the service of presumed eternal truths is the functional equivalent of theology. And like theology, in turning attention away from human issues, it helps perpetuate the status quo.

If, as positivism thus assumes, the "objective" world is the arbiter of truth, then a "value-free" science must seem the best road in the search for truth. But which truths? Certainly not the truths about the quality of life of different classes within society, but rather some never-specified idealist truths that are given more value than the lives of real men and women. This sort of value-free positivism purports to be empirical, to be dealing with the real world, but it does so only to mystify it, to direct attention away from issues and contradictions within society which the ruling (read "research-funding") class prefers to keep unexamined.

Max Horkheimer (1972:10–46) argues convincingly that in addition to having the same ideological function as metaphysics, positivism also has comparable epistemologic assumptions. About this, Stanley Aronowitz says the following.

The two sides of bourgeois thought, positivism and metaphysics, are the unified world view of the bourgeoisie, split according to the prevailing division of labor between science, which serves industry, and religions and secular spiritual ideologies, which serve social domination. On the one hand, positivist thought denies the relevance, if not the existence, of universals. It asserts the rationality of the given surface reality and documents its permutations. On the other hand, metaphysics abolishes the positivist enslavement to the concrete and searches for a teleology to give meaning to human existence. Science offers no transcendent meaning to men; it simply asserts facts. Its immanent viewpoint is the unity of thought with outer reality. Metaphysics is the other side of positivist nominalism. Its universals are abstract. If not God, then the absolute idea informs its search for purpose so resolutely denied by empirical science. (Aronowitz 1972:xv)

In its infancy as a product of the Enlightenment, positivism had a progressive function as the outlook of liberal philosophers of the emerging bourgeoisie who were in need of a practical ideology to promote the development of capitalism and to legitimize their struggle against the traditional authority and power, which were shrouded in spiritualism. However, in the current phase of mature capitalism, positivism has assumed ideological duties formerly fulfilled exclusively by theology.

Whereas idealist concepts are timeless and unchanging and are therefore conservative ideological forces, materialist views are inherently more likely to be subversive of conservatism in that they turn attention to the material world, which is in constant flux. An awareness of past history and large-scale processes in nature erodes the hegemonic view that the material world-in-place is natural. To combat this tendency, idealist ideology directs attention to the heavens, away from the realization that the world is constantly coming into being, and the even more subversive realization that humans have the power to create their own material realities. The evolution of the material world teaches that truth is to a very great extent contingent upon what people make it. By engaging in praxis we create realities, and to the degree that we do this consciously we do so intentionally. This realization, tutored to us by the material world, is anathema to a ruling class that wishes to cling to its privileged position as though this dominion over others were an eternally divine or natural state of affairs.

Thus, just as idealism comes mainly from the top of society, materialist philosophies and world views spring from the bottom. There are several reasons for this. First among them is the predisposing nature of the division of labor into mental and manual. Just as intellectuals are inclined to idealism because it overvalues and glorifies the products of their work—ideas—so thinkers whose identities are rooted in the working classes are inclined to stress the importance of their concrete creations. It is not surprising, then, that historical materialism is the main expression of the intellectual and political struggles of the proletariat. Close personal identification with nineteenth-century industrial workers shaped Marx's and Engels's consciousness in this direction. It is also significant here that historical materialism has developed for the most part outside of rather than in the universities, where mental labor is overwhelmingly nurtured and supported by conservative and liberal forces.

But there are more important practical reasons why materialism is a world view most associated with the bottom strata of society. It is in the interest of the dispossessed, the exploited classes to overthrow the existing social order. To do so effectively requires an empirical science of revolution, based on an accurate view of reality. Whereas the social function of the ruling-class philosophy, ideology, and science is to mystify and direct attention away from issues of real concern to the lower classes, and in doing so to perpetuate business as usual, the purpose of proletarian consciousness is to demystify and bring about change. This requires a valid analysis of the existing state of affairs, including the sociology of knowledge. These are the first steps in the founding of a revolutionary program. A materialist view of history and society is thus a practical necessity for the lower classes.

The equation of idealism with conservative ideologies and materialism with progressive ones is valid in the long view. In the short run there are of course many exceptions. Most notable is the recurrent appearance of social protest expressed as sectarian religious movements that derive their plan and legitimacy from a divinely inspired prophet. Until the Enlightenment in Europe and the modern scientific socialism which grows out of it, almost all social protest movements were clothed in a religious guise. In a society saturated with religion, the language of supernaturalism is the only idiom available for dialog. The function of revolutionary prophets in such a situation is to short-circuit the priesthood and establish direct communication with God. This provokes not only physical repression by the state, but also ideological warfare in that the prophet and his followers are branded as heretics. The greater truthfulness claimed for the official religion is justification for suppression of the upstart one with its inevitable new chosen people. The great innovation of modern socialism was to restructure this ideological dialog by opposing supernaturalism not with supernaturalism but instead with scientific principles.

Currently the most significant religious protest movement in the West is occurring in Latin American countries with peasant-based movements of national liberation. In these countries conservative Catholic dogma is giving way to a "theology of liberation" (Gutiérrez 1973) that is ideologically compatible not with the reigning oligarchs, but instead with socialist revolutionaries who often as not are themselves practicing proponents of the theology of liberation. Apart from the materialist-idealist debate, which is not a major issue in the theology of liberation, clerics who identify with the political and social goals of their impoverished parishioners share basic world-view assumptions with Marxist revolutionaries. Like the Marxists, they seek the transformation of social structures that perpetuate gross inequities and human suffering, and like Marxists they have a vision of a human potential for altruism and productive work that are their own reward (Miranda 1974).

Conservative forces are also capable of occasionally utilizing materialist ideologies in their class interests. The most notable example in modern history is the distortion of Darwinian evolutionary theory to legitimize

nineteenth- and twentieth-century laissez-faire capitalism and its sociological correlate, racism. This was done by twisting the principles of natural
selection so as to give undue emphasis to intraspecies competition as the
condition promoting progress. Darwin actually did not talk about progress,
only adaptation, which resulted from some individuals in a population
having more surviving offspring than others, due to small and random
differences in their morphology or behavior which tended to allow them
to live longer than other less "adapted" forms. The conservative social
Darwinists argued that differences, viz., social and economic inequalities,
were a necessary and desirable result of such a "natural" process. Any attempt to interfere with it by social reforms would thus go against the laws of
nature. What the social Darwinists did was to focus on the presumed end
result of evolution in the present as a justification of social conditions. What
they did not discuss was the future course of evolution, which implies that
present forms will be transformed with time. This evolutionary aspect of
Darwin was exactly what most interested Marx, who said that Darwin's
Origin of Species was "a basis in natural science for the class struggle in
history."

A current variant of social Darwinism in the service of conservative
ideology exists in the arguments that differences in the intelligence-test
scores of ethnic minority students as compared with the majority white
population are due to inherent differences in psychological capacities
among these different populations, rather than to environmental or cultural
differences (the argument from the left opposes this). Current conservative
sociobiology also purports to find an instinctual basis for human territori-
ality, psychological differences between the sexes, social hierarchy, and
aggression. These qualities presumed to be founded in genetics are rather a
recent conjunction of materialism and conservative ideology in the service
of the status quo, the cold war, ethnocentrism, sexism, and the arms race.

Lewis Feuer (1975) has masterfully shown how virtually any philosophical principle and ideology can serve the needs of both the left, the
right, and the center. He demonstrates how ideologies have a wavelike
motion as they oscillate back and forth across the political spectrum, generation by generation. But from a larger perspective, these waves are but rip-
ples on the flow of history. To transform this river metaphor into a pun we
can say that history has a left and a right bank. There are many eddies and
backcurrents in this river, but because of the structural reasons discussed
above, the main currents sweep idealist ideologies to the right and materialism to the left.[3]

Cultural anthropology is the prevailing style of anthropology in North
America. It is based on the premise that culture is a subject suitable for investigation in its own right. Culture by its very nature is idealist—it ultimately consists of the images, rules, plans, preferences, and fears that people

have in their heads, and that they have learned for the most part from others in their society. None of this is to be denied or diminished. And there is no doubt that culture in this sense is the immediate, proximate determinant of people's behavior in society. The prevailing strategy in cultural anthropology is to take culture as such as a given and then to analyze it for the most part internally. The task that most cultural anthropologists set themselves is to take the content of a culture and analyze it much as textual criticism is done in the study of literature. The results in both cases, while often interesting and even brilliant, are equally sterile in that they have little relevance to the lives of the bearers of culture so dissected. Insofar as analysis extends to behavior, and this is rare in cultural anthropology, behavior is seen as a result of culture. In this paradigm there is no theory for investigation of the practical forces shaping culture. This is idealism in a virtually pure form.

IDEALIST APPROACHES TO WORLD VIEW

From the perspective of radical world-view theory, cultural idealist theories and studies are seen as being mainly concerned with static and internal aspects of world view defined solely as a set of ideas or categories that transcend individual cognition. Since the model presented here also is concerned with the internal nature of world view—both its universal structure and the contents of particular world views—it is worthwhile to review the idealist contributions to this issue to see what is available for developing this aspect of the present model.

In attempting to describe similarities and differences among societies of the world, anthropologists of the cultural idealist tradition pose a number of problems. One that is characteristic of many cultural anthropologists of the twentieth century is the attempt to discover and describe the underlying "pattern," "configuration," "basic personality," "ethos," or "world view" of a society. What all of these concepts have in common is that they refer to an hypothesized mental principle that organizes in a distinctive way nonmaterial elements—such as perceptions, values, folk concepts, and emotions—of a given society. These mental constructs are assumed to shape social and cultural behavior and the material and nonmaterial results of this behavior—e.g. social organization, government, art styles, architecture, and literature. This shaping is assumed to be unconscious in that a typical member of the society in question is unable to describe it fully.

This style of anthropology is idealist first of all in its main concern with the ideational, summed up most generally as culture. This bias is expressed by anthropologists of this persuasion by identifying themselves as "cultural" anthropologists. Cultural anthropology is also idealist in that this cultural knowledge, once analyzed, is held to be useful in explaining behavior; ideas are deemed primary, their visible outward expression secondary. In practice, however, there is little interest in the use of culture as an explanation of behavior. This situation is comparable to that in linguistics where linguists interested in theories of language have little concern with the practical use of speech in everyday life. Cultural anthropologists practice their art in its pure form, by limiting their interests to chunks of culture that they analyze internally. In doing so they have discovered a great deal about how culture is structured. Since one of the three main problems in radical world-view theory is to analyze the internal content of world view (see in Chapter 4, Internal Causes), there is much to be learned from the work that has been done in this area by cultural anthropologists. However, when we go on to the more important questions of how world view affects and is affected by environmental and practical considerations, we must return to the historical materialist perspective. This discussion of world-view studies in the cultural idealist tradition is both part of the critique of cultural idealism and an exploration of useful concepts which can be salvaged from it.[4]

Antecedents of the contemporary world-view concept appear in the writing of various nineteenth-century cultural historians. Jacob Burckhardt offers a good example; in his *The Civilization of the Renaissance in Italy* he attempted to write a new kind of culture history in which he explained such diverse things as the festivals, dress styles, etiquette, folk beliefs, and science of Renaissance Italy in terms of one paramount theme—individualism. As Barnouw has said, "To find an index of 'individualism' in such disparate areas as fashion, crime, and the writing of biography was a brilliant departure" (1963:30).[5]

The German historian and philosopher Oswald Spengler developed perhaps the most well-known example of this monothematic cultural historical approach. Spengler demonstrated his theory by looking at how cultures selectively borrow traits from one another, and how the accepted traits are transformed when introduced into a new cultural setting. The way in which a people reject alien cultural traits or borrow and transform them tells us something about their basic values. As one example, Spengler showed how Egyptian art, architecture, and so forth were altered when incorporated into Greek culture. Similarly, these aspects of Egyptian culture that the Greeks rejected were also diagnostic. The main point here is that Spengler saw an underlying world view as responsible for such transformations and rejections. In Spengler's interpretation, the classical Greeks lacked a concern with inner development, due to a poorly developed sense of time and history. He pointed out that although the historical chronology and almanacs of the Babylonians and Egyptians were available to the Greeks, they nevertheless retained a "shallow" concept of time in which people essentially lived for the moment. Accordingly, such Greek historians as Herodotus and Thucydides wrote that no important events had happened before their own age. Spengler also argued that these attitudes were consistent with Pericles's decree banning the propagation of astronomical theories.

Spengler saw a sharp contrast between these Greek attitudes about time and those of the Egyptians. He argued that in constrast to the Greeks they showed great concern for time. They built with granite, chiseled their archives, kept detailed records of past events, and had elaborate administrative and irrigation systems. Whereas the Greeks merely burned their dead, the Egyptians developed elaborate methods of mummification.

Spengler also characterized modern Western culture by a single leitmotif—"Faustian." He defined the Faustian man as having an "existence which is led with a deep consciousness and introspection of the ego, and a resolutely personal culture evidenced in memoirs, reflections, retrospects, and prospects and conscience" (Barnouw 1963:33, quoting Spengler). As with Spengler's ancient Egyptians, this culture is concerned with planning and history, and by a desire to dominate space and seek mastery. Spengler pointed to the invention and widespread use of clocks and chimes in bell towers as reflecting a concern with the passage of time. Western musical instruments such as the organ, a "space-commanding giant," were expressive of a desire to fill infinite space with sound. Western mathematics similarly revealed this Faustian tendency with its irrational numbers, decimal fractions, negative numbers, all unrealized by the Greeks. Classical mathematicians were not so much concerned with abstractions as with what they could tangibly see and count.

He also drew similar conclusions from drama, art, and even language. For example, the Latin *sum* is replaced by *ich bin, je suis, I am,* viz., a word for "I" is introduced. In architecture the Faustian feeling for depth and the infinite was expressed in soaring Gothic cathedrals which contrast with low, flat Greek temples.

Within American anthropology there are two principal traditions of world-view studies. We may refer to these by the names of the individuals most responsible for shaping them: Franz Boas and Robert Redfield.

The Boas Tradition

The tradition of Germanic idealist scholarship that produced Burckhardt and Spengler (and against which the young Marx and Engels reacted, most notably in *The German Ideology* and *The Holy Family*) was carried into American anthropology by the immigrant ethnographer Franz Boas (1858–1942), where it culminated in the concept of culture.

The emphasis on the concept of culture in Boas's anthropology is explained in large part by his constant use of it to assault racist assumptions and arguments present in much of nineteenth-century and early twentieth-century social evolutionism and physical anthropology (see Stocking 1968:110–233). This use of culture against a conservative biologizing was consistent with Boas's identification with the revolutionary ideals of 1848. "He wanted to 'live and die' for 'equal rights for all, equal possibilities to learn and work for poor and rich alike.' So also he could only be happy as 'a member of humanity as a whole,' working 'together with the masses toward high goals'" (Stocking 1968:149, quoting young Boas). In this role the culture concept was and is a powerful progressive force against spurious biological reductionist arguments. But outside of this dialog it tends to assume a conservative function typical of idealist beliefs in general.

Boas's impact on world-view studies is indirect in that as the most influential individual in the formation of American anthropology he established an intellectual milieu in which the study of world view was an almost inevitable outcome. The roots of this concern with world view can be traced to fundamental epistemological issues with which Boas grappled as a physics student doing his doctoral research in Germany on the color of distilled water, in which he was both subject and experimenter. After becoming aware of the large subjective factor involved in his laboratory observations he realized the necessity of taking into account the situational conditions that influenced the mental state of the subject. This problem evolved into a broader project concerning the influence of environmental conditions on perception in general and was the objective of his first ethnological field trip to the Arctic. Thus Boas, who began as a student of physics —the most materialistic of sciences—moved successively from it through cultural geography to what eventually became a predominantly idealist anthropology.

Other roots of the American concern with world view are in the particularistic historical reconstructionism of Boas and his students. This school of anthropology, if we may call it that, has often been typified as a reaction to the evolutionary theories of Lewis Henry Morgan, Karl Marx, E. B. Tylor, John F. McLennan, and other nineteenth-century evolutionists. Instead of attempting to determine the overall plan of social evolution as these theorists had done, the Boasians set about reconstructing the cultural history of discrete local cultural traditions by an exhaustive compiling of cultural elements in each one. Another similar application of this method was the objective delineation of specific "culture areas." The concept of culture area is most associated with Clark Wissler. Although he received a Ph.D. in psychology at Columbia University in 1901, early in his career Wissler turned to anthropology, largely under the influence of Boas and

Livingston Farrand, who had already established the essential features of the culture area concept. Wissler offered the first large-scale demonstration of this method in his book *The American Indian* (1917) in which he marked off and described eight culture areas for the entire Western Hemisphere on the basis of the prevalent food resources utilized in each one. Each of these areas was further defined in terms of a large number—a complex—of other culture traits. The traits typical of an area were, according to Wissler, most common near the center and decreased near the periphery as one approached adjacent culture areas. In this way the Indian societies of the Northwest Coast region of North America, for example, could be distinguished from others located in say the Southwestern United States by their respective list of material and nonmaterial cultural traits. Other students of Boas identified comparable areas in Africa and Oceania. Each such cultural area was seen as exhibiting a particular combination of traits, and on this basis questions of historical affinities and differences could be posed and tested.

Although this method began as a particularistic and objective research strategy, another and more abstract question began to capture the attention of Boasians working on these problems. From the beginning of this method it was subjectively apparent that each cultural area so delineated had certain qualities that typified it. Each culture was, in some sense, not just a random assortment of traits, but an integrated, coherent constellation that manifested a distinct style. There was, in effect, some underlying "pattern" or "configuration" that orchestrated the individual traits. Typically, "patterns are those arrangements or systems of internal relationship which give to any culture its coherence or plan, and keep it from being a mere accumulation of random bits" (Kroeber 1948:311). It was thus possible to analyze how this implicit configuration "accepted" or "rejected" alien traits, and how the form, function, and meaning of accepted traits might be altered so that they would more compatibly fit into the basic configuration.[6] This idealist approach to culture and culture change was essentially the same as Spengler's, only on a smaller scale. It also differed from Spengler's in that Spengler had a rather fatalistic notion of recurrent cycles in history.

Franz Boas is often said to have been an anthropologist who was strongly antitheoretical. This is a surprising criticism when one considers that he produced several generations of American anthropologists who developed variations of this basic configurational method. One of the first of his students to make explicit use of it was Edward Sapir. Indeed, culture as he defined it was a *world outlook*, and in his own work he wished

> to embrace in a single term those general attitudes, views of life, and specific manifestations of civilization that give a particular people its distinctive place in

the world. Emphasis is put not so much on what is done and believed by a people as on how what is done and believed functions in the whole life of that
people, on what significance it has for them. (Sapir 1949:11)

But by far the most sweeping use of this method was that of Ruth
Benedict. As did most of Boas's students, she cut her teeth on a particularistic trait-list approach to culture-area problems, yet even her earliest work
reveals a concern for underlying configurations. Her first published paper,
written as a second-year graduate student, was "The Vision in Plains
Culture" (1922). It is an analysis of the distributions of three traits among
Indian cultures of the North American plains: infliction of self torture, lack
of a laity-shamanistic distinction, and the attainment of a guardian spirit.
Using familiar Boasian methods, Benedict plotted the distribution of these
traits and then examined the patterns in which they occurred. But in analyzing how the various groups in her sample crystallized these specific traits
into characteristic patterns she argued that these patterns were reflections of
the prevalent *psychological attitude* of the different societies.

Benedict's work of this kind culminated in *Patterns of Culture* (1934).
In an obituary of Benedict, Margaret Mead refers to it as "one of the great
books of the second quarter of the twentieth century" (Mead 1949:460). It is
also one of the clearest instances of the paradigm that we are discussing.

For those who are unfamiliar with this book, it is a contrasting study of
three cultures—Dobuan, Pueblo, and Kwakiutl. Her main theoretical
premise is that each culture is analytically reducible to a single psychological rubric: the Dobuans are paranoid, the Pueblos are Apollonian, and the
Kwakiutl Dionysian. In developing this psychological idiom Benedict was
influenced by several authors whose works were already more or less based
on the same configurational paradigm. One of these nonanthropological
sources was Spengler's way of looking at history. She also read the works of
the German philosopher and historian Wilhelm Dilthey, who explained any
particular historic period in terms of its *Zeitgeist*, or "spirit of the times." A
Zeitgeist was similar to Spengler's leitmotifs in that it was an underlying
motif that gave a special quality to a period and was associated with a particular *Weltanschauung*, or world view (Dilthey 1957, 1961).[7] Benedict also
seems to have been influenced by Gestalt psychology, which developed out
of experiments with perception. It is based on the hypothesis of stress systems in individuals that predispose them to combine perceived elements into
complete forms, doing which reduces the stress. In other words, the theory
is that the mind inherently tends to form coherent structures, patterns, or as
they are called in German, *Gestalten*. Like Spengler's civilizations, Dilthey's
Weltanschauungen, and Benedict's patterns, *Gestalten* are held to be greater
than the sum of their parts.

Since *Patterns of Culture* was published in 1934 a large critical literature has grown up around it. There are four main criticisms, which are worth looking at since they are also implicitly criticisms of the underlying configurational paradigm: (1) *Psychological reductionism.* Speaking in a psychological metaphor, as she did, Benedict said that a culture was a "personality writ large." Many anthropologists object to this, arguing that cultural and social phenomena cannot be explained in terms of individual psychological traits. (2) *Cultural particularism.* Benedict adopted an extreme cultural relativism in arguing that each culture was a unique configuration of traits which was valid and complete in itself. Critics have argued that if this is so, how then can cultures be compared; what can serve as a basis for comparison? Aside from limited problems in analyzing how a culture rejects or accepts and modifies alien traits, there is no analytic framework here for an historical or evolutionary examination of a culture, nor a scheme for looking at its relationships with its geography or its productive system. (3) *Oversimplified diversity.* A number of papers have been written demonstrating exceptions to Benedict's characterization of the three societies. They argue that a culture is too complex and has too much internal variation to be summed up under a single rubric. (4) *Neglect of personality acquisition. Patterns of Culture* was written before Benedict's later interest in childrearing, and offers no explanations of how the members of a given culture acquire its characteristic personality.

These are valid criticisms of *Patterns of Culture,* and of the configurational paradigm in general. I list them here so that the reader may keep them in mind while assessing the usefulness of the world-view model presented in the following chapters.

Benedict's star student, Margaret Mead, was one of the first to respond to the last of the above criticisms, and along with various psychiatrically oriented researches began to examine the problem of cultural influences on personality formation. In this way another variation of the configuration paradigm developed as a new speciality in anthropology. Its aim was to study the "basic personality" of the members of a society. Whereas Benedict's methods were largely literary and intuitive, the new "culture-and-personality" school drew heavily from psychoanalytic theory and attended especially to the problem of personality formation.

While culture-and-personality theory has much in common with world-view theory, there is one fundamental difference: culture-and-personality theory, deriving largely as it does from psychoanalysis, is concerned mainly with the expression of affect. It is consistent in this regard with Freud's so-called hydraulic model of personality, which accounts for the channeling and transformations of libidinal energy. In contrast, the study of world view is more concerned with the rational functions of the mind. Rather than attempting to analyze the influence of culture on needs and emotions, it seeks to understand cross-cultural variations in the logic, structuring, and content of systems of thought having to do with the general nature of reality.

One cultural idealist who leveled the third criticism mentioned above was Morris Opler. Unlike Benedict, Opler (1945, 1968) argues that it is improbable that an entire culture can be dominated by a single pattern, and so in his work he attempted to surmount this problem of oversimplification by describing multiple "themes." These themes are "dynamic affirmations," "which are found, in limited number, in every culture and which structure the nature of reality for its members" (Barnouw 1963:104). Opler thus departs from the classic configurational paradigm by identifying multiple configurations, or "themes" as he calls them. Another important distinction is that he sees themes as interacting and balancing one another. Opler, however, does not elaborate on these dynamic relationships that exist among themes, but treats them minimally in a commonsensical way. For example, one theme among the Chiricahua Apache is valuation of long life and old age. "But there is another theme, 'validation by participation,' which limits the first. An old man is admired and respected as long as he is active and fit, but when he can't keep pace with younger men, his years and knowledge do not prevent his retirement" (Barnouw 1963:104).

Similar to Opler's themes are what E. Adamson Hoebel (1954) calls *postulates*. He used this concept in a study of primitive law to explain the logic and workings of different legal systems by showing how they are understandable once the underlying legal postulates are understood. Hoebel also isolated 16 postulates that organize Cheyenne culture (Hoebel 1960: 98–99). For example, Postulate 1 states, "The world (universe) is fundamentally a mechanical system with a limited energy quotient which progressively diminishes as it is expended." And Postulate III is, "Man is subordinate to supernatural forces and spirit beings. These forces and beings have superior knowledge concerning the operation of the universe and are benevolently inclined toward man." This postulate has a corollary: "Tribal well-being and individual success are abetted by the tutelage or blessings of the supernaturals" (ibid.: 98). And in another ambitious attempt to discover cultural postulates Francis L. K. Hsu (1981) has derived postulates of the total culture of China and the United States.

Hoebel's postulates are similar to Opler's multiple themes, but are more formalized and have their corollaries. In my study of world view in the Mexican village of Ixtepeji (Kearney 1972) I also derived a set of interrelated propositions that organize sociocultural behavior and beliefs. It is in this study of Ixtepeji, in Opler's discussion of how themes balance one another, in Hoebel's corollaries, and in Foster's "cognitive orientations" (see below) that we can see a suggestion of what I refer to below as *logico-structural integration*. Benedict and the other monothematic configurationalists that I have mentioned were also concerned with explaining how cultural traits were integrated. But their approach was more what we can refer to as aesthetic-stylistic. That is, their analyses were based primarily on the presence of a pattern of cultural traits whose existence could be subjectively apprehended much as we recognize the particular personality of a friend or of an art style. Following this strategy in his later work, Alfred Kroeber attempted to identify the "super-styles" of various civilizations and trace their growth. As for methods, "The mental processes called for in dealing with styles are somewhat different from those ordinarily used by the historian or scientist" (Kroeber 1963:70). This perception of a style is a "total, immediate and final judgement," which "is neither inductive nor deductive."

A recent successful use of a monothematic analysis of large areas of Mexican peasant cultural behavior, and of peasant behavior in general, is Foster's (1965a, 1967) "Image of Limited Good" (see Chapter 7). Foster's model is more strictly a world-view approach in that it deals with a major "cognitive orientation," as contrasted with Benedict's and Kroeber's stylistic and aesthetic configurations. By referring to this one *idée fixe*, i.e., that many desired things in the community are seen existing in finite supply insufficient to satisfy the wants of all members of the community, Foster accounts for such diverse things as economic behavior, folktales, medical beliefs and practices, friendship patterns, and mother-child relations. Although based on one fundamental proposition, Foster's model does contain an internal logic that generates corollary orientations. Most notable is one which has to do with a principle of equilibrium that regulates certain folk concepts of causality in physical and biological phenomena, and reciprocity in interpersonal relations.

WORLD VIEW AND ETHNOSEMANTICS

In recent years several offshoots of the configurational paradigm have developed, which may be referred to generally as "ethnosemantics." These new approaches to cognitive anthropology share some important similarities and differences with the concept of world view presented in the following chapters. It is therefore worthwhile to examine this related but different field.

The primary task of any science is to discover orderly arrangements and patterns among the observed phenomena, and then to describe them adequately. The description of human cultural phenomena presents a problem that is not present in the physical sciences and the natural sciences that study nonhuman animals. In these disciplines there is only one apparent way to describe, and that is according to principles and in a language that are of the investigator's own choosing. But in cultural anthropology, the nature of the phenomena studied—human psychology and behavior viewed cross-culturally—introduces another dimension—the existence of the "natives' " ideas about *their* environments and themselves as *they* see them, and their ability to talk about them.

In the 1960s and early 1970s ethnosemantics was concerned primarily with perception and thought about the world as reflected in culturally specific labels—names. A basic assumption here is that the naming of things is an important indicator of cognition. Ethnosemantics as such has been essentially the study of the internal ordering of groups of nouns—mainly folk taxonomies and paradigms—in different languages. Ethnosemantic studies also have several other general features in common: (1) They take as their subject matters areas of culture content that are defined as such by native criteria, rather than by analytic categories of theoretical anthropology. (2) They attempt to discover units and dimensions of meaning within these domains, again according to principles inherent in the native systems. (3) As of yet, most of the applications of these approaches have been to relatively small and finite ethnosemantic domains, such as kin terms, aspects of folk medicine, ethnobotany, or ethnocuisine. (4) They do not, for the most part, investigate how the idea systems relate to behavior, nor how they change through time.[8]

Like the ethnosemantic approaches, world-view theory is also concerned with how the perception and organization of reality vary cross-culturally. But it differs from them in several important ways. First of all it deals with much larger domains, viz., the total perceived reality, or the "world" itself, as it is apprehended and cognitively organized in culturally specific ways. It thus represents an attempt to describe the perception and experiencing of life by peoples of other cultures. And, as noted above, one of the main assumptions of ethnosemantics is that naming is a basic way of imposing order on perception. Ethnosemantics therefore tends to be limited to semantic domains for which the natives have existing named items and relationships among them that the anthropologist can verbally elicit. In contrast, informants are far less likely to be capable of verbally expressing their world view. It is in effect a deeper structure, and one that the anthropologist seeks to reconstruct from nonverbal as well as verbal behavior.

Another distinction between world-view study and ethnosemantics is that the ethnosemanticists limit their search for meaning to dimensions that are internal to the domains being analyzed. These orderings of culture content are essentially diagrammatic and static, but do imply certain formal logical relationships (Tyler 1969b:16–18). In world-view study, however, in addition to analyzing internal, or what I call logico-structural relationships (see Chapters 2 and 5) that exist among the contents of a world view, there is also an interest in the dynamic three-way relationship that exists among a world view, associated behavior, and the sociocultural and geographic environment in which they occur.

Ethnosemanticists, like all cultural idealists, insist that they are attempting to describe the cultural knowledge, rules, or norms that will account for appropriate types of behavior in general, rather than specific acts. This strategy ignores the fact that much human social behavior involves breaking and manipulating rules and norms and creating new ones. Appropriate behavior is often an ideal that is observed in the breach. The cultural idealists counter this observation with the need to study rules for breaking rules. But to follow this line of investigation leads us into the world of practical affairs. Arriving here, we find that one of the ways people advance their interests as individuals and groups is by devising strategies to do so. An important aspect of this infighting is the attempt to impose norms of your making on your adversaries, to get them to play the game according to your rules. This amounts to a reversal of the causality the cultural idealists describe: instead of the behavior being a result of the rules, the rules are artifacts of behavior.

As Harris (1979:269–278) points out, only limited success can be achieved in attempting to account for behavior by analysis of cognitive rules. But, "in principle, the great bulk of rules can be predicted from a sufficiently detailed knowledge of behavior stream events—especially, of course, those involving the . . . infrastructure" (ibid.: 270). This predictability has more than one cause, but one is the causal priority of behavior and of context over their mental reflections. There is feedback between the two realms, but the cognitivists give priority to the tail of the dog.

The prevalence of idealist assumptions in ethnosemantics and cognitive anthropology in general is due in large part, aside from the conservative ideological bias of this strategy, to the close association of American anthropology with linguistics. Linguistics has served as the main model for the idealist conception of culture in general. The first major breakthroughs in modern linguistics were in phonetics—the sound system of a language. Phonetics is the only aspect of culture which has an internal dynamics that functions with a high degree of autonomy from behavioral and environmental contexts. For several generations mainstream linguistic theory has been built on the assumption that all other levels of language could also be successfully reduced to rules that do not take into account conditions external to language. The limitations of this strategy have become most apparent in contemporary semantics, which only in the last generation has been generally accepted as a legitimate branch of the discipline. The inclusion of semantics in idealist linguistics did not come about, however, out of any great concern to relate linguistic theory to practical affairs, to language use in daily life. Instead, linguists were driven to incorporate semantic rules because they are necessary to adequately model grammar. It is now apparent that just as syntactic rules must include semantic rules, so semantic rules must take into account completely nonlinguistic features of the environment. Language, which was once thought to be a totally self-contained mental world, has been found to be largely dependent on the social and material setting in which it functions.

Unfortunately for the development of American anthropology, contemporary Boasians not only pattern the study of culture on linguistics, but moreover the linguistics they choose is the "synchronic" linguistics of Saussure (1966). This type of structural linguistics is logico-structurally comparable to metaphysics in its ideological import, in that for the most part it disregards both individual and social change. "Thus, the object of study is not the language-using individual (who is, of course, continuously changing within changing sociocultural conditions) but an abstract being removed from or fixated upon a particular point in individual and historical time" (Riegel and Rosenwald 1975:xi). Saussure also proposed a "diachronic linguistics," which was supposed to describe historical development, but all this did was study language at different points in time, and therefore it was not fundamentally different from synchronic linguistics.

> A design of this type, a time-lag design, compares different generations or cohorts with one another. Thus it merely explores historical differences but not as claimed "historical development through time." To study such changes, the investigation would have to be combined with longitudinal methodology. . . . Subsequently the individual would have to be reintroduced into the analysis, the individual who through his own changes with and within his cohort or generation has made historical development possible at all. However, introducing the individual into the analysis would be contrary to Saussure's primary goal: to establish the autonomy of linguistics by eliminating psychology. Unfortunately, by liberating linguistics from psychology, Saussure also eliminated the most important object of study, the language-using individual. (ibid.: xi–xii)

It is interesting to speculate how ethnosemantics would have developed in American anthropology if instead of being based on idealist linguistics it had been built on models of language consistent with historical materialism, such as those of Lev Vygotsky and Jean Piaget. Vygotsky and Piaget (both born 1896) developed models of language as aspects of their general theories of cognitive development and functioning. These general theories are materialist in that both start from practical motor activities, pass from them to the concrete, and then to the abstract. They are interactionist (dialectic) in that instead of being based on either empiricist (priority given to the environment) or rationalist (priority given to "mind") premises, they assume that knowledge arises from the organism interacting with and changing its environment. Thought and language both have their origin in motor action. "Indeed, knowledge does not start in the subject (through somatic knowledge or introspection) or in the object (for perception itself contains a considerable measure of organization), but rather in interactions between subject and object and in other interactions originally set off by spontaneous activity of the organ as much as by external stimuli" (Piaget 1971:27–28). "Rational, intentional conveying of experience and thought to others requires a mediating system, the prototype of which is human speech born of the need of intercourse during work" (Vygotsky 1962:6). This general model is in broad outline the same as the model of world view presented here. It is especially Vygotsky (1962, 1978) who recognizes the practical and social functions of language as that which most shapes it (see also Volosinov 1973). In this respect language is analogous with tools. Following Engels's discussion of the transforming power of tools, Vygotsky shows how language develops because of its mediating position between humans, and between humans and environment. From this perspective the study of knowledge systems (ethnoscience) in the abstract is plowing a sterile field. A more fertile strategy would seem to be to investigate how systems of knowledge arise out of activities and how they in turn organize behavior.

Recently some cognitive anthropologists have become more concerned with action, or praxis, as Marxists prefer to say. Thus, whereas I noted above that ethnosemantics has dealt primarily with nouns, there is presently, within this general field, a growing concern with verbs. This is apparent in recent anthropological studies of the cognitive processes involved in decision-making and action plans in such areas as economics (Gladwin and Gladwin 1971; Randall 1977), social structure (Quinn 1975), law (Quinn 1976), medical anthropology (Young 1981) and migration (Stuart and Kearney 1981).[9] Because decision-making theory is concerned to dialectically relate cognition to action it is consistent with world-view theory, and the relevance of world-view theory to the study of decision-making is obvious. People make decisions on the basis of their images and assumptions about their life situations. These include their ideas about cause-and-effect relationships, time and space, and other culturally specific variants of the other world-view universals. World view is thus the cognitive background that influences the perception of alternatives and choices made among them.

A world view is the greater conceptual framework within which exist the smaller domains studied by ethnosemanticists. World-view studies seek to discover, at much greater levels of abstraction, underlying assumptions about the nature of reality, assumptions that can then be stated by the anthropologist as formal propositions. The theoretical bias here is that these assumptions are systematically interrelated, and that they form a basis for culturally patterned decision making (influenced by values which also derive from these existential assumptions), and for other culturally specific cognitive activity.

Ethnosemantics, because it has dealt mainly with relatively small domains, has been able to achieve considerable rigor, but at the same time, because it does tend to deal with such discrete cognitive areas and disregards nonverbal behavior, it tends to have limited explanatory power. World-view studies, on the other hand, ask questions that have more relevance to the quality of life and to strategies for making a living. But because they are broader, world-view studies are less precise and harder to verify. In other words, in choosing between ethnosemantics and world-view study, as they are both currently developed, a choice must be made between rigor and relevance. One of the objectives of this book is to advance the study of world view such that it can attain greater rigor, while retaining its traditional humanistic objectives.

We can sum up this discussion by saying that ethnosemantics and world-view studies constitute the ends of an academic continuum. The ethnosemantic end is characterized by the identification and analysis of the contents of culturally defined semantic domains, while world-view study takes all of the culturally specific cognition of a people as its subject and attempts to represent it in terms of a set of logically interrelated and structurally consistent propositions and corollary statements that are assumed to model native perception and thinking. World-view theory and ethnosemantics are both concerned with internal ordering of cultural content, but whereas ethnosemantics has for the most part confined itself to this type of problem, the world-view theory presented herein seeks also to discover dynamic interrelations between cognitive structure and content and between external environment and behavior. In this formulation, then, world-view theory corrects the cultural idealism of ethnosemantics and of cognitive anthropology in general (see Chapter 4).

I have so far focused on the differences between ethnosemantics and world view. But this is not meant to imply that they are incompatible. The relationship between them is more correctly seen as one of inclusion: ethnosemantics falls within the larger domain of world-view theory, and as a set of techniques has much to offer world-view theory and study, although as of the present most of this promise is yet to be realized.[10]

The Redfield Tradition

The work of Robert Redfield (1897–1958) is largely independent of the Boas tradition and parallel to it. Boas and his students were associated mainly with Columbia University, where Boas founded the Department of Anthropology. Redfield, associated with the University of Chicago and the Carnegie Institution, had more intellectual affinities with American sociology and British social anthropology than with the Boasian configurationalists. He was not part of the culture-and-personality movement, nor was he affected by the strong influence that linguistics had on the Boasians. His own approach to world view is in its general conception more similar to that of the British social anthropologist Bronislaw Malinowski, who confessed that

> What interests me really in the study of the native is his outlook on things, his *Weltanschauung*, the breath of life and reality which he breathes and by which he lives. Every human culture gives its members a definite vision of the world, a definite zest of life. In the roamings over human history, and over the surface of the earth, it is the possibility of seeing life and the world from the various angles, peculiar to each culture, that has always charmed me most, and inspired me with real desire to penetrate other cultures, to understand other types of life. (Malinowski 1922:517)

In the 1950s Redfield began to analyze world views in a more systematic manner than had previously been done. He maintained the total culture approach of Benedict, but his solution to the problem of oversimplified total patterns was to break a world view down into what I prefer to call world-view universals. Chapter 3 is a discussion of this problem, and therefore as an introduction to it we can review Redfield's ground-breaking work.[11]

Redfield was concerned with one basic question: *How do a people characteristically look outward upon the universe?* His aim was to be able to make comparative statements about different world views, and so in order to do this he set about identifying their common features—what I have just referred to as universals—that could serve as a basis for comparison. Although Redfield used other language, we can state his ideas as follows: He asked, What are the fundamental ways in which all people everywhere conceptually divide up and categorize the phenomena that they perceive? Once this universal structure of world view, this metamodel, is established, then the task would be to fill in the content of specific world views of different societies.

What then are the universal aspects of world view according to

Redfield? First of all he assumed that all men are conscious of a Self within them. The Self is the vantage point from which the "world" is observed; it "is the axis of world view." In addition to this sense of Self, which is defined primarily in contrast to that which is seen as not-Self, there are divisions within the Self. This is an idea that Redfield borrowed from the philosopher George Herbert Mead who distinguished within the individual Self an "I" and a "me." The "me" is that part of the Self that an individual perceives and objectifies within himself, and is largely socially determined. The "I" is the unknown, impulsive, and creative aspect of the Self that results in the ability of an individual to surprise himself; it influences changes in the "me."

Against the Self with its I and me is all else that is perceived in the universe. This general not-Self is in turn split into two fundamental realms, that of the human and that of the not-human. In other words, Redfield assumes that all peoples generalize the sense of Self to at least some other humans, whom they thus distinguish from nonhuman forms of life. Inherent in this dichotomy are attitudes about human nature and about the not-human. Within the set of humans there are invariable distinctions made by all peoples. For example, all societies recognize major differences among sexes, usually dividing them into at least two subsets, and sometimes into more than two. These sexual groupings are also inevitably crosscut by age. Thus, although there are wide cross-cultural variations in ideas and attitudes about aging and the human life cycle, they are all based upon recognized differences in age.

In addition to these dimensions of the human set there are other bases of recognized inequality. While the nature of these inequalities varies from society to society, the notion of inequalities based on other than sexual or chronological differences appears to be universal in human societies. Thus some peoples may pay special attention to power differences of a political, physical, or economic nature whereas others may be more concerned with differences in knowledge or in supernatural powers that exist among the members of the group. These dimensions of the human set may be seen as applying to all humans everywhere, but most typically they are held to be peculiar to one's one group, which is seen as unique and therefore distinct from all other humans (who, according to many world views, may be considered not-human, or not as human as those of the group in question). The human set is thus cleaved into at least two major subsets: We and They. From the individual's point of view then, there are those who belong to his group and those who do not. Obviously an individual may belong to various different groups, which may or may not overlap. Most likely he will strongly identify with one or more of these groups (clan, tribe, nation), and will identify with it largely in the sense that he sees that group in opposition to another group or other groups.

Within the large realm of the nonhuman there is a major cleavage which Redfield felt was best indicated by the terms "God" and "Nature." Using this major tripartite division in world view—Human, Nature, God—Redfield wished to know in what characteristic way different peoples "confronted" the nonhuman (Nature and God). He noted that there is much variation in the central concerns of peoples, with some attending more to the Human, some more to Nature, and some more to God, while others more evenly divide their concerns.

Redfield also reasoned that in relating to the universe all people must take into account extension in space, and duration and periodicity of time, and therefore included space and time as world-view universals. We will discuss these concepts in detail in the next chapter.

So far we have outlined Redfield's universal features of world views, which he proposed as a framework for analyzing and describing them. We can represent this scheme as a three-dimensional diagram (Figure 1) if we do

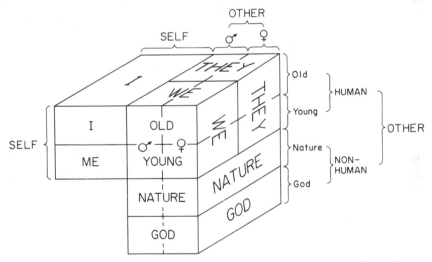

Figure 1. Redfield's World-View Universals (Space and Time Omitted)

not include the last-mentioned universals of Space and Time. The way in which the diagram is compartmentalized thus represents the way Redfield argued that reality is minimally cognitively organized by normal adults of any given society.

Redfield's concept of world view is mainly descriptive. Insofar as he speculated on the causes for differing world views he did so very generally. There were for him two basic types of world views and they were related by historical processes. On the one hand there was the primitive or folk world view characteristic of simple, nonliterate societies. Primitive world view contrasted with that of complex urban societies, and Redfield argued that the former gradually evolved into the latter. But except in this general way he did not attempt to explain why a certain type of society may have one world view, nor how world views change. Nor did he attempt to explain what connection there is between world view, environment, and behavior. These are questions we must attempt to answer if the world-view concept is to be something other than a mere descriptive scheme.

Chapter 2

BASIC CONCEPTS

This chapter begins in earnest a systematic definition of what a world view is, and continues the discussion of how world views, as systems of knowledge, are formed by the interaction of humans and their environments. Concepts presented here, along with the world-view universals of Chapter 3, provide the materials for construction of the world-view model presented in Chapter 4.

WORLD VIEW

The world view of a people is their way of looking at reality. It consists of basic assumptions and images that provide a more or less coherent, though not necessarily accurate, way of thinking about the world. A world view comprises images of Self and of all that is recognized as not-Self, plus ideas about relationships between them, as well as other ideas we will discuss.

From a purely physical point of view we can assume that the phenomenal world is a single continuum of energy and matter in motion. The anthropological study of comparative philosophy (and here we must take notice of the hundreds of cosmologies of nonliterate peoples as well as those of literate peoples) readily demonstrates that there is no general consensus about the nature of reality. Assumptions about reality vary considerably from one group to another, and at bottom they depend upon and affect the actual perception of it. There is now ample evidence that human perception "does not present the human being with a 'picture' of an 'objective' world

41

which, in all its attributes, is 'there' only waiting to be perceived, completely unaffected by the experience, concepts, attitudes, needs, and purposes of the perceiver" (Hallowell 1955:83–84).

Consider for a moment a society as a communication system whose main function is the receiving and sending of information (and energy) among its members and between them and their environment. For such communication to occur there must be conventional agreement regarding codes. This problem is solved for the most part in nonhuman societies by having such conventions genetically encoded into the species as instincts. Among humans, however, codes are far more arbitrary in that they vary from group to group. Rather than inheriting codes per se, the individual inherits the capacity for coding and decoding. Any normal child is thus capable of learning the verbal language and all other communication skills for relating to other humans of its group and to its environment. The important point here is that there must be some conventional agreement among the members of an intercommunicating group as a prerequisite for communication. Each human society has thus, as it were, chosen a particular system of communicating, in the broad sense used above. In other words, each society is a particular arrangement of ideas and behavior. The overall cognitive framework of these ideas and behavior is that society's world view. Another way of stating this is that a world view is the collection of basic assumptions that an individual or a society has about reality.

These assumptions, which can be stated as propositions, are as much a result of the nature of the brain as of the reality to which they refer. That is, there are certain modes of conceptualization necessary for people to interact with themselves and with their environment. We will refer to these as world-view universals. In other words, one theoretical assumption of mine is that world-view categories are universal within the species, and as such constitute fundamental categories of human thought (see Chapter 3). But although these categories are fixed, their contents are not, wherefore there is considerable leeway for filling them with contents which, although different, may be equally, or more, or less adaptive. We will refer to the contents of these categories as *images* or *assumptions,* as defined in the next chapter.

PERCEPTION AND WORLD VIEW

Any complete theory of world view must account for how such a stable, useful representation of the physical and social environment is constructed. All world views must be founded in the real world, though one of the most notable features of human thought is its relative autonomy from reality. The senses provide this contact between mind and reality. World view thus has one of its roots in sensory processes, for the senses are the portal through which the brain receives information about external reality. Hence the problem we now address is the way in which information acquired by the senses is transformed into images and assumptions. To do so we must examine several distinct but related issues.

First: The senses can only receive information which is compatible with physical and structural aspects of the nervous system. Both the potentials and limitations of human world view depend to a great extent on the neuroanatomy and neurophysiology of the sensorium. For example, as Piaget notes somewhere, if we had eyes with facets without the ability to focus, like those of houseflies, or if we were unable to manipulate objects or move ourselves, we would live in a very different cognitive universe. Thus, for example, the world as dogs perceive it is quite different from the world as sensed by humans. This difference is entirely apart from the fact that human and canine nervous systems process information differently after it is sensed. It results instead from the fact that dogs rely on smell to a much greater extent than do humans. Indeed, when speaking of dogs it would be more appropriate to refer to "world smell." And one can further speculate on what the implications would be if we were, for example, sensitive to ranges of electromagnetic wavelengths other than those of normal vision.

Second: Apart from the physical abilities and limitations of the nervous system there are aspects of what, borrowing from computer science, we might call its "software." Here I am referring to such considerations as the presence of principles of logic, of the world-view universals (which organize thoughts into fundamental categories), and of any other innate or acquired structures that determine perceptual selectivity and serve to organize received information and recombine it in new patterns (below, such structures are referred to as anticipatory schemata).

A third and equally important link between thought and reality is action, by means of which thought affects the external environment, the effects of action themselves in turn being perceivable. We will return below to interrelations within this perceptual triad of thought, world, and action.

Sensation and perception are the most discrete aspects of cognition. It is here that information from the outer world impinges on the sensory organs in the form of matter and energy. In some way, which is not yet well understood, over time some of this sensory information becomes generalized and recombined with previously acquired knowledge stored in memory in such a way that it enters into world view and macro thought in general. There are no clear demarcations among these levels of this abstraction hierarchy. In other words, beginning at the level of sensation we have a continuum in which knowledge becomes progressively removed from immediate sensory experience. One consequence of this is that there is relatively greater potential for variation at the upper end of this continuum than at the lower, hence the marked cross-cultural differences in world views. However, even at the lower end, the sensory level, there is a potential for individual and cross-cultural differences.

Although world views differ in the way they represent reality, to be successful, they must have some connection with it. It is therefore theoretically desirable that the approach to macrothought be consistent with that taken to sensation and perception. One such link is via the world-view universals that provide the basic structure of world view, as discussed in Chapter 3. These universals are also for the most part present at the bottom of the abstraction continuum, at least insofar as object, space, time, motion, change, causation, etc., are traditional categories examined by perceptual psychologists. It is therefore possible to follow transformations in these basic categories at different levels along the abstraction hierarchy.[1] Another link is the following: Chapter 4 discusses the way in which a world view is related to the environment. This relationship is essentially dialectical or circular, that is, a partial-feedback model. Briefly, the argument is that experience is the main force shaping the contents of world view, but that environment is only one aspect of experience. The other is the nature of the mind itself—its inherent basic structure, viz., the universals, plus their existing contents resulting from previous experience. The way in which new experiences are perceived and conceptualized depends on how they can be related to or fitted into existing images and assumptions. Similarly, the way in which internally stimulated cognition (such as decision making and imagination) proceeds also depends on existing images and assumptions that are the result of the logico-structural ordering of past experiences.

The dialectic relations between knowledge, action, and environment are represented in Figure 2 by the arrows between different levels of these respective elements.[2]

The circular features of the macrothought aspects of this general model are readily apparent to anyone who has been concerned with individual or cross-cultural differences in behavior and cognition. Until recently, however, they have not been so apparent to cognitive psychologists working on sensation and perception. The traditional empiricist paradigm in psychology for discussing the inputting of sensory information into an organism has been to break sensory stimuli down into elemental aspects (e.g., hue, intensity, temperature). Once having isolated such elemental stimuli, the problem is then to discover how they impinge on the sensory apparatus, and how they become combined into percepts and ultimately concepts. This approach is analogous to the synthesis of complex chemical compounds from atoms. According to this model, various percepts and the memories of others also recombine and form yet more complex mental structures—concepts or images—now far removed from sensation.

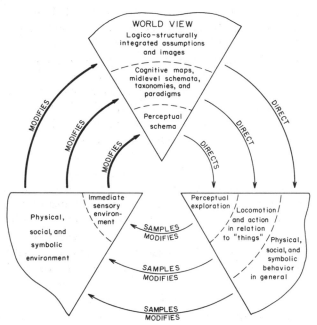

Figure 2. Perceptual Cycles: Schemata and Cognitive Maps Embedded in World View

Recently Neisser and Gibson (see Neisser 1976) have criticized this information-processing approach. They demonstrate that knowledge is organized at all levels—from perception to cognitive maps and images—by anticipatory schemata that determine the selection of new information and the manner in which it is incorporated into these schemata, which in turn become altered in the process. "The schema accepts information as it becomes available at sensory surfaces and is changed by that information; it directs movements and exploratory activities that make more information available, by which it is further modified" (Neisser 1976:54).[3]

It appears that some anticipatory perceptual schemata are present at birth. For example, newborn infants are soon able to focus on and visually track moving objects, look in the direction of sounds, and respond to change in general. But beyond such elementary structures, cognitive schemata are shaped to a large extent by experience, which, because it varies from individual to individual, results in distinct schemata in different individuals. And conversely, insofar as individuals of particular cultures have common perceptual experiences, variations in such structures are identifiable cross-culturally.[4]

Horkheimer points out that since its beginnings materialism regards as real only that which is given through sensory experience, and that it shares this attitude with positivism. " 'What we contemplate in mind has its whole origin in sense perception,' says Epicurus" (Horkheimer 1972:42). But unlike positivist empiricism, historical materialism "does not absolutize sensation." "The requirement that every existent manifest itself through the senses does not mean that the senses do not change in the historical process or that they are to be regarded as fixed cornerstones of the world" (ibid.). Perception results from the dialectic relation of subject with object. This model of perception has, of course, not yet been accepted by most cognitive anthropologists, who still adhere to one form or another of an information-processing model. For example, Spradley (1972:8–11) describes perception and concept formation as nothing more than a one-way process beginning in an object or event, passing through some medium to a sense organ, then through nerves to the brain, where it registers as percept (ibid.: 9, Fig. 1). Percepts are then described as being abstracted and combined into concepts (ibid.: 10, Fig. 2). This model of perception is consistent with the epistemology of idealist anthropology. Ideas and culture in general are assumed to emanate in some vague way from the world, but there is no concern with how they return to and affect it.

Most work in cognitive psychology has focused on the lower or sensory-perceptual end of the abstraction continuum. Insofar as cognitive psychologists have been concerned with higher-level problems the concern has been mostly with cognitive maps and spatial imagery of rather circumscribed fields (see Figure 2). There has also been sporadic work at this mid level on the cognition of time and causality, and anthropologists along with psychologists have been concerned with the investigation of classification at all levels, but again primarily at the mid and lower levels of the domain "universe." Also, most recent study of decision making attempts to model cognitive processes at this level. Since most work on ethnosemantics is done within this range, it is here that the terms "taxonomies" and "paradigms" are commonly used. But as was noted in Chapter 1, this cognitive anthropology has been idealist in conception and therefore has not employed the interactionist methods we are here discussing. Work in perception has also been characterized by attention to only one or two modalities or relationships at a time (e.g., vision, hearing). In contrast with these mid- and low-level examinations of isolated modalities, world-view study entails concern with the formation, mutual influence, and significance for behavior of multiple and higher-level cognitive structures. A world view is, from this approach, an integrated combination of concepts, typical of a particular society, having to do with the nature of things human beings need to know to behave successfully. For the most part, insofar as they are aware of them, humans tend to regard their world-view images and assumptions about time, space, causality, etc., as absolute and true knowledge of reality. Another way of saying this is that most people do not critically analyze the processes whereby their fundamental ideas arise from their senses and past experiences and thereby gain insight into how they might change.

To sum up, what we are dealing with is a set of hierarchical processes which at one end have to do with the physical reception of information from the environment and, at the other end, with the highest abstraction of these primary sensations. At every level information from the environment is received and fitted into pre-existing structures (schemata, cognitive maps, images, assumptions, etc.) that determine how much information can be received and how it is to be organized, and are themselves altered by the received information. At every level the organization of these cognitive structures depends on their previous state, which is as much a given as is the sensory information. Perception and world view are thus products of reality, mind, action, and history.

IMAGES, ASSUMPTIONS, AND PROPOSITIONS

The term *image* is used herein with two meanings. One is the more literal sense of a visual representation in the mind, such as, for example, an image of the earth as an island floating in an immense sea above which are suspended the stars and planets. Mental images may also be experienced in words, or in sensory modalities other than vision, such as auditory or tactile images. Visual imagery is thus only one form of mental representation, but it is no doubt a major one. Thus, we say "I see" to refer to an intellectual "insight" in any mode of representation, and use a metaphor such as "world view" to sum up a general "outlook" on life.

In the history of thinking about thinking, the concept of image has been a central subject. Aristotle regarded such images as the basic units of thought, and argued that thinking consisted of series of images linked together by associations. This idea was popular among psychologists until the twentieth century, when it was demonstrated that much of what is called thinking occurs somewhere outside of consciousness and is therefore "imageless thought." But whether thought is organized into conscious imagery or not, its most notable attribute is an internal organization of sensations, percepts, concepts, and emotions. These organizing principles have been variously called schemata, Gestalten, plans, structures, and so on. Here I will be using the word "image" to refer to such fundamental general perceptions and concepts of reality. Taken together, the total of such primary images constitutes a world view.

Images are thus more or less synonymous with world-view *assumptions*. However, in some contexts it is more convenient to refer to one or the other, so I shall therefore use both terms interchangeably. It is important, however, to distinguish images and assumptions from *propositions.* Assumptions are images of reality that the anthropologist hypothesizes as existing in the world view of a particular individual or group. He states these hypothetical statements as propositions, which he infers from any and all social behavior and expressive productions of the people whose world view he is studying. This means that the location of an image or assumption is in the mind of the people whose world view is being analyzed, while the proposition is in the model that the anthropologist constructs to replicate that world view.[5]

World-view propositions are "as if" statements in the sense that much of social behavior and cultural phenomena (e.g., social organization, myths, folklore, enthnoscience, fantasy, figures of speech, economic decisions) can be explained as if they were predicated on these statements, as I demonstrate in Chapters 5, 6 and 7, and in Kearney (1972). Thus, whereas propositions are explicit formal statements, the assumptions that they presumably replicate are perhaps never consciously formulated by the people who bear them.

In general there are two types of images and assumptions, and corresponding propositions, which we can refer to as first-order and second-order, respectively. The first-order assumptions exist at the core of every world view as the contents of the universals about which I have already hinted and which are discussed at length in Chapter 3. Thus, every world view, as a functioning system of knowledge, must have come to terms with categories of thought such as Time, Space, and Causality. For the most part, these fundamental attitudes are tacit knowledge. That is, although they order much specific content of thought, they are normally not explicitly articulated, and indeed, the native language may lack words to indicate them. Second-order images and assumptions are those that people can readily describe (assuming that they have the appropriate role-specific expertise). These are what we usually call beliefs or folk knowledge. In many ways they can be seen as permutations of the underlying culturally specific forms of the universals. Thus, someone can inevitably describe such things as a people's understanding of creation, human nature and reproduction, and proper behavior. Such explicit, second-order images and assumptions are usually more easily cast as propositions (cf. Tyler 1969b:16–18), while the underlying first-order images and assumptions tend to be more abstract, less explicit, and therefore more elusive.

Presupposition

Within anthropology there is almost no systematic discussion of the concepts which grew out of the Boas tradition that are relevant to world-view theory. I am referring here to the "patterns," "configurations," "themes," "mazeways," "postulates," etc., mentioned above and in Chapter 1. Philosophers, however, have addressed similar issues, and especially the basic understandings which organize different sciences and on which more formal statements and questions rest. R. G. Collingwood is the main advocate of this task. From his *Essay on Metaphysics* (1940:162–171) we learn that he agrees with the logician A. J. Ayer's observation that it is impossible to verify the "propositions" of traditional metaphysics. But rather then accept this impossibility as ground for defining metaphysical issues out of philosophy, Collingwood gives a novel definition to metaphysics. He argues that what Ayer took to be unverifiable propositions are really "absolute presuppositions," which are by their nature neither true or false. This being so, Collingwood says, metaphysics is not a field of philosophy concerned with the truth value of absolute propositions. Instead it is the historical investigation of beliefs about the nature of reality—absolute presuppositions —that scientists have "had" or "made" in different periods, even though they may not have consciously stated them.[6] Collingwood was mainly concerned with the presuppositions of science and other traditions of consciously systematic thought, but there is much in his work which indicates that he was also interested in the prevailing absolute presuppositions of different ages. The metaphysician, as Collingwood defines him,

> . . . has as many worlds to conquer as any conqueror can want. He can study the presuppositions of European science at any phase in its history for which he has evidence. He can study the presuppositions of Arabic science, or Indian science, of Chinese science; again in all their phases, so far as he can find evidence for them. He can study the presuppositions of the science practiced by "primitive" and "prehistoric" peoples. All these are his proper work; not an historical background for his work, but his work itself. (Collingwood 1940:71)

Collingwood desired to subsume philosophy to history as a way of linking theory with practice so as to return to the practical aims of classical philosophy and employ it to avoid human folly such as war. This was to be possible by a proper understanding of the human mind. He is thus resolutely idealist in assuming that we live in "a world which is *essentially* one of thoughts" (Rubinoff 1970:7), in which ideas determine history. He rejects positivism and behaviorism because whereas they treat human nature as only an aspect of nature in general, he approaches it under the problem of freedom.[7] In this regard he is Hegelian and dialectic in rejecting traditional positivistic and metaphysical assumptions about the fixity of the mind or of human nature. These are fascinating aspects of his historical philosophy, but here we are concerned with the relevance of his ideas on presuppositions to what I am calling world-view assumptions.

What are presuppositions? Collingwood's analysis of them proceeds by arguing that every statement that is ever made is made in answer to some question (1940:23), and that all questions are based on presuppositions, which may also have presuppositions that the original question therefore also presupposes. "Whenever anybody states a thought, there are a great many more thoughts in his mind than are expressed in his statement. Among these there are some which stand in a peculiar relation to the thought he has stated: they are not merely its context, they are its presuppositions" (ibid.: 21). Statements as answers to questions are "propositions," but in giving rise to further questions they are "presuppositions." At the base of these chains of questions and answers are "absolute presuppositions," which although generating questions are not themselves answers to prior questions, as are the "relative presuppositions" which derive from them.

> Thus if you were talking to a pathologist about a certain disease and asked him "What is the cause of the event E which you say sometimes happens in this disease?" he will reply "The cause of E is C"; and if he were in a communicative mood he might go on to say "That was established by So-and-so, in a piece of research that is now regarded as classical." You might go on to ask: "I suppose before So-and-so found out what the cause of E was, he was quite sure it had a cause?" The answer would be "Quite sure, of course." If you say, "Why?" he will probably answer "Because everything that happens has a cause." If you are importunate enough to ask "But how do you know that everything that happens has a cause?" he will probably blow up in your face, because you have put your finger on one of his absolute presuppositions, and people are apt to be ticklish in their absolute presuppositions. But if he keeps his temper and gives you a civil and candid answer, it will be to the following effect. "That is a thing we take for granted in my job. We don't question it. We don't try to verify it. It isn't a thing anybody has discovered, like microbes or the circulation of blood. It is a thing we just take for granted."
> He is telling you that it is an absolute presupposition of the science he pursues; and I have made him a pathologist because this absolute presupposition about all events having causes, which a hundred years ago was made in every branch of natural science, has now ceased to be made in some branches, but medicine is one of those in which it is still made. (Collingwood 1940:31–32)

Collingwood's absolute and relative presuppositions are comparable to what I prefer to call first- and second-order assumptions. I prefer to retain my terminology, which I settled on before stumbling across Collingwood, for several reasons. Although there are intriguing similarities with aspects of my model of world view and Collingwood's historical metaphysics, there are important differences. Most notably there is the inherent idealism of Collingwood's general philosophical system. Apart from this is my attempt to analyze first-order assumptions within a framework of world-view universals. Although Collingwood does at times come close to a Kantian position, there is in his work no attempt to formally locate absolute presup-positions within such categories. As regards this point, I maintain that each of the world-view universals contains one or more first-order assumptions (about, e.g., Time, Self, Causality) which themselves may differ from one world view to another. In this strategy the question of invariant features of all human world views is shifted from the issue of possible universal beliefs or assumptions to that of invariant categories of understanding, namely the world-view universals, the contents of which—absolute presuppositions, first-order assumptions, or whatever they be called—may differ from world view to world view. This is not to deny that there may be some universal world-view assumptions. But whether or not there are any is an empirically answerable question, whereas the set of world-view universals is justified on theoretical grounds. Finally there is the important issue, which critics of Collingwood have pounced on, of whether or not presuppositions are con-nected by relationships of question and answer. My lack of commitment to this essential feature of Collingwood's scheme is itself sufficient to warrant a separate terminology.[8]

Ketner (1972) has investigated the relevance of Collingwood's work on presuppositions for world-view theory.[9] He proposes that basic world-view concepts be called "principia" (singular "principium"), which he sees as "the basic, most important beliefs in a world view" (1972:23). He regards them as similar to Collingwood's absolute presuppositions, but prefers to distin-guish them because the essential nature of principia is that they are beliefs. Furthermore, assuming, as Collingwood implicitly seems to, that some beliefs (principia) are more basic than others, he finds need of a term to replace relative presuppositions; for this purpose he proposes "reasoned belief" (ibid.: 71). There are, however, two major liabilities inherent in investing so much in belief as a central feature of presuppositions, principia, or what have you. For one, as Rodney Needham (1972) has persuasively argued, it is quite possible that belief is not a universal human resemblance, but rather a concept peculiar to the Western world. Needham's arguments for this are too complex to go into here, so suffice it to say that they bring into serious question any theoretical interpretation or ethnographic account that purports to deal with belief in non-Western society as if belief were a universal human experience. Any theory of world view that sees world view as a belief system is also seriously called into question by Needham's inquiry. The second reason against defining the basic components of a world view as beliefs is that "belief" implies a consciously held idea. To believe is consonant with saying "I believe." Such a stricture therefore automatically excludes any unconscious content from world view. As both Ketner and Collingwood demonstrate elsewhere, this is not what they in-tend to do.

LOGICO-STRUCTURAL INTEGRATION

The discussion above leads us to the concept, that I refer to as *logico-structural integration*, which is concerned with the ways in which the assumptions of a world-view are interrelated and with how they in turn affect cultural behavior. Chapter 5 deals more fully with this concept, but it can be explained briefly as follows. The organization of world-view assumptions is shaped in two ways. The first of these is due to internal equilibrium dynamics among them. This means that some assumptions and the resultant ideas, beliefs, and actions predicated on them are *logically* and *structurally* more compatible than others, and that the entire world view will "strive" toward maximum logical and structural consistency. The second and main force giving coherence and shape to a world view is the necessity of having to relate to the external environment. In other words, human social behavior, social structure, institutions, and customs are consistent with assumptions about the nature of the world. Therefore, in given environments, some such assumptions are more functional than others, and are therefore more subject to positive selective pressures. Logico-structural integration refers primarily to the first organizing force just mentioned. In the analysis of a world view, such relationships are identified in terms of parallel relationships among the world-view propositions, which presumably replicate those that exist among the assumptions.

The theoretical bias behind the concept of logico-structural integration is that a world view is a dynamic, more or less internally consistent system which demonstrates logical and structural regularities. Furthermore, these regularities persist through time. That is, just as a world view ideally consists of a set of logico-structurally integrated assumptions at any given time, so perturbations in that integration will be influenced by logico-structural principles. The examination of such moving equilibria among assumptions is thus tantamount to an analysis of culture change. Boulding expresses this same idea by saying,

> The stability or resistance to change of a knowledge structure also depends on the internal consistency and arrangement. There seems to be some kind of principle of minimization of internal strain at work which makes some images stable and others unstable for purely internal reasons. (Boulding 1956:13)

Anthony Wallace has also worked on this problem of the integration of culturally constituted cognitive structures. His position, which is basically the same as mine, is that at any given time, every human brain contains "a unique mental image of a complex system of dynamically interrelated objects" which he calls a "mazeway" (Wallace 1970:15). "It consists of an extremely large number of assemblages or cognitive residues of perception and is used by its holder as a true and more or less complete representation of the operating characteristics of a 'real' world" (ibid.). The ways in which such "knowledge structures" are integrated is a problem we must take up below.

So far we have discussed invisible world-view assumptions and abstract theoretical concepts, but always we must return to behavior. Our link from these abstractions to behavior is the theoretical bias that specific world views result in certain patterns of action and not others. Therefore, knowledge of a people's world view should explain aspects of their cultural behavior. The objection might be raised, Would it not be better to merely observe the behavior in question? The answer is that many different kinds of behavior are predicated on relatively few world-view assumptions, such that once the assumptions are understood we are in a position to predict many other different behaviors and meanings, and to understand relationships among them. This is possible because

> a world view is not merely a philosophical by-product of each culture, like a shadow, but the very skeleton of concrete cognitive assumptions on which the flesh of customary behavior is hung. World view, accordingly, may be expressed, more or less systematically, in cosmology, philosophy, ethics, religious ritual, scientific belief, and so on, but it is implicit in almost every act. (ibid.: 143).

No claim is made that this modeling of world view is in itself capable of always predicting logical or structural symmetries among different types of behavior. Environments obviously shape behavior in different areas of life in ways often contrary to ideologies, ideas, or world view. This model assumes, however, that there is an inherent economy of basic cognitive orientations—world view—that tend to result in logico-structural uniformities in all spheres of sociocultural behavior. Where environmental forces shape behavior contrary to these orientations, the world view also in part determines the response. Furthermore, assuming that these cognitive orientations are the single feature common to all the various environment-organism relationships present within a given society, the modeling of these orientations is thus the most readily available way of building conceptual bridges among the otherwise isolated domains studied by cultural anthropologists.

In talking about world views we have stressed their systematic nature and internal consistency. We could not properly approach world views in a scientific manner if they did not have such properties. But in so speaking of them, I have used such qualifiers as "more or less" and "tends to be." This is necessary because it is unlikely that any world view has ever been entirely consistent. Indeed, one of the most intriguing problems in world-view studies is to identify such inconsistencies, of which there are two basic types: external and internal.

External Inconsistency

"External inconsistencies" in a world view result when its images or assumptions are maladaptive or otherwise inappropriate for the reality that the world view presumably mirrors. Thus, at a given point in its history a world view may be a satisfactory cognition of the environment. That is, the culturally patterned perceptions of that environment and the organization of those percepts into concepts are not only internally consistent as discussed above, but also serve to organize behavior such that it is meaningful and adaptive. The study of culture change in general and of the history of science in particular is fundamentally the analysis of this fit or lack of fit between world view and environment.

Let us take as an example a geocentric cosmology such as that which existed in Europe before Copernicus and Galileo. Given the development of astronomy and other sciences at that time, this model was an adequate explanation of the heavens. As this model was applied to more and more astronomic phenomena it had to be continually tinkered with to make it conform to them. It became so cumbersome by the end of the mid-Renaissance that some astronomers began to doubt whether the Ptolemaic model was in its broad outline isomorphic with nature, and they began to seek radically different solutions to explain astronomic and related terrestrial events such as the movements of the sun, the stars, the planets especially, and the changes of the seasons. The result was a shift to a new heliocentric astronomic paradigm.[10] It must also be noted that this particular instance of an external inconsistency reverberated through virtually the entire world view. Thus the shift to an explicit heliocentric image of the universe was not just a new image of astronomy, but one that also had profound implications for the prevalent images of humanity, God, creation, cosmic space, and the millennium. Above we mentioned that world views have a tendency to strive toward consistency. A dramatic example of this is seen in the medieval church branding as heretics those who proclaimed a heliocentric image that was in so many ways incompatible with other images upon which the Christian world view rested. A more cynical interpretation might be that the church authorities were eager to proclaim proponents of this new image as heretics and burn them alive because it threatened the political power of the church. But the point remains that we are still dealing with world-view images, which in this case served either to rationalize or diminish ecclesiastical power. We will return to a fuller comparison of the integration of these two cosmologies in Chapter 5.

The example just offered is an external inconsistency concerning a single image being out of line with reality, reality being that the sun actually does not revolve around the earth. But sometimes it appears that many different images of a world view may become grossly out of line with reality in the sense that they are maladaptive for the people who bear them. For example, anthropological literature contains many examples of what happens to native peoples when they are overrun by the destructive representatives of more powerful societies, such as those of Europe or the United States. Historically, such contact has often resulted in the ethnocide of the native peoples. From the point of view of individuals within such disrupted societies, this experience is apt to create "an image of a world that is unpredictable, or barren in its simplicity, or both, and is apt to contain severe identity conflicts" (Wallace 1970:189). Often when such a society is in its death throes, or "period of cultural distortion," what seems to be a last-ditch collective attempt to survive occurs. Characteristically these "revitalization movements," as Wallace calls them, involve in certain individuals an extensive cognitive reorganization which is essentially an attempt to create a new world view that is more consistent with reality.

A variant of the external inconsistencies we have been discussing occurs when people with differing world views come into contact with one another. Just as holding world-view assumptions in common allows members of a community to understand one another, so does the holding of disparate assumptions create problems in cross-cultural communication. The ethnographic literature on contact between culturally different societies is filled with examples such as the following. In the late 1800s, in response to disintegration of their societies and economies due to disastrous intrusion of white people, many North American Indian peoples accepted the tenets and practices of a revitalization movement (see above) known as the Ghost Dance. A basic idea in this new political and religious movement was that the white people would disappear in some catastrophe and the dead relatives of the living Indians would return and usher in a general state of well-being. Most Indian people who had suffered in their confrontation with the whites readily accepted the ideology and practices of the Ghost Dance. But due to phobic attitudes about death, the Navaho rejected the Ghost Dance out of hand.

> For the Navaho with his almost psychotic fear of death, the dead and all connected with them, no greater cataclysm than the return of the departed or ghosts could be envisaged. In short, the Navaho were frightened out of their wits for fear the tenets of the movement were true. (Hill 1944:525)

Contradiction and disparities between world views are an important force affecting the historic development of world views. The tensions among them and resultant changes are comparable to the ideological strains and struggles that occur within a complex society as an aspect of class struggle. This is an important but complex issue in world-view theory to which a separate study must be devoted. Except for a brief look at some of the inconsistencies and ideological implications arising out of the differences between biblical and scientific world views (Chapter 5), we will not deal with it further in this one.

WORLD VIEW AND TRUTH

Apart from the functional value of a world view in allowing its bearers to successfully adapt to their environment is the question of whether or not it is an accurate representation of that reality in some absolute sense. For, as we shall see in more detail in Chapter 5, it is possible for people to live effectively with world views consisting of erroneous images and assumptions of physical reality—as compared with the images and assumptions of some other world view that is presumably more valid. If world-view theory is to advance beyond the limp relativism which now dominates cultural anthropology, this issue must be confronted. Such an attempt to assess the validity of world views is to cross the artificial threshold between ethnology and philosophy. Our exploration of this nether world will be made easier by a few observations on some of the terms we have so far established.

World-view assumptions have only one type of truth value while world-view propositions have two: assumptions in some sense either coincide with (are true statements about) reality or they do not. Similarly, world-view propositions when they accurately replicate assumptions (make them explicit) can be judged against reality in the same way. But in addition to this there is the question of whether or not the proposition is in fact an accurate representation of the assumption. The verification of this type of validity when dealing with tacit assumptions is a central issue in world-view methodology. Verification of the first type of truth is primarily the task of natural science and philosophy, while verification of the second is the task of anthropology.

As regards my distinction between assumptions and propositions, there is in Collingwood's terminology a parallel distinction between "absolute presuppositions" and "metaphysical propositions." "It will be clear that the true metaphysical propositions are true historical propositions and the false metaphysical propositions false historical propositions. It is the proper business of a metaphysician to answer [for example] the question what absolute presuppositions are or were made by Newtonians, Kantians, Einsteinians, and so forth. These are historical questions" (1940:55). Collingwood quite rightly maintains that metaphysical propositions may be true or false, depending on whether or not they accurately replicate what the person or persons in question actually presupposed. He also argues quite strongly that absolute presuppositions are neither true nor false. Part of the reason for this, Collingwood says, is because they are not formal propositions, and as such their logical effectiveness for the relative presuppositions based on them does not depend on their being true. Collingwood's reasons for exempting absolute presuppositions from all tests of validity is also explained by his view of history as a dialectical process in which truth is arrived at historically. Thus, it is not a question of the absolute presuppositions of particular persons at a particular time in history being true or false when judged against reality, as it is of them doing the best that they could with the ideas given them by history. "An absolute presupposition cannot be undermined by the verdict of 'experience', because it is the yard-stick by which 'experience' is judged" (Collingwood 1940:194–195). I am unwilling to accept this philosophical skepticism, however congenial it may be with cultural relativism. Even though the truthfulness of someone's absolute presuppositions (first-order assumptions) must of necessity be judged against the yardstick of someone else's, still at our own point in history we have the advantage of looking back and making educated judgments about features of other world-views which simply do not coincide with reality as we see it from our position where possibly we are the beneficiaries of more comprehensive and exacting observations, which are dialectically involved with more valid world-view assumptions. [11]

It appears that Collingwood is taking this position in part as a reaction to the realism of the logical positivists and positivistic behaviorists who, as he points out, are consciously unaware, and therefore naively uncritical, of their own absolute presuppositions. Since his epistemology is historical, the question for him is not whether someone's absolute presuppositions are true or false, but whether they are fruitful negations and therefore an advance over those that precede them, in a word, whether they are effective. There is a solution to this impasse between Collingwood and his positivist adversaries, which avoids both the naive realism of the latter and the skepticism of the former. We may evaluate different world-view assumptions as more-or-less accurate representations of reality, as judged by some presumably more valid historical perspective. This is quite consistent with both Hegelian and Marxist dialectic views of history, the epistemology of which assumes a progressive movement of knowledge.

Such a view of comparative epistemology does two things. First, it allows for a modified version of Collingwood's insistence that the question of validity does not apply to them. Second, it rejects the simplistic either-or requirements of logical positivism, which holds that all propositions are either true or false. This view, when applied to absolute presuppositions, comes from not accepting most of them as the highly metaphoric statements that they are. In other words, I think that the logical positivists' insistence on absolute testability of statements to qualify as propositions depends on a failure to recognize the metaphoric nature of ordinary language. Metaphors are such that if taken literally they are usually not true, but this is not cause for rejecting their intended meaning or all aspects of the presuppositions that underlie them, albeit that they are stated in a hazy manner. We can take an example from Collingwood, which he uses for a different purpose. At one point he discusses how the absolute presuppositions underlying the concept of monotheism were necessary logical and temporal precursors to modern natural science, based as it is on the absolute presuppositions that "in any realm of nature there are certain laws which hold good not only there but in all other natural realms without exception . . ." (Collingwood 1940:205). The germ of this idea occurs in monotheism. By contrast, a polytheistic assumption is analogous to disparate natural sciences in which each science consists of the study of phenomena that obey natural laws not operative in the other sciences. In such a situation, discoveries in one science would be of no relevance for the others. Viewed this way, monotheism is in part false and in part true: it is false in presupposing the presence of a humanlike but suprahuman being somehow superior to human will and knowledge, but it is true that its presupposition of uniform causes in nature coincides with modern scientific presuppositions.

This comparative and relative (in the sense of more-or-less) attitude to world-view validity is conducive to an understanding of the historic process whereby knowledge asymptotically approximates reality. An assumption —an absolute presupposition, as Collingwood would say—of this attitude is that human consciousness is progressive. Consciousness at some time in the past differentiated from matter and is in the course of human evolution becoming more and more conscious of itself and its material substrate. Or if you prefer a different metaphor, we can say that matter is becoming progressively more conscious of itself. This process is dialectical in the various senses used in this book. It is the absence of any understanding of this dialectical nature of knowledge that cripples modern positivist philosophy and science.

Internal Inconsistency

The second type of inconsistency that may exist in a world view, what we may call *internal inconsistency*, results from contradictions among its assumptions or images. Such inconsistencies often result from assumptions of one historic period being retained into another in which a new social order has generated a different set of assumptions. Certain conflicting assumptions embedded in the Old and New Testament are a case in point. For example, to an agnostic, it appears that there is a fundamental logical contradiction in some of the major premises of modern Christianity. There is one set of basic premises which maintain that God is omnipotent and benevolent. At the same time, another basic belief is that the Devil, or some less personified source of evil, is loose on the earth causing sin and suffering of the most excruciating sort. A moment's speculation reveals a contradiction here in the existence of a presumably benevolent God who allows such suffering which He has the power to prevent.[12] Now above, I referred to world views as having a tendency to strive toward consistency. This means that internal contradictions of this kind are bothersome and that the "system" strives to resolve or minimize them. Thus for example, the history of Christian theology and Scholasticism can be seen as mainly a vast intellectual gymnastic feat attempting to resolve this inconsistency. Another such contradiction in medieval and Calvinistic Christianity existed between the doctrines of divine predestination and free will. Such contradictions may exist in various degrees of conscious awareness. Thus, whereas the ones mentioned just above are of great conscious concern to theologians, common people may never reflect upon them, even though they permeate the fabric of their religion. When the student of world view discovers such implicit inconsistencies, ". . . a key task will be to show how this incoherence does not appear as such to the members of the society or else does appear and is somehow made tolerable" (MacIntyre 1970:71).

The problem of identifying internal inconsistencies is not as straightforward as it might appear. Let me give an example. Once, while living in the Mexican peasant village of Ixtepeji, I became interested in the way that Ixtepejanos conceived of their *santos* — the wood and plaster statues, or paintings of saints that they keep in their church, as well as other miraculous *santos* that they know of elsewhere in Mexico. For the Ixtepejanos, the actual figure itself is the *santo*. That is, rather than thinking of the figure as a representation or reminder of the *santo's* ethereal substance, they deem the actual tangible statue or painting the unique abode of that *santo's* essence and power. Each *santo* is regarded as a distinct individual spiritual being with its own distinct personality. Thinking about this, I was struck by an apparent logical inconsistency: throughout Mexico, the most important *santos* are various highly revered "representations"[13] of the Virgin Mary. Individual Ixtepejanos thus may enter into special relationships with, say, the Virgin of Juquila, as opposed to the Virgin of La Soledad or the Virgin of Guadalupe. I then asked how could these separate, unique *santos* also each be the mother of Christ, or God, as the Ixtepejanos also maintain? When I have explicitly posed this problem to Ixtepejanos, they have not been overconcerned. They are certainly able to recognize the formal nature of the contradiction (i.e., "Jesus can have but one mother," versus "There are many holy Virgins who are each the mother of Jesus"), but for reasons which are too involved to go into here, I am convinced that this contradiction is not meaningful or real within their world view.[14]

Above we have been talking about logical consistency, which represents the logical aspect of logico-structural integration. We must now specify more exactly what we mean by this term; first let us examine the logical aspect of it.

Although logicians and mathematicians have devised various formal logics, and anthropologists, especially linguistically oriented ones, have asserted that different languages and cultures consist of different logical systems, it seems safe to assume that underlying all systems of logic, both native and formal, there are invariable logical principles, or what Boole called "the laws of thought": (1) the principle of identity, (2) the principle of contradiction, and (3) the principle of excluded middle. These principles can be formulated as: (1) If anything is A it is A, i.e., if any proposition is true, it is true. (2) Nothing can be both A and not-A, i.e., no proposition can be both true and false. (3) Anything must be either A or not-A, i.e., any proposition must be either true or false (Cohen and Nagel 1962:181–182). To this list might be added the principles of the syllogism, tautology, and others.[15] Although many anthropologists have asserted that peoples of different cultures think differently,

> the evidence to support [such] logical pluralism has so far been unconvincing. Some "different" logics appear to be merely variants comparable to contrasts in emphasis on class products as opposed to relative products or preferences for probabilistic versus true-false truth values. And some appear to be based on mistaken assumptions about the primitiveness or irrationality of non-Western or ancient thinking. (Wallace 1969:538)[16]

An important distinction to note is that the above presumed logical universals have to do with consistency and inconsistency among propositions and not with thoughts. Failure to realize this distinction has caused most of the confusion regarding so-called "prelogical mentality," which among other things was assumed to lack a clear notion of identity.[17] To illustrate this type of confusion we can examine the thinking of a Mexican spiritualist friend of mine who occasionally tells me that a neighboring *bruja* (witch) has come as an owl to molest her. Now, her thinking might be interpreted as asserting that a human being can also be an owl, which would seem to violate the principle of identity. But this is not what she means; she means that the witch comes in *the form* of an owl, which is one of the forms that this witch can take. Human form, owl form, and coyote form are simply different forms of something called a witch that has underlying essential features and continuity. Such an assertion is logically no different from asserting that water can also appear as ice or steam. The confusion about the presumed lack of the principle of identity results from confusing the content of such statements as my friend's with their logic. The creature hooting at her may or may not be a witch, but this is an empirical, not a logical issue. Given my friend's folk concepts about witches, it is not illogical for her to assume that an owl form, under certain circumstances, is a witch.

As the above example demonstrates, there are two types of truth in a world view. First, there is absolute truth having to do with empirical facts, for example, assumptions about the shape of the earth or whether witches exist. Second, there is formal truth having to do with the relationships among assumptions, which are either consistent or inconsistent with each other according to basic logical principles. For example, if it is assumed that the world is a spheroid, then it follows that it is potentially possible to travel around it, and vice versa. Assessment of the truth value of the first type is a scientific and philosophical problem and is not the central concern of world-view study. Investigation of the formal consistency of world-view assumptions is also an empirical problem in that the content of native thought must be inferred from observations and elicitations, and then formalized as propositions; but here we are concerned with the native view of reality rather than the reality that the native view cognizes. Once we have established such a set of propositions we can then examine them for internal consistency. This is not to say, however, that the formal truth value of all possible combinations of propositions in our model can be determined since many will be logically unrelated, for example the propositions that the earth is the center of the universe and that time repeats itself.

When I say that the logical consistency among propositions of a world-view model can be analyzed, I mean so in the same sense that formal logicians do. But also, in a less formal sense, world-view propositions are consistent or inconsistent in the same way that a well-constructed novel is "logically" consistent. For example, if it is a basic proposition of some particular world view that the phenomena of the world tend to be more or less erratic and nonpredictable, then it is logically inconsistent for the same people to assume that the future is foreseeable, or that natural processes are basically orderly and regulated by uniform natural laws. Likewise, in such a society, one would not expect to find well-developed folk methods for telling fortunes. If the proposition about randomness and unpredictability is an accurate statement about this aspect of a world view, then, within the logic of this hypothetical world view, fortune telling is ipso facto impossible. By the same token, an outside observer who had been informed of this proposition might expect that games of chance would be present in this society.

Analysis of logical relationships within a world view takes us only so

far in understanding how it is integrated. To further reveal the architecture of a system of knowledge one must avoid what Dykstra (1960:67)
calls the characteristic tendency of philosophers to "overrationalize" human
behavior by assuming that presuppositions are linked only by entailment or
some other principle of formal logic, when they in fact have some
psychological, biological, or sociological cause. It is these other systematic relationships existing among world-view assumptions which I refer to
by the catchall term "structural," and hence the term "logico-structural
integration."[18]

The "structural" aspect of logico-structural integration refers to various
types of replications in the forms of world-view images and assumptions
that can be seen as permutations of more primary ones. Speaking figuratively, we can say that whereas logical integration results from rules that
order the fitting together of assumptions, structural integration results from
the way in which images are formed by templates, such that although they
have different content, they are structurally analogous. Whereas logical
integration has to do with formal relations—such as whether or not Jesus
can have one or more than one mother, or an omnipotent benevolent god
would allow suffering—structural integration has to do with such things as
the similarity between, say, images of physiological and social processes
(Douglas 1966:114–128). Another instance of such structural replication
occurs in an analysis of cultural themes in North India by Morris Opler.
Among the various themes that Opler identifies is one having to do with
hierarchy, whereby such disparate things as castes, supernaturals, and parts
of the body are all hierarchically ordered in accord with what, in my
terminology, appears to be an underlying image of hierarchy (Opler 1968).
In this instance there is no logical necessity that castes, gods, and body parts
be conceived as so ordered; there is simply an apparent replication of a
common image.

In some instances it is significant whether we treat world-view contents
as assumptions or images, since it is often possible to translate from one
idiom to the other. In general, speaking of assumptions implies that logical
integration is at work, whereas imagery implies structural integration.

As an example of how it is possible to transform a world-view statement from a structural to a logical form we can anticipate a concept developed in the next chapter. There I propose the idea that some distinction
between *Self* and *Other* is the fundamental structure of all world views. The
cosmos is in effect divided into these two paramount domains, and this
division, in turn, results in a number of potential relationships between Self
and Other. For example, it may be that the image of Self is one in which it is
relatively powerless and ignorant. These characteristics of the Self are

meaningful of course only when contrasted against the Other, which must have the antithetical qualities. The images of Self and Other are thus structurally complementary, such that given either one, the other could be described by simply inverting the given one. Now the same results could be obtained by dealing with hypothesized assumptions, rather than hypothesized images. Thus, given my basic theoretical bias that Self and Other are the primary poles of a world view, we could write this as a universal proposition: *The world (universe) consists of two dynamically interrelated parts—the Self and the Other.* Then going to our culturally specific case we have a proposition about the Self: *The Self is relatively ignorant and powerless to affect the Other.* Now if we are given only these two propositions, we should be able to infer something about assumptions regarding the Other: given that the Self and Other are all that exists, and are dynamically interrelated, and given that the Self is relatively ignorant and powerless to affect the Other, then it follows that the Other must contain knowledge and power to affect the Self. (It might be objected that it is logically possible for both Self and Other to be ignorant and incapable of affecting each other. This argument of course disregards the unitary nature of the first proposition and the semantics of the qualities denoted by the words "ignorance" and "powerless," which are meaningful only if we assume the existence of their opposite qualities.)

Anthropologists, sociologists, cultural historians, and art critics have recognized other types of cultural integration. Just as logical integration has much in common with structural integration, structural integration fades imperceptibly into *stylistic integration,* which is a variant of the type of configurationalism typified by Benedict and other Boasians, as we discussed in Chapter 1. Stylistic integration is much like structural replication, but is often more subtle and more akin to artistic style. It is possible, for example, for some people to distinguish composers one from another by comparing their personal graphic styles with their music (see Barnouw 1973:10–11). That is, there is a recognizable similarity between a man's penmanship and the kind of music he composes. Similarly, it is often not a difficult task for someone to identify some material artifact, bit of folklore, or other cultural product as to the cultural tradition it comes from, even though he may never have been exposed to the particular item in question. Its identity is revealed by its style. Most of the concern with stylistic analysis centers on the fine arts, but styles have also been described in phenomena more like world view, such as science and philosophy (Kroeber 1948, 1957), social thought (Mannheim 1936), and political and economic behavior (Riesman 1970).

Style, then, in this sense is something that is often basic in a culture, transcends different domains of the culture, and imprints some perceptible similarities on them. From a world-view perspective, the assumption here is that underlying all of these cultural products are some common mental image(s) or structures(s) that account for replications of cultural forms.

Let me give an example which, as are most such examples, is difficult to support but is nevertheless quite real to me. I have been struck by similarities in certain aspects of Mexican peasant personality and certain aspects of their architecture. As Ixtepejanos often say, *somos cerrados*, we are closed (Kearney 1972). Living as they do in a world perceived as having many dangers, they try to present an impenetrable exterior to the threats and attacks of others. One way that a potential enemy can gain power is by acquiring knowledge of his victim's state of affairs, especially of his emotional states and weaknesses. Accordingly one defends himself by attempting to present a neutral and ordinary countenance to the world. One reveals his true feelings only in appropriate settings, among people he can be reasonably sure of trusting. The Ixtepejanos build their houses in similar ways. Ideally they present a solid, plain adobe wall to the street. This wall has no windows, or if it does have windows they are usually shuttered. In the interior or at the back of the house there is ideally a patio and a kitchen, which are areas of security where one may relax and let down defenses. To me, this parallel between Ixtepejano personality and architecture contrasts with a parallel between, for example, middle-class Anglo-American personality and contemporary middle-class houses with their front yards and picture windows, which serve not only for the inhabitants to look out of but also for the world to look into.

Although cultural styles are often intuitively quite apparent, we will not further deal with them in this book. To exclude them we must impose some admittedly arbitrary limits in deciding when we have come to the limits of structurally integrated phenomena, and not trespass into problems of style.

We will further examine logico-structural integration in Chapter 5, in conjunction with concepts introduced in Chapter 4. We therefore temporarily leave the subject at this point.

Chapter 3

WORLD-VIEW UNIVERSALS

In order to establish a model of comparative world view on solid theoretical ground we must deal with three fundamental problems. The first of these is, What universal cognitive categories are necessary dimensions for cross-cultural comparisons of world views? The second, What kinds of forces determine or shape the contents of these categories? And third, What relationship exists between these world-view universals and sociocultural behavior?

This chapter examines the first of these questions, and attempts to establish a framework with which we can describe and compare world views. The basic requirement of this framework is that it be applicable to any human world view without greatly distorting it. It is in this sense analogous to the diagnostic categories of doctors. When a doctor examines patients he has in mind definite notions about human anatomy and physiology that allow him to describe the patient's state of health. Although the doctor is confronted with a wide variety of patients, he can presumably describe the most significant medical facts about them in terms of dimensions and features that are common to all patients, e.g., blood pressure, pulse, respiration. In a similar manner we must discover a universal set of diagnostic categories to describe world views. Other possible universal dimensions of world view can be derived or posited for various purposes, but the ones that I present here appear to me to be the minimal ones for adequately analyzing and describing a world view as a dynamic logico-structurally integrated system of knowledge.

My approach to the issue of world-view universals and their respective assumptions presupposes that more than anything else they serve the pragmatic necessity of communication, and that accordingly world view is preeminently a practical and social phenomenon. This way of dealing with these concerns contrasts sharply with the prevailing way they are dealt with in an academic philosophy that tends to presuppose that most ordinary people have the same concerns as speculative philosophers engaged in idealist conjecture—which, rather than returning to the world of practical affairs, dissipates into a rarefied atmosphere like a hot gas. In contrast, the historical-materialist approach considers world-view universals as analogs of physiological principles necessary to maintain life. The contents of particular universals are comparable to tools; they vary cross-culturally, but are adapted to local environments for the most part for pragmatic purposes. Speculative philosophy differs from ordinary human thought not only in being more self-conscious but also in not having to submit to the test of how to get meat and potatoes on the table and successfully reproduce the next generation. Most anthropological concern with world view has had this same sort of bias. This is especially evident in Redfield, who seemed to assume that most people sit around and speculate at length on existential issues. He had little concern with how the contents of a world-view shape people's behavior in everyday life, and how this conduct of their lives constructed their world. Referring to the world-view model as represented in Figure 7, we can say that mainstream anthropology has been preoccupied with the bottom half of the model to the neglect of the top half: its epistemology is unidirectional and nondialectic. From the perspective of historical materialism, a world view is above all a practical necessity and for the most part is a more or less adequate reflection of the world, but one in which there is tremendous potential for variation.

With regard to this difference in emphasis on the pragmatic versus the speculative aspects of world view, Ketner (1972:159) exemplifies the latter in saying that, ". . . there seems to be a need in the mental life of all men, a need to bring coherence and unity to the world in response to what Dilthey called 'the enigma of life.' Or to paraphrase Aristotle, *all men* by *nature* desire to understand." From the perspective of this book I would rephrase Aristotle by saying that all people *need* to understand—understand not only the world as matter existing in space and time, but equally important, they need to understand one another. These common understandings evolve day-to-day, through generations, adapting to and shaping (when manifest as action) their social and physical environment. Formed as they are in this manner, these understandings then are pressed into service—their basic functions are extended—to answer the "enigma of life." Idealist anthropologists and speculative philosophers would have us believe that the "big questions" come first, and that world view is a response to them. This is the bias of the intellectual who, secure in his study, analyzes human knowledge apart from the so-called real world in which common human knowledge arises.

Although it does not frequently occur in contemporary writings, not long ago anthropologists often referred to the "psychic unity of mankind." This concept, made popular by E. B. Tylor and Adolf Bastian, was one of the most important contributions of nineteenth-century anthropology. Briefly, it referred to the tenet that all living peoples, regardless of their level of technological development or their social customs, possess the same innate human qualities and potentials resulting from a common evolutionary past. Tylor's argument was that it was "no more reasonable to suppose the laws of the mind differently constituted in Australia and in England, in the time of the cave-dwellers and in the time of . . . sheet-iron houses, than to suppose that the laws of chemical combinations" would vary from one age to another" (Tylor quoted from Stocking 1968:115). That this expression is not frequently uttered today is an indication of the degree to which it has permeated the thinking of contemporary anthropologists. Individual anthropologists may in their private lives act as racists and behave as though they believed in the inherent superiority of their own group. But their professional work is for the most part predicated on an assumption of psychic unity, especially insofar as they perform cross-cultural studies based on a random sampling of the societies of the world. In other words, if generalizations are to be drawn from such studies, it must be assumed that the societies selected are subject to the same psychological and social laws, and that although they are in some respects different, nevertheless, in more fundamental ways they are comparable.

It is rather amazing that such an important concept as this has not been given more attention. Although virtually all living anthropologists accept it as true, there is almost no discussion about exactly what psychic unity refers to in a psychological and especially a cognitive sense. Most definitions of psychic unity are in fact behavioral descriptions of how different peoples respond similarly to similar conditions. But for a comparative science of world view we need a theory of the mind, and in particular one about how it conceptualizes the phenomenal world.

Let us begin by asking what are the necessary conditions for a world view, and in this way we may define at least some of its features. In doing so

we must be careful to distinguish between those conditions and characteristics that are necessary requisites and those that may be possible, but not
necessary, for obviously we can only be assured that the former are
universal.

THE SELF AND THE OTHER

The first requirement for a world view is the presence of a *Self*—
discernibly distinct from its environment, which I refer to as the *Other*.
There are two reference points for viewing this organism-environment
distinction. One is that of the external observer who is interested in studying the world view of the organism in question, and apart from that there is
the requirement that the organism itself be sensitive to its surroundings.[1]
Also, for reasons that will become apparent below, another characteristic of
such an organism is that in addition to being able to gather information
about its environment, it must be able to alter its behavior on the basis of
this information.

Using these two characteristics, we could speak, for example, of the
world view of a type of flatworm called planaria.[2] Suppose we observe
planarians while we alter conditions in their surroundings. We will note
that they consistently crawl toward some objects or conditions, and crawl
away from others. In other words, we can assume that they are receiving
information about their surroundings and responding on the basis of such
information. At this point we would be able to venture some statements
about the "world view" of these flatworms. From our observations we
would note that there are three kinds of conditions and objects which flatworms predictably react to: they go away from some, go towards others,
and do not appear to react at all to yet others. We could thus hypothesize
that in flatworm world-view, reality consists of three types of qualities or
conditions, namely positive, negative, and neutral. In doing this we have
said nothing of the ontology of flatworm world-view; we have only written
an *as if* statement: it appears as if flatworms regard their environment as
consisting of these three qualities.

Upon analyzing the notion of the Self, we can see that it consists of two
aspects. One is the "awareness" of Self as distinct from surroundings; the
second is the notion of relationship between Self and surroundings. It is difficult to conceive of an organism that might somehow float freely suspended in some environment without having to respond to it in at least some
minimal way. One way of looking at life forms is to consider them as systems that exchange energy and matter (e.g., food and information) with

their environments. There is no known life form on earth that does not exist in such exchanges with its surroundings. To be an organism is thus to be in a necessary relationship with things external to Self. But these relationships may not be arbitrary, that is, they must exist within certain limits of say temperature, salinity, and light, and if these limits are exceeded for a sufficient length of time, the organism's vital processes break down and it ceases to exist. An organism thus has an interest in the nature of its relationship with its surroundings such that, insofar as it is able, it can affect that relationship. Our flatworm, for example, can use muscular action to move about in its surroundings so as to alter its relationships with local conditions (e.g., move towards food, or move away from a toxin).

Such coordinated activities imply an ability to be aware of two general conditions—those of constancy and those of change. In the example of the flatworm seeking food, it must have an awareness of the food's relatively enduring presence, and at some location, as well as an awareness that the relationship between Self and food can be altered so that Self's body can eat the food. Awareness of change and constancy is not, however, limited to the relationships between Self and external surroundings, but it also an attribute of the relationship between Self and Self's internal physiological environment. Physiologically, the organism is a complex set of interrelated biochemical processes, which must be maintained within narrow ranges. There are essentially two types of processes—recurrent ones, such as those having to do with alternations of night and day, reproductive cycles, and longer nonrecurrent processes that are synonymous with the life cycle. Thus again, this time in the perspective of internal physiological management, it is necessary that the organism in some sense be "aware" of constancy and change, although here we refer to process rather than to physical location.

Let us now examine what is specifically characteristic of the Self and Other universals in human world view. We can first inquire about the locus of the Self. As a first approximation we might assume that it is coterminous with the individual's body. This is reflected, for example, in the speech of a man who misses a nail with a hammer and hits his thumb: "I hit myself." But there is also reason to assume that sense of Self may be experienced as less than coextensive with the body. This appears to be the case in Ixtepeji, where Self and body seem to be joined together in less than an always harmonious alliance, the body being as it were a shell for the Self, and not always under its control such that it often acts so as to inconvenience or pain the Self apart from the Self's intentions. This orientation of Self to body is expressed in the frequent use of Spanish reflexive-verb constructions such as "my tooth hurts me," or "my body does not wish to heal itself."

But it is also readily apparent that many people consider some vital aspect of their Self to be not necessarily contained in their physical body. On numerous occasions I have heard spirit mediums in Mexico speak while in trance as their bodies told of sights and events reported back to it by their "souls" as they "traveled" to other locations (Kearney 1977; 1978a; 1978b). The point here is that these individuals "experience" the flight out of their bodies of what in my terminology here is an aspect of the Self. Similarly, many peoples assume that in dreaming the soul-Self's departure from the body is evidenced by the experiences it has in other settings. There is also the common belief that the soul-Self leaves the body at death. And conversely, in the widespread phenomenon of spirit possession, it is assumed that the soul-Selves of other humans or creatures temporarily enter into the person's body. The belief that the Self is restricted to the body is a notion of Self perhaps most typical of people of modern technologically advanced societies, but more of that later.

Ethnographic literature reveals many other possible ways of conceiving of the Self. For example, there is a concept among various Indians in Mexico that each individual has an animal counterpart, a *tonal*, who lives apart from the individual, and that the human's well-being is dependent on the counterpart's. Should, for example, an accident befall the *tonal*, a similar accident will happen to the human. The individual's sense of Self is thus bound up with the external creature, which is most likely never even seen. Another example: many people who have incorporated modern psychological theories about the unconscious into their own thinking have a rather unusual self-image. In accord with these beliefs they may recognize within themselves a large dynamic area outside of their conscious awareness, but a part of themselves that exerts strong influence on their ideas, feelings, and actions.

When we examine variations in the sense of Self we find that it varies between two limits. At one extreme are the experiences of mystics who describe how all discontinuities between their normal Selves and all the rest of the world dissolve so that they are left with the experience of being continuous and identical with the cosmos. At the other extreme there are the reports of psychotics and individuals experiencing extreme anxiety in which they feel that their Self is shrinking to a vanishing point at which they will cease to exist. Psychiatrists refer to this as "depersonalization."

In building his theory of personality, Freud was also concerned with the Self-Other distinction, and put forth ideas about its genesis, which although not verifiable, nevertheless seem reasonable. He argued that the newborn baby would be unaware of such a distinction. Because its existence in the mother's womb was completely parasitic, it had no functional need to be consciously aware of objects external to it. This absence of a Self-Other distinction, or nirvana principle, was according to Freud comparable to the selflessness of mystics. Shortly after birth, however, the infant experiences its first deprivation. At this point its "world" begins to be cleaved into two nebulous realms—all that is Self and all Other that is the source of comfort and pleasure. It soon begins to perceive also that the Other is further composed of perhaps cold, pains, and visual and auditory things that appear and disappear. Presumably, too, it becomes aware that parts of its body, its fingers and skin, are in some sense parts of itself. But all of these other discriminations are elaborations of the paramount distinction between Self and Other. And like Freud, Piaget also bases much of his model of cognitive development on the progressive elaboration of this distinction between Self and Other, as is discussed below in the section on Causality.

The way in which the two categories of Self and Other become elaborated in the adult are for the most part determined by the cultural heritage of the individual. We have seen in this brief discussion that there is considerable potential for cross-cultural variation in the concept of Self. The same is true for notions of the Other, although it appears that this image of some totality that comprises all that is not-Self is not as well developed. But since the distinction between Self and Other is the primary conceptual cleavage of perceived reality, the Other must exist as a complement to the Self. It is, however, not denoted by a term in many languages, but rather, as in English, the most inclusive terms for all that is not Self refer only to large domains within the Other, e.g., nature and society. (The use of "Other" as employed here is obviously a technical exception that does not exist in ordinary spoken English.) But when we go to the level of ultimate inclusiveness, viz., the universe, we find that there is almost invariably a comparable term, and therefore presumably a corresponding image. Thus, although we will retain the category of Other as a world-view universal, it must be remembered that, like the Self, it often refers to an unnamed domain that is composed of several named domains, each of which has a taxonomic status on the same order as the Self, all of these domains being subordinate to the ultimate domain of "universe." This domain has an empirically verifiable status in that many societies reveal, at least in their myths, an awareness of such a concept, if only to recount how the world (universe) came into existence.

These possible cultural variations in the status of the Other as a world-view universal are represented in Figure 3. In (a), the first of these three hypothetical cases, there is a well-developed folk notion of Other vis-à-vis the Self. In other words, there is linguistic or other evidence to assume that for adults in such a society there is a conscious psychological reality to the Other. In societies of type (b), this notion would *appear* to be absent insofar as there are no folk concepts or terms to indicate it. In such cases we would therefore have to assume that it is an implicit, unnamed category, which amounts to a situation represented in (c). In the absence of any linguistic or psychological evidence to assume the existence of the Other, as in (c), the most powerful argument for its retention as a world-view universal is the genetic argument advanced above. Since it was a necessary implication of the emergence of the Self—Self being defined in contrast with it—it did have a status at some point in the cognitive development of all humans. It seems unlikely that such a fundamental awareness would totally disappear and we would expect it to persist as an implicit category of thought.

We can now sum up what we have so far established as universal dimensions of world view. There is first of all the notion of cosmic totality, which is the most inclusive domain. There is also the notion of a Self in contrast to all that is not-Self (Other), and there is the notion of dynamic interrelationship between Self and Other, plus the ability to be aware of constancy and change.

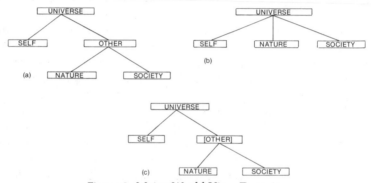

Figure 3. Major World-View Domains.

RELATIONSHIP

Let us now look at this notion of Relationship between Self and Other. As we have already indicated, our planarian flatworm is aware of three types of relationships vis-à-vis objects and conditions external to it (positive, negative, and neutral). These same basic relational awarenesses are also apparent to the human child soon after birth. But whereas we can legitimately say only that the flatworm exhibits positive and negative behavior, it is possible to speak of the child's behavior as responses to pleasure and pain. Also we can argue, given the Self and Other universals, that the child soon comes to realize that the sources of pleasure and pain originate to some degree from the Other. When such aspects of the Other as food, mother, warmth, physical contact are present, the Self experiences pleasure; when they are absent for some time, it experiences pain, which it may also come to associate with such aspects of the Other as cold, loud noises, or not-mother. It learns then that both pleasure and pain emanate in part from the Other.

Given just these simple polar notions of pleasure and pain, ranging as it were from a neutral point of neither, it is possible to imagine some possible variations in the general world views of recently born children depending on the relative prevalence of these three types of awarenesses. Should the child be well-tended and protected by loving arms and tender care it may experience a minimum of pain; an awareness of well-being and security would then predominate. Thus at this early stage the child's view of reality would be colored by a predominance of pleasure. Conversely, if the baby experiences many deprivations and traumas, its general image of the Other would necessarily be one in which all that is not-Self is mainly a source of frustration and pain. Other possibilities exist. Pleasure and pain may alternate predictably in such a manner that the Other is seen as regularly fluctuating between these values. Or they may alternate in some proportion, but do so unpredictably. In the first mixed case the child would come to perceive the Other as regular, ordered, and predictable, and it might even perceive regularities between its own states of being or behaviors and whether or not pleasure, pain or neither emanate from the Other. Acting so as to elicit such responses from the environment, the child develops an image of Self as having an ability to affect the Other, and thus in turn affect its own condition. Conversely, if the child be subjected predominantly to unpredictable experiences it will come to see itself as relatively powerless and incapable of affecting either its own state of being or aspects of the Other.

The Relationship universal is given by the necessary interaction of Self and Other. As we have just seen in the case of the child, there are various forms that this interaction may take and in turn be so cognized by the individual. The particular manner in which individuals perceive their relationship vis-à-vis the Other is in effect a stance toward the world. Redfield was thinking of something like this when he said that a person may regard the Other, or parts of it, as existing to be maintained, obeyed, or acted upon. That is, is the Relationship between Self and Other one of harmony, subordinancy, or dominance? For Redfield, however—consistent with the idealist assumptions of his anthropology—these attitudes are taken more or less as givens. He is little concerned with their formation nor with their role in social action. But within the model of world view being developed here, these dialectic aspects of the Relationship universal are equal in importance with the images and assumptions possible within it. Images of Relationship are on one hand the result of past collective experience. On the other they shape strategies for interacting with social and physical aspects of the Other.[3]

Ecological Relationship

The way in which people see their relationship to the Other affects the way they act toward it. If a people see themselves as intimately interconnected with the Other in general, then they see their well-being as dependent on its well-being. In such a case it might be appropriate to speak of an "ecological consciousness." Chapter 6 describes such an image of Relationship as it existed among California Indians. Here we can anticipate that discussion with some general observations about this attitude, which is common in band and tribal societies. For the sake of discussion we can consider two aspects of this type of image: relationship with other humans and relationship with "nature." To illustrate these I shall, relying on Lowery-Palmer (1980), take examples from the Yoruba of West Africa.

The corporate kin-based social structure is the most immediate source of this image when it is present in tribal and other societies. Indeed, this image of Relationship results from an image of Self which is seen as an aspect or feature of the group. Lowery-Palmer notes that this attitude is reflected in Yoruba accounts of creation in which group relations are a central theme.

> Man is not created to be alone. He is created to be a being-in-relation. The whole existence from birth to death is organically embodied in a series of associations, and life appears to have its full value only in those close ties. Those close ties will include extended family members, the clan and village, the various societies and organizations in the community together with the close ties to the ancestors and gods who are interested in the day-to-day life of man. These ideas accord with those of [the Nigerian psychiatrist] Lambo . . . who observes that the basic need of the Yoruba individual is that of attachment to other human beings. The need to belong rules his entire attitudes throughout his life. (Lowery-Palmer 1980:63)

This image of Self as an aspect of and as dependent on the group is consistent with Yoruba assumptions of Causality. As is common in tribal societies, all visible and invisible phenomena are assumed to result from the presence of varying concentrations and forms of ubiquitous energy (see sections on Causality in this Chapter and in Chapter 6). All persons and things are part of a web of relationships that depend on this energy. It is contrary to this image to think of people or things in isolation; they exist only as aspects of relationships, linked together by this pervasive power. As Mbiti (1970:141) puts it, "I am because we are; and since we are, therefore I am." One of the forms of this power is human thought, which is assumed to be effective in the sense that wishes and emotions can have an effect at a distance. What another may think of you can potentially affect your personal condition. The individuals of the local community are intimately connected in this way. And it follows that you are concerned about how others regard you, for your state of well-being is dependent not only on how they act toward you but also on what they think about you.

Yoruba attitudes toward nonhuman aspects of the world are consistent with assumptions about interpersonal relationships. Here too the image of pervasive power is central.

> The unity of "wholeness" of the universe is dependent on man who is at the center, relating himself to natural phenomena, including other men, in a manner which facilitates balance or harmony. The underlying principle on which balance is achieved and maintained is that of proper respect for the unifying principle of power or energy exchange between all created forms. In order to understand and make use of power, the Yoruba individual seeks knowledge by continuously improving his skills and abilities in deciphering the meaning of the invisible as manifested by the visible. To the Yoruba natural phenomena, including the physical body, are a source of knowledge and wisdom. The dynamic relationship of Self and nature is characterized by knowledge seeking activities in a cooperative harmonious manner. (Lowery-Palmer 1980:75–76)

This view of perceptible forms as but manifestations of a more fundamental "spiritual" principle is logico-structurally consistent with Yoruba world-view classification.

> To the Yoruba, while particular persons (or entities) appear outwardly different, behind surface appearances they are only manifestations of an underlying power which unifies all creation. As in the Yoruba image of Self-Other, in which the Self is completely identified, in an undifferentiated way, with the group, so is person/not-person not qualitatively different from all life; it is a visible aspect of the underlying process of interactions and interdependence of all living systems. Living beings—man, plants, animals, spirits—are viewed as a continuum of beings differing only in amounts of power. The Yoruba image of life is that of an energy system that can maintain itself as a self-centered, self-regulating, balanced unity irrespective of the form in which it inheres. . . . (Lowery-Palmer 1980:84)

Individualism

Contrasting sharply with the image of Relationship in Yoruba world view is the individualism prevalent in modern Western industrial society. Individualism is at base an image of self, and as with any image of Self, it is only in relationship with the Other that it is understandable. Speaking in the most general terms, it is permissible to say that individualism arises with the transition from tribal to class society (see Leacock 1972; 1978). In the

Western world it becomes even more prevalent with the decline of kin-based agrarian communities that occurred during the gradual transition from feudalism to capitalism. Two of the critical—perhaps the most critical—changes which conditioned this new image was the ascendancy of the concept of private (i.e., individually owned) property and the growth of a market-based economy. These were the essential features defining the social classes that emerged in capitalism. On the one hand the rising bourgeoisie came to "own" the basic means of production and to control their distribution. They did this for the most part as individuals and as corporate groups of individuals whose relationships were contractually defined. It was in this historic context that individualism as an image of Self become consciously expressed by bourgeois philosophers and theologians of the Renaissance and Enlightenment. These new principles had then, as they still do, an ideological component advancing the interests of the propertied classes. This new concept of private ownership of the wealth-producing resources required a new form of legitimation, and the new social relationships that emerged with capitalism provided the raw materials for the manufacture of this new ideology.

> Capitalist ideology, replete with the language of "freedom" and the "worth and dignity" of each "individual" and "the inalienable rights of man," is finally only a support for vested property interests in capitalist society. Freedom is the freedom to exploit. The "dignity of the individual" really means the rapacious, rugged individualism of the entrepreneur. Jeffersonian democracy is "bourgeois democracy," which is simply justification for state protection of bourgeois interests. (Wogaman 1977:290, referring to Marx)

At bottom, as all ideologies have, this one has assumptions about human nature. These images are simultaneously the reflection of and a justification for the competitive individualized economic relationships in capitalist economy. By false analogies with the animal kingdom, humans are said to be locked into the "struggle for existence" in which only the fittest survive. Humans are different, however, in that they have formed social contracts among themselves to control this brutishness. The idea of social contract could only have been conceived in a market economy. This attitude is a basis of bourgeois political theory in which "democratic" decisions are arrived at by peacefully agreeing to weigh political forces by elections. And until very recently in the bourgeois "democracies" of England, Europe, and the Americas, the right to vote was limited to male property owners; working people and women gained the franchise only by long political struggle.

Whereas the individualism among the propertied classes was re-enforced by the struggle for private profit, among the propertyless it was re-enforced by having to enter the labor market as a lone person. In a communal classless society one's well-being is dependent on the well-being of the group. Norms of reciprocity demand that resources be shared. "Good" persons are those who share with others when they can. This arrangement is adaptive for individuals, because it insures that when they are without, others will share with them. This is the essence of reciprocity as the fundamental form of exchange in classless society. Because it is adaptive for individuals, it is adaptive for the group. A necessary presupposition here is that major productive resources are communally owned. Or perhaps a better way to say this is that in this type of society all individuals have equal access to the main productive resources.

Relationships in a market economy are completely different. Here it is possible to enter into economic relationships only if you have money to buy or if you have commodities to sell. In capitalist society the main sources of wealth have become property. These productive resources are now concentrated in a relatively few hands. The majority in capitalist society are therefore dependent on the propertied classes in that they must sell to them the only commodity they possess, which is their labor. They sell this for the most part as individuals, and doing so diminishes whatever sense of commonality they may have with others. Their economic behavior becomes egocentric rather than group-centered. In a word, they have become alienated. "Alienation" is a major theme of nineteenth- and twentieth-century critical thought, especially in the writings of existential philosophers and psychologists and of any number of social commentators, beginning with Marx. This intellectual tradition speaks to the dark underside of the ideology of "individualism," "freedom," and "private property."

Individualism (read alienation), as an aspect of Relationship, appears in two forms. One, which is prevalent in North American society, is associated with an active Self that sees the Other as existing to be manipulated and exploited for personal gain. This is epitomized in the "rugged individualism" of the entrepreneur. The other is a passive form of individualism in which the Self sees itself as subjugated to and at the mercy of the Other. This second type in capitalism is associated with a Self lacking power, which is to say, lacking wealth in private property. This constellation of images of Self, Other, and Relationship is also especially characteristic of peasant societies (see Chapter 7). In both forms of alienation the individualistic Self is predisposed to competition and struggle with other persons and with the Other in general. The "ecologic" Self is not. Viewing other persons as aspects of the Other, the "ecologic self" image predisposes one to be altruistic.

In the bourgeois image of human nature as based on a calculus of egoistic maximizing of pleasure and minimizing pain, altruism is a conundrum that has been as much resistant to satisfactory explanation as the paradox of a benevolent omnipotent god who allows evil and suffering. A person who acts in the interests of others' Selves with no perceivable self-gain is, from the perspective of this economistic utilitarian psychology, behaving irrationally. But the notion of altruism as a paradox is presupposed only in the assumptions of hedonism and individualism contained in this impoverished bourgeois view of human nature. And here egoism and altruism are logico-structurally integrated. Only an isolated self can act selfishly and egoistically vis-à-vis other selves. In the case of an ecologic self, the discreteness of distinct individuals is considerably reduced and therefore acting in the best interests of others, and in the interests of the world in general, is consistent with self-interest — not just of a discrete, alienated self, but of the system of which one is an inextricable part. From this set of assumptions about Self, Other, and Relationships, altruism is not an issue.[4]

CLASSIFICATION

One of the most important subjects of Western philosophy is the notion of class and the process of classification, and it is to these concepts that we are now in position to turn. That the idea of class is universal is verifiable in that all peoples name objects and conceptually include them into larger more general groupings. The study of world view is to a great extent the analysis of the major categories of reality recognized by a people and the criteria by which they group the contents of these categories together. The way in which a people categorize the major areas of their conceptual world constitutes an important part of the framework of their world view. And, as we will see, the arrangement of the major categories in the Classification universal depends on and in turn influences the contents of the other worldview universals.

The Origins of Classification

Depending on one's philosophical predispositions, the notion of class is either an innate capacity of the mind or in some other way acquired from the outside world. Still a third type of solution to this problem of the origin of the ability to classify sees it as arising out of the mind's interaction with the external world, and to me a solution of this type seems the most convincing. What I would like to suggest is that this presumed category of thought is neither *a priori* nor, much less, an ability that derives from without, but rather that it results from the necessary awareness of Self versus an empirical Other that must be present in all organisms if they are to function in exchange with their surroundings, as we discussed at the beginning of this chapter. The cleaving of existence into these two realms is thus the first instance of classifying, and results from the necessary opposition

and integration of Self and Other. At the lower phylogenetic levels of proto-
zoans or of our flatworm, the awareness of this distinction is inherent in the
organism's ability to maintain its integrity vis-à-vis its surroundings. The
conscious awareness of this distinction is nothing more than an abstraction
and elaboration of this underlying biological awareness.

One of the main advances in philosophical and scientific attacks on the
problem of Classification as a category of thought was in a small book by
Emile Durkheim and Marcel Mauss (1903/1963). Their great insight was to
link the ability of the individual human mind to reduce the phenomenal
world into classes of like things with the social categories of human
societies. Durkheim (1965) later developed this idea in his *Elementary
Forms of the Religious Life* (1912), and although he professed to be neither a
rationalist nor an empiricist, but rather to be resolving the opposition
among them, one can see upon reading him carefully that he attributes primary importance to the social groupings. The first mental classes are thus
somehow reflections of these groupings, and once formed are generalized to
other areas of the world and serve to organize them. Durkheim and his followers thus actually argue for a social empiricism.

In Durkheim's scheme, social groupings are taken as givens that serve,
as it were, as a template to impress the notion of class onto the mind. This is
the weakest part of his theory, for we are left with the nagging question of
how this imprinting actually occurs.

Actually, two issues are confounded here. One is the origin of the
concept of the unitary group; the other is the origin of the notions of sub-
groups in opposition to one another, i.e., classificatory thinking per se.
Noncultural gregarious animals are constituted into groups in which their
intragroup social behavior is largely instinctively determined. Thus a flock
of birds or a school of fish need not have an image of their group to collectively behave as a group. But Durkheim is mainly concerned with the problem of the component groups, which while in opposition to one another are
also united into the larger group, for example the clans of a tribe. Such
lesser groupings are cultural and therefore artificial, and the question is:
how could these have existed without a social structure, which is of course
an ideal image in the minds of the people, an image which is dependent on
the ability to artificially categorize? Therefore this ability must have had
other than a social-group origin.[5]

Durkheim and Mauss advance their argument for the origin of the classificatory ability by simply taking social groupings as given "social facts."
But what they also would have realized had they pushed their ideas farther
was that the primary social fact is the opposition and interrelationship of
Self and Other. Durkheim at one point comes close to this idea in his argument that the concept of class arises from social groupings and from these is
generalized to other collections.

. . . if conceptual thought can be applied to the class, species or variety, howsoever restricted these may be, why can it not be extended to the individual, that
is to say, to the limit towards which the conception tends, proportionately as its
extension diminishes? (1965:480)

For Durkheim, the realization of individual as a class (note that he is
not referring to the Self) derives from a prior recognition of social groupings
as classes. But, as I see it, the generalization process runs in the reverse
direction, and begins not with the individual but with the more discrete Self
that is apperceived as such in contrast to the Other. Ontogenetically this
Other is first of all perhaps an inchoate sense of mother or some such care-
taker, and it is out of this given relationship that the primary classes of Self
and Other derive. Thus where Durkheim says that "the category of class
was at first indistinct from the concept of the human group" (1965:488), we
can now say that it was at first indistinct from the concept of Self and
Other. This is a more plausible way for the notion of class to arise in the
human mind. Once it is so established, we can allow that it generalizes as
Durkheim assumes.

In dealing with the notion of totality, Durkheim argues, society is again
the model since

there is no individual experience, howsoever extended and prolonged it may
be, which could give a suspicion of the existence of a whole class which would
embrace every single being, and to which other classes are only co-ordinated or
subordinated species. This idea of *all*, which is at the basis of the classifications
which we have just cited, could not have come from the individual himself,
who is only a part in relation to the whole and who never attains more than an
infinitesimal fraction of reality. (1965:489)

But following the argument that I have made about the primacy of
the Self, we can say that everything that is not Self is simply all else.
Durkheim's *all* is thus synonymous with the Other, whereas in my terminology it is the universe, which includes both Self and Other (see Figure 3).
Within a cognitively differentiated universe the most fundamental classification categories are Self and Other; this is the reason they are treated as
universals.

World-View Categories

In terms of the Classification universal, a world view is the broadest
and most fundamental cognitive organization of reality. We have an example of one such fundamental classification of reality in the preceeding dis-

cussion of Self and Other. Again, I should emphasize that such world-view categories are not necessarily named.

Given the wide variety of cross-cultural classification schemes, it seems that there is a large element of arbitrariness to them, that the fundamental categories in different world views are all distinct but more or less adequate solutions to the problem of cognitively organizing the phenomenal world. The point is that some order, however arbitrary it is, must be agreed upon. "Without some starting point, some initial schema, we could never get hold of the flux of experience. Without categories, we could not sort our impressions. Paradoxically, it has turned out that it matters relatively little what these categories are" (Gombrich 1969:88). However, once world-view categories become established, they organize many other classes.

One implication of this arbitrariness of classification is that the largely implicit categories of Self, Other, and Universe may be the only universal categories. But the way in which a particular world view orders these major categories and further compartmentalizes them is revealing and has implications for other dimensions of that world view. Examination of a world view's Classification universal yields two types of information that provide insight into that world view. One of these is the contents of the domains, and the other is the criteria or attributes by which these contents are grouped together into common domains.

Two common major contrasting domains in many world views might be referred to as real and unreal. "Real" and "unreal" are actually attributes of domains, which may be named by the same terms insofar as they are explicit domains. If it is established that such domains do exist in a world view, then their contents may be quite revealing. The existence of an "unreal" domain results from the presence of images that have no presumed objective correlate, such as, for most people, the image of a unicorn. For many people dreams, images of demons, angels, astrological influences, or an international communist conspiracy, would also fall within their unreal domain. For others these are images with assumed objective correlates, and are therefore a basis for acting toward these "real" phenomena. Dreams are one type of common experience where there is wide cross-cultural variation in this regard. For some peoples they are comparable to hallucinations, for others they are real experiences in that the dreamer assumes upon awakening that in some sense he actually visited and encountered the places and things that he experienced in the dream.

Another set of contrasting domains that often exist in world views is that of the natural and supernatural. You will recall that although Redfield assumed that such a distinction occurred in all world views, there is reason to believe that it is not universal. It does result in two major domains in European thought: one is the province of science (originally called natural science), the other of religion and witchcraft. For some people, atheists perhaps, this distinction corresponds to the real-unreal. For others, these two dichotomies are cross-cutting. For example, one who is otherwise imbued with a "scientific" outlook on life might have a traditional notion of God as able to perform miracles that contravene natural laws, yet this same person might reject as fanciful a belief in ghosts. The intersection of these two domains would appear as in Figure 4.

	REAL	UNREAL
SUPERNATURAL	God	ghosts
NATURAL	dogs	dreams

Figure 4.

What this simple example demonstrates is that the attributes of domains are as important in defining them as are the contents. For example, it is possible that two people may conceptually group the following items: ghosts, spirits, the Devil. Knowing this grouping alone tells us little about their respective world views. However, if we know that for one person these items are grouped together as elements of folk tales and superstitions, while for another they are sources of sickness and sin, we then gain insight into the associated dimensions of Causality and Relationship in their respective world views. As an additional illustration we can examine the domain of "persons" as it exists in the thinking of the Ojibwa Indians. In discussing the term "grandfather," Hallowell explains that it applies not only to human persons, but also to spirit beings who are nonhuman persons.

Thus if we study Ojibwa social organization in the usual manner, we take account of only one set of "grandfathers." When we study their religion we discover other "grandfathers." But if we adopt a world-view perspective no dichotomization appears. In this perspective "grandfather" is a term applicable to certain "person objects," without any distinction between human persons and those of an other-than-human class. Furthermore, both sets of grandfathers can be said to be functionally as well as terminologically equivalent in certain respects. The other-than-human grandfathers are sources of power to human beings through the "blessings" they bestow, i.e., a sharing of their power which enchances the "power" of human beings. A child is always given a name by an old man, i.e., a terminological grandfather. It is a matter of indifference whether he is a blood relative or not. This name carries with it a special blessing because it has reference to a dream of the human grandfather in which he obtained power from one or more of the other-than-human grandfathers. In other words, the relation between a human child and a human grandfather is functionally patterned in the same way as the relation between human beings and grandfathers of an other-than-human class. And, just as the latter type of grandfather may impose personal taboos as a condition of a blessing, in the same way a human grandfather may impose a taboo on a "grandchild" he has named. (Hallowell 1964:52)

Another linguistic clue to the class of "persons" in Ojibwa thought is the term *windigo*. *Windigowak* are fabulous terrifying giant men that live on human flesh. Hallowell and others have collected accounts of how particular individuals have heroically fought threatening *windigowak* and have killed relatives whom it was thought were becoming the dread monsters. The point here is that again, as with the Ojibwa "grandfather," we have an unusual entity that Ojibwa thinking defines as a "person." And Hallowell notes,

The more deeply we penetrate the world view of the Ojibwa the more apparent it is that "social relations" between human beings *(anicinabek)* and other-than-human "persons" are of cardinal significance. These relations are correlative with their more comprehensive categorization of "persons." Recognition must be given to the culturally constituted meaning of "social" and "social relations" if we are to understand the nature of the Ojibwa world and the living entities in it. (Hallowell 1964:52–53)

Since Hallowell's Ojibwa material is so useful for this purpose I shall cite one more example. The grammar of the Ojibwa language expresses a formal distinction between "animate" and "inanimate" nouns. One peculiarity of this classification is that stones are classed as "animate." About this puzzling fact Hallowell says,

Since stones are grammatically animate, I once asked an old man: Are *all* the stones we see about us here alive? He reflected a long while and then replied, "No! But *some* are." This qualified answer made a lasting impression on me. And it is thoroughly consistent with other data that indicate that the Ojibwa are not animists in the sense that they dogmatically attribute living souls to inanimate objects such as stones. The hypothesis which suggests itself to me is that the allocation of stones to an animate grammatical category is part of a culturally constituted cognitive "set." It does not involve a consciously formulated theory about the nature of stones. It leaves a door open that our orientation on dogmatic grounds keeps shut tight. Whereas we should never expect a stone to manifest animate properties of any kind under any circumstances, the Ojibwa recognize, *a priori*, potentialities for animation in certain classes of objects under certain circumstances. The Ojibwa do not perceive stones, in general, as animate, any more than we do. The crucial test is experience. Is there any personal testimony available? In answer to this question we can say that it is asserted by informants that stones have been seen to move, that some stones manifest other animate properties, and . . . Flint is represented as a living personage in their mythology. (Hallowell 1964:54–55)

The above examples show the kinds of insights into world view that can be obtained from analysis of culturally specific ways of classifying. In doing so, however, there is one major caution that must be observed, and that is to not merely assume that the existence of classifying patterns necessarily represents deeper cognitive orientations. For it may well be that the classifying features of a particular domain of things may be no more than an artifact of the language. In each of Hallowell's examples cited above there is ample behavioral evidence to assume that the linguistic categories mentioned do in fact reflect underlying attitudes and assumptions about the nature of things.

CAUSALITY

It is in the Self-Other relationship discussed above that we find the source of another universal category of thought, that of Causality, the following examination of which also elaborates the nature of the Self-Other relationship.

As I see it there are two arguments for the universality of the notion of causality. One is empirical; the ethnographic record does not seem to indicate any peoples who lack such a notion, as is implied from their economic and ritual beliefs and practices. The second argument is a common-sense one; it is impossible to conceive of a human society in which there do not exist some concepts of an orderly relationship between acts (causes) and desired ends (effects). The notion of causality—of cause and effect—has, however, disappeared from modern physics, where it has been replaced by a probabilistic analysis of random events at the subatomic level and by a view of macroevents as occurring within complex interrelationships that are nondeterministic parts of some large dynamic system (see Russell 1981). In other words, as Collingwood (1940:69) puts it, "the idea of causation is not presupposed in modern physics." This is not sufficient reason, however, to question the Causality universal, for there are in modern physics models of process in nature, and such images are one of the essential features of the Causality universal. What I mean by causality is well defined by Durkheim:

The first thing which is implied in the notion of the causal relationship is the idea of efficacy, of productive power, of active force. By cause we ordinarily mean something capable of producing a certain change. The cause is the force before it has shown the power which is in it; the effect is this same power, only actualized. (Durkheim 1965:406)

Durkheim developed an argument for the category of Causality, viz., effective power, as arising from the functional necessity of society having to have its members believe in the efficacy of its communal rituals, the practice of which was part of the glue that holds society together. I am inclined, however, to see it as arising out of the Self and Other universals as they emerge in the world view of the child. This approach is well supported by Piaget's study of the development of causal thinking in children.

In an attempt to understand the course of its development in the child, Piaget (1969:258-281) has done the most thorough psychological study of causal thinking. On the basis of his clinical studies, he identifies seventeen principles of causality that appear to be implicit in the reasoning of children of various ages. He then combines these seventeen types into three groups that correspond, according to him, to three developmental periods. In the first period, "Causality, like the whole of reality, is at first teeming with subjective elements" (ibid.: 267). In this period, there is, for example, no conception of physical causality in a Newtonian sense of objects acting on each other through spatial contact. Instead, because the notions of subject and object—Self and Other—are weakly developed, the child has "a dim sense that the inchoate feelings of effort, longing, etc., which saturate [its] actions are somehow responsible for external happenings" (Flavell 1963:142). Thus, mountains exist, clouds move, and dreams come to us because people or gods wish them. Or things are as they are out of pure finalism: "it is much the same when we say, in accordance with ordinary common-sense, that ducks have webbed feet so as to swim better" (Piaget 1969:259). Or else two events that occur together are uncritically assumed to be causally connected, in much the same way that careless social scientists impute causal relations to things that are merely correlated. Also characteristic of this stage is a notion of participation and of magical causality. In the notion of participation,

two things between which there subsist relations either of resemblance or of general affinity, are conceived as having something in common which enables them to act upon one another at a distance, or more precisely, to be regarded one as a source of emanations, the other as the emanation of the first. Thus air or shadows in a room emanate from the air and shadows out of doors. (ibid.: 260-261)

This notion underlies astrological beliefs in the power of celestial bodies to influence earthly events, and is involved in the concept of witchcraft discussed in Chapters 6 and 7. We might also include here folk notions of gravity and magnetism, for which no verifiable theory exists. Magical causality is a special case of participation in which "the subject regards his gestures, his thoughts, or the objects he handles, as charged with efficacy, thanks to the very participations which he establishes between these gestures, etc., and the things around him" (Piaget 1969:261). This principle underlies belief, for example, in the efficacy of charms and spells, and in the evil eye (see Chapter 7), in which a person's mere thoughts and feelings may harm another.

Related to the above types is moral causality. "The child explains the existence of a given movement or a given feature by its necessity, but this is purely moral: the clouds 'must' advance in order to make night when men go to bed in order to sleep; boats 'have to' float, otherwise they would be of no use, etc." (ibid.: 261).

In Piaget's second period, principles of a more objective nature appear, objective in the sense that they are disassociated from the subject. By the principle of artificialist causality, things are explained as due to human creative activity. In animistic causality, "the existence of a character or form is explained by an internal biological tendency that is both alive and conscious" (ibid.: 262). In other words, things are animated, are alive (see discussion of spirits in Chapters 6 and 7). Closely related to this is the idea of dynamic causality, in which rather than imputing life or spirit to objects, their behavior is attributed to nonliving forces or dynamic mechanisms, or internal motors (see the discussion of "power," Chapter 6).

Whereas all of the previous forms "appeal either to motives or to intentions, either to occult emanations or to mystical manufactures" (ibid.: 263), in the third period the child's notions come more into accord with principles of classical physics. Now there are explanations in terms of reaction of the surrounding medium and in terms of mechanical causality in which mechanisms are posited that physically transfer effects from one thing to another. Also now, more or less realistic generative concepts are recognized —rain comes out of clouds, clouds come from air and smoke, rocks are composed of smaller rocks, etc. Piaget also indicates the appearance of spatial explanations in this period, but the culminating principle is that of explanation by logical deduction based upon previously observed phenomena. This kind of explanation presupposes the existence of natural laws.

Now, what does this rather long discussion of children's notions of causality have to do with Causality as a dimension of adult world view? Piaget argues that in the mental development of the child, the formation of this objectivity is a slow continuous process that is never entirely completed, for there always remain "adherences" or "fragments of internal experience which still cling to the external world" (ibid.: 244). These adherences are participation, animism, artificialism, finalism, and force, five notions which we have just discussed. As explained above, in feelings of *participation*, there is an assumed affinity of Self with external objects, such as that the sun and moon follow us, or that "things around us notice us and obey us, like the wind, the clouds, the night, etc.; the moon, the street lamps, etc., send us dreams 'to annoy us,' etc., etc. In short, the world is filled with tendencies and intentions which are in participation with our own" (ibid.: 245). As we saw, closely allied with this is the notion of *animism*, which endows things with consciousness and life. In the third form, *artificialism*, there is the uncritical assumption that objects obey will and intention, and in doing so are organized and act for the good of men. This notion that things exist for and are organized for man is the *finalistic* assumption. To the extent that this notion exists, the world is seen as teleological. The fifth type of adherence is the notion of *force* or *power*, which is attributed to things such that they make efforts as do muscles.

In Piaget's scheme, "the better the child succeeds in dividing off the internal world from the external, the less stubborn are the adherences" (ibid.: 246). But from our anthropological perspective we want to ask, is this scheme perhaps culture-bound and representative of French Swiss world view as manifested in the children who were Piaget's experimental subjects? In other words, might it not be that these adherences which Piaget assumes to drop away in the "general process of evolution which leads the child from a dynamic to a mechanical view" (ibid.: 246) remain as strongly developed orientations in normal adults of other cultures? There is ample ethnographic evidence that these adherences are widespread in the thinking of traditional peoples.

Given the prevalence of these notions among peoples of the world, we are faced with several ways of reconciling them with Piaget's developmental scheme. Piaget himself has suggested and cross-cultural research has demonstrated that certain cognitive skills will develop at a later age and will be less developed in nonliterate societies (Dasen 1974). This research goes beyond the Durkheimian concern, best exemplified in the work of Evans-Pritchard (1937, 1940), with how cross-cultural variations in thought are conditioned by social structure. But certainly social structure is a powerful force shaping cognition. For a discussion of how this traditional anthropological concern with the relationship between social structure and cognition could be advanced by being informed by Piagetian developmental psychology see Hallpike (1976); conversely, D'Amico (1972) examines the lack of attention to social structural influences on cognition inherent in Piaget's ahistorical psychology. This is a fascinating issue, but our main concern here is merely to introduce these "adherences" of Piaget as aspects of the Causality universal that will serve us in describing and comparing world views.

Psychological Sources of Idealism

This is a convenient point to resume our discussion of idealist world-view assumptions begun in Chapter 1. There we examined political and sociological functions of idealism. The propensity for this form of false consciousness rests at bottom on the state of development of the Causality universal.

Above we discussed how the Self and Other universals are the backbone of a world view. A world view comes into being as an individual begins to achieve awareness of himself or herself shortly after birth. This awareness develops as the Self becomes more and more distinct from the Other. The realization of this separateness can take many forms and progress or be inhibited at various stages. When this distinction is less than complete there is a tendency to attribute to the Other, to the natural world, thoughts and feelings that are internal to the Self. This inappropriate causal attribution, which Piaget has studied at length (see above), is similar to what psychoanalysts refer to as projection (see Chapters 4 and 7). This tendency is greater in the absence of a well-developed empirical physics and biology that explain phenomena in terms of natural laws. In such a situation humans are especially prone to attribute — to project — internal feelings and ideas onto things in the world, thus imputing will and volition to events such as the weather and accidents. In extreme forms of projection inner contents are not attributed to external things but become reified symbols that are, however, assumed to be real objects in the Other. What occurs here is that what is inherently human's is separated from them, split off, and assumed to exist apart from them. In terms of the Self and Other universals, what is really a product of the Self is falsely assumed to part of the Other.

In classless societies this propensity to confuse internal states with external reality often results in belief in spirits, the sociology of which is minimally organized. But in more complex societies these spirits are elaborated into a pantheon that constitutes a separate society inhabiting a realm to which ordinary people do not have access under normal conditions. An inevitable part of this belief system is that the well-being of humans in the ordinary world is dependent upon the dispositions and actions of the imaginary beings in the spirit world. This situation thus gives extraordinary power to that segment or class of society which has assumed the responsibility and prerogative of having access to the spirit world. Indeed, those in that class not only control access to the divine, they inevitably elaborate and otherwise glorify it, thus making it more significant in the lives of the common people of society. Needless to say, access to the sacred, in such a situation, becomes a valuable commodity, control of which is readily wielded as political power. The irony of this is that what is being controlled and dispensed by the priesthood springs from the inner nature of the very people to whom it is dispensed. Symbols and sentiments that people themselves have created are alienated from them, elaborated by a priesthood (who may themselves be ignorant of what they are doing), and then given back to these same people, at a price. Sentiments and vague apperceptions of Self in the form of dreams, hallucinations, fears, and desires are not recognized for what they are. They are assumed to exist outside the Self as aspects of the Other. This mystification of what is properly man's own creations results in the reification of these creations. People are thus alienated from that which is properly their own.

This alienation of man's mental creations is parallel to the alienation of the products of his labor under capitalism. In the case of labor, what he has produced is taken from his possession and control and then sold back to him at a profit. In the case of religion, sentiments and symbols that spring from his own partly self-conscious mind are accumulated, as it were, by a priesthood and as such are direct analogs of the private property owned by capitalists but created by the labor of workers, and then sold back—at a profit—to the un-Self-conscious producers of them.

This form of psychological exploitation, indeed the possibility for religion to exist at all, is dependent on a Self-consciousness in which the distinction between Self and Other is poorly developed. As Tyler, Freud, Engels, and Piaget so clearly showed, the fundamental problem in attaining intellectual maturity is learning to distinguish what is properly an aspect of the Self from what is external. The immature mind has a strong predisposition to confound these two domains and to attribute contents and characteristics of the former to the latter. Not only does this propensity provide the psychological basis for the belief in spirits in simple societies and for religion in general in class societies, but it is also at the same time a basis for all idealist ideologies, which also find their most elaborate expression in class societies.

SPACE AND TIME

Let us now examine further the two notions of constancy and change (see The Self and the Other above), awareness of which is a necessary ability of all organisms. There are, I argued, two aspects each of organismic awareness of constancy and change, and these are process and location.[6]

Our flatworm must have some awareness of its physiological states and how they fluctuate according to their characteristic rhythms, and also it must be aware of its locational relationship with food, danger, and other environmental conditions. At first we are tempted to equate process with time and to assume that there is a necessary temporal dimension in world view. Similarly, awareness of location seems to imply a spatial dimension. Are not things located in space? They are, but they are also inextricably located in time, such that it is impossible for a flatworm to know the position of something without knowing it in time. When, for example, it senses a bit of food in its surroundings, its ultimate knowledge of it will be in eating and assimilating it. This involves crawling to it, ingesting it, and digesting it, acts which are processes. Given the neurological development of flatworms, it seems safe to assume that its locational awareness is entirely dependent upon sensory stimuli—in other words, that it is aware of the location of objects or conditions only while it is being physically affected by them (smell, light, temperature, etc.). Its image of the food's location is thus sensory-dependent, and since sensation is a process, we are hard pressed about how to distinguish flatworm awareness of location from process, and by the same token, about assuming an ontologic distinction in flatworm world view between space and time. Our lowly flatworm might in this sense have a world-view dimension of space-time, perhaps not dissimilar to that of modern physicists.

Things are different with humans, for they truly appear able to abstract two dimensions—space and time—where our flatworm is perhaps aware of only one. That in doing so the humans have a distorted or relatively unreal perception of reality compared to those of flatworms and physicists is irrelevant, for it is primarily their images with which we are concerned. The main question is, do normal adult humans characteristically segregate Space and Time into two distinct categories of knowledge?[7] In answering this question we face a great danger of merely reflecting one of the bedrock assumptions of Western philosophy and Western world view in general. Since Aristotle the notions of Time and Space have been accepted by Western philosophers as necessary attributes of human thought. And in the more modern philosophy of Immanuel Kant, the most influential idealist philosopher of Western Europe, Space and Time are held to be the only *a priori* categories of thought, having their seat and origin wholly in the mind.

Thus whereas Space and Time are aspects of one kind of knowledge for flatworms, they are quite distinct for Kant, and no doubt most of the readers of this book. How could this be so? It is possible because of the human ability to abstract locational and temporal relationships apart from sensory knowledge of them. The distinction here is analogous to two of the periods that Piaget marks off in the development of human cognition. In the first, or sensorimotor period, knowledge of surroundings is sensory-dependent in that the child does not appear to form images of them which can serve him as maps or plans apart from the actual perceived setting. At a later period, what Piaget calls the formal-operations period, the ability for imaging is well developed, such that the child, unlike our flatworm, is able to hold images of his surroundings even when he is not receiving physical stimuli from them. Needless to say, this is knowledge of a greatly different kind in that it is removed (abstracted) from sensations. One of the qualities of these abstracted images is that they are relatively static. Whereas the flatworm's image of the location of food is necessarily a product of direct interaction (process) with his surroundings, the abstract image of humans is, once formed, more closely analogous to a diagram, which once drawn, does not change. For humans then, a spatial image can exist out of time, or at least that is how we conceive it.

Similarly, we are able to abstract temporal images that are independent of space. For the flatworm, time is a function of physical motion and chemical process. Presumably it does not envision a tomorrow, or taking a nap after eating. Rather, its sequences of behavior are the results of immediate interactions of its internal states with conditions in its surroundings. The flatworm does appear to have a temporal awareness divorced from immediate sensory awareness in that it is capable of memory and learning. But this is a temporal knowledge only of what humans refer to as the past. They alone are able to conceive of a future in addition to having knowledge of the present and the past, plus the notion of time itself.

But we are still faced with the possibility that this discussion is biased by our own underlying culture-specific notions of Space and Time. Might it not be that other peoples have notions of space-time in some ways more similar to those of flatworms or physicists? One answer to this is the empirical one that no one seems to. The main evidence here is linguistic. All known languages indicate a concern with directions per se, which can be discussed out of time—notions of up, down, east, west, upstream, downstream, forward, backward, etc. Also, all known languages are able to abstractly discuss temporal relations, although the means by which they do so varies. Another argument for the reality of Space and Time as human categories of knowledge is that all languages appear to have nounlike words and verblike words. Nouns, in referring to "things," imply an awareness of the continuity and the constancy of those things. Thus when I put my shoes in the closet, I expect them to be there the next day. (Although time changes, the shoes do not.) But verblike words imply actions or process, and therefore time.[8]

We are thus prepared to admit the dimensions of Space and Time to our list of world-view universals with the proviso that they are perhaps only genuinely attributes of human-world views. We can summarize this analysis diagrammatically in Figure 5.

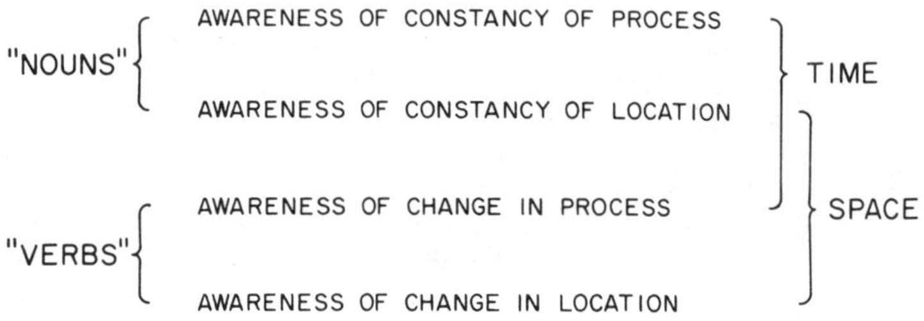

Figure 5. Time and Space.

Now that we have established Space and Time as world-view universals we can discuss ways in which they can vary cross-culturally.

Perception of Space

The term "space" is used to refer to many different concepts, ranging from an easily measurable geographical space to more metaphorical usages such as psychological, life, and mathematical space (Downs and Stea 1973: 5). When, as we are doing here, we deal with the world-view aspects of space, we are concerned with the relationship between the environmental space of a people and their images of it. In analyzing spatial images of a given people, their folk cosmology often offers valuable clues, since cosmologies are by nature pre-eminently statements about space. Cultural conventions for measuring and mapping space and for indicating directions also provide valuable clues about spatial images. Since behavior in physical space is presumably predicated on the images of that space, we should be able to read back to those images by observing how people utilize their physical space. Settlement patterns, house construction, architecture in general, the arrangement of furniture, folk dances, and so forth, all involve action in space. The actual uses of space that a people make from those potentially available to them are affected by their spatial images.

The inhabited landscapes of the earth differ tremendously and we would expect them to affect the cognition of space. A dramatic example of this occurs in Colin Turnbull's book about the Pygmies of the Ituri Forest in Zaire. Once Turnbull took a Pygmy friend of his named Kenge on his first excursion out of the forest. In the forest one cannot see for great distances due to the denseness of the foliage, and at most one sees only small patches of sky through apertures in the forest canopy. It is visually a very closed-in space, and one in which the Pygmies feel secure and at home. Traveling by motor car, Turnbull and his friend left the forest and went onto a hill above an expansive savannah that stretched off to the horizon. A herd of about 150 buffalo were grazing several miles away, and seeing them Kenge asked Turnbull, "What insects are those?" Turnbull comments,

At first I hardly understood; then I realized that in the forest the range of vision is so limited that there is no great need to make an automatic allowance for distance when judging size. Out here in the plains, however, Kenge was looking for the first time over apparently unending miles of unfamiliar grasslands, with not a tree worth the name to give him any basis for comparison. The same thing happened later on when I pointed out a boat in the middle of the lake. It was a large fishing boat with a number of people in it but Kenge at first refused to believe this. He thought it was a piece of floating wood. (Turnbull 1961:252)

The above example illustrates environmental influences on the perception of space. Apart from this is the closely related question of how environmental setting shapes culturally conventional ways of dealing with direction and the underlying notions of space upon which they are based. In discussing spatial orientations of the Salteaux Indians of Canada, Hallowell shows how they have a directional schema such as ours which is based on the four cardinal directions, but which differs from it in important respects. One difference is that the Salteaux equivalents for north, south, east, and west are place names rather than abstract directional terms or coordinates. A directional schema such as that of the Salteaux also persists in Western civilization along with the more abstract system of geometric coordinates. "We say, 'He lives in the West,' or 'The South grows cotton.' The terms 'Occident' and 'Orient' are also used as nouns denoting places or regions. The latter arose at a period when, like the Salteaux, the people employing them thought that the earth was flat" (Hallowell 1955:191).

Another difference between Salteaux and Western spatial orientations is that the Salteaux take their directional cues from nature rather than from scientific instruments or a system of fixed coordinates. Their main reference points are the North Star, the movements of the sun, and the "homes" of the four winds. But it is only by reference to the four winds that they linguistically refer to the cardinal directions. The Salteaux dependence on natural phenomena for directional orientation is analogous to the Nuer's reliance on environmental and social phenomena for a temporal frame of references (see Chapter 4); in this regard they both differ from urban industrial peoples who rely more on artificial abstractions of space and time.

Western man has been freed from the direct observation of nature insofar as he depends upon mechanical instruments for the determination of directions, or does not need to maintain his orientation with respect to compass points at all so far as the pursuit of daily life is concerned. The latter is particularly true of urban populations where such directional orientation may be almost completely ignored. (Hallowell 1955:192)

In contrast to this, Hallowell says that the Salteaux "constantly maintain a directional orientation. Traveling in the open as they do at all seasons of the year, across lakes and through a network of waterways in summer and over snowclad wastes in winter, the direction of the wind in particular is always noticed and their principal activities adjusted accordingly" (ibid.: 192). Modern city dwellers no doubt get around as efficiently as the Salteaux, but they do so for the most part by thinking about going "left" and "right" or "uptown" and "downtown," rather than about east, west, north, and south. Indeed, often they do not know their route in terms of the points of the compass. In the United States rural people, however, do tend to orient themselves in terms of the cardinal directions. These different images become apparent when directions are being given.

Perception of Time

Compared with space, time is a more complex and abstract concept. This is no doubt due to the fact that whereas perception of spatial relations is dependent upon immediately sensed information (object location, body position, motion, etc.), time as a percept is not so directly tied to objects. There is linguistic evidence that cognition of time is influenced by images of space; talking about temporal relationships relies heavily on metaphors of space. For example, temporal prepositions and particles in many languages are marked forms of spatial locatives. Thus, in English when we make temporal statements we almost invariably use words which are primarily terms for space, e.g., *after* an hour, *ahead* of time, *at* noon, *before* the election, *by* tomorrow, *over* an hour (Traugott 1975:210). The unmarked spatial meanings of such prepositions in English are primary in that historically their temporal use developed after the spatial; there is also evidence that the temporal meanings develop after the spatial in children's speech, and in pidgin and creole languages (ibid.: 209, 225 nt.). Language tenses and sequencing are also expressed by using spatial metaphors in which the past or earlier is associated with what is back of the speaker and the future or later with that which is in front: we *come from* the past and *go ahead* into the future. Temporal sequencing can also be ordered vertically, e.g., move a date *up*, pass traditions *down* (ibid.: 221–224).

Just as spatial orientations are influenced by the interaction of our senses with the three-dimensional environment, so do events and objects in our environment affect concepts of time. Ways in which environmental conditions shape temporal concepts are discussed in the next chapter; here we can indicate some of the dimensions of temporal perceptions that must be analyzed for an adequate understanding of the perception of time in any given individual or culture.

There are two basic problems to deal with in analyzing and describing a people's perception of time. First, With what sector of time are they most aware and concerned—the past, the present, or the future? Second, What are their dynamic images of time, of time as process? We can now examine each of these problems.

PAST, PRESENT, OR FUTURE

In examining the temporal orientations of various cultures, it is apparent that they implicitly consider one area of time—the past, the present, or the future—more important than the other two. For example, a cross-cultural study of value orientations in five societies in the Southwestern United States asked, "What is the temporal focus of life?" (Kluckhohn and Strodtbeck 1961). In this study, one of the strongest contrasts was between "Anglos," who tested as having a strong "future orientation," and "Spanish-Americans," who are described as living in a "timeless present." And in contrast to both of these orientations, and using the same test as well as ethnographic examples, I have described Ixtepejanos as having primarily a temporal orientation to the past (Kearney 1972:81–88).

Future Orientation. To have a future orientation means that one thinks of future events and conditions that have not yet come to pass more than one senses the immediacy of events that are actually occurring, or than one thinks of past times. This orientation appears, for example, to have been strongly developed among Calvinists who placed great importance on doing good works in this life such that they would demonstrate their place in heaven in the next. Hard work, success in business, and austere living were the ways in which future salvation was to be demonstrated. This attitude is expressed today in billboards and graffiti exhorting sinners to "Prepare to meet thy maker." Freud described a personality type characteristic of this temporal orientation and referred to it as anal retentive, arguing that even the pleasure of defecation is deferred to a latter time by such a personality. He argued that such a personality, symbolically equating feces with money, also tends to save money for future needs or pleasure rather than indulge in immediate gratification. This orientation thus tends to promote success in business insofar as accumulation of capital is necessary. Similarly, it is compatible with scholastic achievement in that such a student is more able to resist immediate distractions and focus energies toward distant goals—good grades, degrees, etc. A future orientation may also serve as a palliative for poverty and misery and as a justification for the status quo, and as such is satirized in Joe Hill's song about how the mine workers should "Work and pray, live on hay"; in other words, accept their low pay and poor working conditions because "There'll be pie in the sky by and by when you die." If they are good workers, resigned to their earthly fate, they eventually will get to a blissful heaven when they "go to their reward."[9]

There is reason to believe that Americans are becoming less future- and more present-oriented. One possible indication of this is the recent decline in their habit of saving money and tremendous increase in debt for purchase of nonessential consumer goods. Saving is done with an eye to the future, whether consuming at a later date or being prepared to deal with unforeseen financial need. Buying on credit is the opposite in that spending for gratification of a desire or filling a need is immediate. It is possible that this shift in economic behavior and the change in temporal orientation which may be associated with it are a contradiction in a senescent capitalism. Capitalist development was in large part associated with a strong tendency to save and invest rather than consume. But the resultant productive power has necessitated ever greater consumption, which has been encouraged by advertising and easy credit. The present decrease in saving is an integral part of the current high rates of inflation that are endemic in the present capitalist world economic system. At some point, of course, this situation feeds back on itself in that when inflation surpasses interest rates on savings it becomes irrational to save.

Present Orientation. To the Spanish-American subjects of the value-orientations study (Kluckhohn and Strodtbeck 1961), and to many Latin Americans, Mediterranean peoples, and others, the future is seemingly unreal, uncertain, and intangible. What matters for them are events and conditions that they are immediately experiencing, now, in the present (see Chapter 7).

Behavior predicated on a present orientation is often misunderstood by someone possessing a future orientation. For example, Anglos often have a false stereotype of Latin Americans as unreliable and oblivious to time. Anglos in Latin America and other countries where there is a prevalent present orientation are often irritated by failure of people to keep appointments and to keep them punctually. For a future-oriented person, a schedule in the future is in some sense a real thing, even before it occurs. But not so for a present-oriented person who may be confronted by another, immediate event demanding his or her attention while en route to an as yet unreal appointment. When immediate concerns are attended to they may then attend to the appointment. In the value-orientation study, the Navajo tested as having a strong present orientation. This is supported by Hall's observation that, "To the old-time Navajo time is like space—only the here and now is quite real. The future has little reality to it" (Hall 1959:33). To illustrate this, Hall quotes a friend of his who was raised with the Navajo.

> You know how the Navajo loves horses and how much they love to gamble and bet on horse races. Well, if you were to say to a Navajo, "My friend, you know my quarter horse that won all the races at Flagstaff last Fourth of July?" that

Navajo would eagerly say "yes, yes," he knew the horse; and if you were to say, "In the fall I am going to give you that horse," the Navajo's face would fall and he would turn around and walk away. On the other hand, if you were to say to him, "Do you see that old bag of bones I just rode up on? That old hay-bellied mare with the knock-knees and pigeon toes, with the bridle that's falling apart and the saddle that's worn out? You can have that horse, my friend, it's yours. Take it, ride it away now." Then the Navajo would beam and shake your hand and jump on his new horse and ride away. Of the two, only the immediate gift has reality; a promise of future benefits is not even worth thinking about. (Quoted in Hall 1959:33).

Past Orientation.   Traditional Chinese culture was strongly oriented to the past. The sinologist John Fairbank has noted that, "No people have been more interested in their past than the Chinese, for to them it was the model for the present and the primary source of information on human society . . . the subject that concerned them most" (quoted from Mathews 1980). Thus, while Americans make the present serve the future, Mao Zedong spoke to the Chinese sense of time when he told the Chinese people, "Make the past serve the present," by which he meant that there was much that could be learned from history in the building of a socialist society. As is typical of first-order assumptions, this past orientation has manifested throughout Chinese culture. It appears in such ways as ancestor worship, filial piety, a strong sense of family traditions, and an almost compulsive concern with record keeping and history. There is also

the Chinese attitude that nothing new ever happened in the Present or would happen in the Future; it had all happened before in the far distant Past. The proud American who once thought he was showing some Chinese a steamboat for the first time was quickly put in his place by the remark, "Our ancestors had such a boat two thousand years ago." (Kluckhohn and Strodtbeck 1961:14)

How different this attitude is from that of most middle- and upper-class North Americans. Implicit in their economic planning, whether at the family or national level, is the assumption that things will be "bigger and better." And even a cursory examination of advertisements for them, by them, reveals a focus on youth and a strong belief in the intrinsic value of change and newness.

Interestingly, the Mormons, who were also tested in the value-orientations study mentioned above, came out as having a strong orientation to the past. This seems to correspond with their strong concern with the historic past of their religion and with their interest in genealogies by which they attempt to discover spiritual links with unknown ancestors.

IMAGES OF TIME

Most people relate to time much as a fish relates to water—uncritically swimming through it, and largely oblivious to it. And yet, they do have rather definite, but unexamined notions of what it is. Time is one of the most abstract and intangible concepts in human thought. Indeed, in many cultures it does not even exist as a consciously expressed idea. Yet, as I argued above, some sense of time, however implicit, must exist in all mobile living creatures. With the realization that we are speaking in metaphors I refer to such notions of time as images. We can in this way indicate what are two general contrasting images of time, which I shall refer to as oscillating and linear. Both images of time are present, no doubt, in all cultures, but most likely one of them is predominant. According to the British anthropologist E. R. Leach, these two types of images derive from two different common kinds of experiences.

> Firstly, there is the notion of repetition. Whenever we think about measuring time we concern ourselves with some kind of metronome; it may be the ticking of a clock or a pulse beat or the recurrence of days or moons or annual seasons, but always there is something which repeats.
>
> Secondly, there is the notion of non-repetition. We are aware that all living things are born, grow old and die, and that this is an irreversible process.
>
> I am inclined to think that all other aspects of time, duration for example or historical sequence, are fairly simple derivatives from these two basic experiences:
>
> (a) that certain phenomena of nature repeat themselves
>
> (b) that life change is irreversible. (Leach 1966:125)

Oscillating Time.   What I am here calling an oscillating image of time has perhaps been the most common in human societies. It is frequently referred to as a cyclical sense of time, but Leach, in the same essay as the one quoted from above, has persuasively argued that a zig-zag image is more appropriate. I agree with Leach, that it is often inappropriate to refer to a primary concern with repetitive events as a cyclical sense of time. The word *cyclical* implies that something is circular and revolves. But in the traditional societies to which a cyclical notion of time is usually attributed, circular motion is virtually absent.[10] Rotary motion is, however, one of the most conspicuous attributes of modern machines. It is understandable then that such a circular image of time would be projected onto primitives by the writers of modern industrial societies which have, to use Mumford's term, a mechanical view of the world. Contrary to this,

> . . . in some primitive societies it would seem that the time process is not experienced as a "succession of epochal durations" at all; there is no sense of going

on and on in the same direction, or round and round the same wheel. On the contrary, time is experienced as something discontinuous, a repetition of repeated reversal, a sequence of oscillations between polar opposites: night and day, winter and summer, drought and flood, age and youth, life and death. In such a scheme the past has no "depth" to it, all past is equally past; it is simply the opposite of now. (Leach 1966:126)

The essential feature of this image of time is that time is seen as rhythmically swinging back and forth between recurrent markers. Such an image occurs most strongly in technologically simple preliterate societies, lacking historiography. Two characteristics of such societies promote this view of time. First, little cumulative change is observable within the life span of an individual. Instead, events seem to repeat themselves with a regular uniformity and periodicity—the passage of the seasons, the succession of generations, the annual round of festivals and ceremonies. Although it is based on speculation, but speculation which intuitively feels correct, it is often argued that such an image derives from close observation of and subjection to natural rhythmically recurring phenomena—solar, lunar, and biological. For example, speaking about how the moon serves as a natural device for marking time, Eliade says, "In the Indo-European languages the majority of terms designating the month and the moon derive from the root *me-*, which, in Latin, in addition to *mensis*, produced *metior*, 'to measure' " (Eliade 1954:nt. 86).

> The phases of the moon—appearance, increase, wane, disappearance, followed by reappearance after three nights of darkness—have played an immense part in the elaboration of cyclical concepts. We find analogous concepts especially in the archaic apocalypses and anthropogenies; deluge or flood puts an end to an exhausted and sinful humanity, and a new regenerated humanity is born, usually from a mythical "ancestor" who escaped the catastrophe, or from a lunar animal. A stratigraphic analysis of these groups of myths brings out their lunar character. This means that the lunar rhythm not only reveals short intervals (week, month) but also serves as the archetype for extended durations; in fact, the "birth" of humanity, its growth, decrepitude ("wear"), and disappearance are assimilated to the lunar cycle. (ibid.: 86–87).

Short-term oscillating time is thus often replicated in cosmological beliefs in which the world or entire universe itself is subject to cycles of creation and destruction. Such concepts were well developed in the cosmologies of Mesoamerican and most Old World civilizations.

Linear Time.   One indication of the presence of linear images of time is in the grammar of many Indo-European languages. As in English, for example, the verb of every sentence must be expressed in a tense, of which there are three general types: past, present, and future. Every utterance in these languages thus makes a statement about an event conceptualized as existing somewhere in a time that extends from the past into the future. As we will see in Chapter 6, this embedding of time in language is not universal. Grammars in which it does not occur appear to be historically related to nonlinear images of time.

When we speak of an image of "linear time," we must again remember that we are employing a metaphor. Within this metaphor time is rather like an arrow coming out of the past, passing by us here in the present, and traveling on into the future. Or you may prefer to transform this image such that time is a line and it is you who are moving along it, going from one segment of time to another. It is interesting to speculate whether these two ways of imaging linear time are logico-structurally consistent with images of Self. Intuitively I suspect that a sense of Self which is passive relative to the Other is also stationary relative to time, which "flows" by it. By the same token, a Self which is active relative to the Other moves forward into time that exists to be "used." In the first case, metaphors of moving time, such as "the coming months" are expected. In the second the active Self is predisposed to use metaphors in which itself moves, such as "the months ahead." Metaphors of the second type suggest an image of an absolute time analogous to the absolute space of Newton, and seem to presuppose a sense of mastery over a regular natural world. These two images are juxtaposed in Marvell's poem, "To His Coy Mistress": "But at my back I always hear / Time's winged chariot hurrying near; / And Yonder all before us lie / Deserts of vast eternity" (quoted from Traugott 1975:217).

Regardless of the metaphor, the essential thing about a linear image of time is that time is one-way and irreversible. Historically this seems to have been an unintentional invention of the ancient Hebrews who had a most unusual image of time for their period. For them, time in effect began with the Creation and progressed unswervingly through the events of the Old Testament, such as the birth of Moses and the Exodus. The early Christians were also imbued with this notion of linear history, and saw the coming of Christ as a midpoint in historical time, which would end with his second coming, the Millennium. For them history was real, and they thought of mythohistoric events as occurring at specific moments they were concerned to identify in terms of temporal succession and duration, such as the idea that the world was created in six days, and so on. Similarly, fundamentalist Christians today refer to Christ's birth, life, and death as part of an ordinal sequence that will continue, as revealed through Revelation, into the future, until at the Millennium time as history will end. How different this forward-looking image of irreversible cosmic history is from that of say the Greeks or the Romans who were less concerned with the dates and order of events in the history of their religion and myths, such as the year in which Odysseus slew the Cyclops, or Romulus and Remus were born.[11]

A well-developed linear time image is most compatible with and most supported by modern industrial urban society. Societies like this usually have a well-developed sense of history; technological and social change in them tends to be rapid and in some respects cumulative. A linear image of time, supported by such conditions, is consistent with the related idea of progress as a desired, if not inherent, aspect of reality. Individuals are thus aware that things will never again be as they were. Also, modern city living insulates one from astronomic and other natural rhythms. Instead of stars, the phases of the moon, and the seasonal movements of animals and growth of plants, one is exposed to clocks, calendars, and history books, which all proclaim the relentless onward march of time. Although the seasons change out of doors, the air-conditioned artificially illuminated interiors, where city dwellers spend most of their lives, monotonously maintain the same atmospheric conditions year in and year out. Having spent much of my life in rural areas, I am astonished from time to time to find someone who does not know the current phase of the moon or the current location on the horizon where the sun is rising and setting.

As with simpler societies' oscillating images of time, the cosmological theories of "linear" societies are conscious elaborations on their underlying temporal images. The current scientific model of biological evolution is based on a notion of irreversible processes, as is the concept of entropy whereby the energy and complexity of the universe are constantly dissipating. True, the Einsteinian theory of relativity describes a time that is neither oscillating nor linear and collapses space and time into a continuum of space-time; this, however, is an esoteric image of time that has not yet begun to enter into the thinking of ordinary people, whose image of time is still logico-structurally consistent with Newton's. Einstein's concepts of space-time are necessary for dealing with high-energy particles and some astronomic phenomena, but such events are outside of the experience of most people. Newtonian physics, in which space retains its dimensions and clocks all run at the same absolute rate, is much more compatible with the experiences of the everyday world, and therefore it seems a safe speculation that such images will persist in our informal thinking.

Also, we can note how a linear image is structurally compatible with a future orientation. Since linear time is irreversible, the past cannot be regained and the present is but a transitory point on a journey to future events. This inherent logico-structural compatibility of a future orientation and a linear image are well demonstrated in the following passage by the intellectual historian J. B. Bury.

> For though we are unable to divine what things indefinite time may evolve, though we cannot look forward with the eyes of "the prophetic soul Of the wide-world brooding on things to come," yet the unapparent future has a claim

to make itself felt as an idea controlling our perspective. It commands us not to regard the series of what we call ancient and mediaeval history as leading up to the modern age and the twentieth century; it bids us to consider the whole sequence up to the present moment as probably no more than the beginning of a social and psychical development, whereof the end is withdrawn from our view by countless millenniums to come. All the epochs of the past are only a few of the front carriages, and probably the least wonderful, in the van of an interminable procession. (quoted by Beard 1932:xx)

In contrasting oscillating and linear time I do not mean to imply that they are mutually exclusive images. To the contrary, as Leach notes (see above), both kinds of experiences are common to all people. Thus it is possible for both to occur in a given world view. In Aztec world view, for example, cosmic time is organized into great cycles, but individuals appear to have been greatly concerned with the fate of their own souls within a shorter perspective. Therefore, in this case, the image of time is dependent upon the scale of times of concern. But in many cultures one of these images appears to predominate and to affect other perceptions of time, such that it is possible to generally refer to them by one term or the other.

Still other culturally prescribed ways of thinking about time affect behavior. One is the perceived *depth* and *range* of time. Future-oriented North Americans have a shallow range of concern with time and tend to think ahead only within the span of their own lifetime, or the next few generations. Thus, although they are good at short-range planning, they are not effective at preparing for the distant future. The current environmental crises in this country are largely the result of very efficient short-term planning for exploiting resources, but without regard for the long-range consequences. Our concern with the past is also shallow. In contrast, English and European cultures in general value tradition and history much more. "Indeed, some of the chief differences between the peoples of the United States and England derive from their somewhat varying attitudes toward *time*. Americans have difficulty in understanding the respect the English have for tradition, and the English do not appreciate the typical American's disregard for it" (Kluckhohn and Strodtbeck 1961:14–15).

Another important question is, How is the *passage of time* perceived? One aspect of passage is the perceived *rate*. Everyone experiences differences in this rate under different conditions, say, the last day of vacation versus time in the dentist's chair. But there also appear to be general cultural differences as well. It has been pointed out that in the United States clocks "run" while in Spanish America they "walk" *(andan)*. One indirect way of assessing differences in perception of rate is by examining native units of time, which vary considerably in length and discreteness from one culture to another.[12]

> As a rule, Americans think of time as a road or a ribbon stretching into the future, along which one progresses. The road has segments or compartments which are to be kept discrete ("one thing at a time"). People who cannot schedule time are looked down upon as impractical. (Hall 1959:28)

Mumford (1963:17) finds that popular concern with timekeeping and scheduling followed the mass production of watches, first in Switzerland and then in the United States, in the mid 1800s. Scheduling and punctuality are necessary to articulate the intricacies of production and transportation in an industrial society, and they in turn require images of an evenly flowing, quantifiable linear time, as mechanically measured by the clock. It is for this reason that "the clock, not the steam-engine, is the key-machine of the modern industrial age" (ibid.: 14).

E. P. Thompson (1967:57) asks, "If the transition to mature industrial society entails a severe restructuring of working habits—new disciplines, new incentives and a new human nature upon which these incentives could bite effectively—how far is this related to changes in the inward notation of time?" As he proceeds to effectively argue, the changes are considerable, and consist of a shift away from a "task-orientation" sense of time prevalent in nonindustrial societies.

> It is well known that among primitive peoples the measurement of time is commonly related to familiar processes in the cycle of work or of domestic chores. Evans-Pritchard has analyzed the time-sense of the Nuer: "The daily timepiece is the cattle clock, the round of pastoral tasks, and the time of day and the passage of time through a day are to a Nuer primarily the succession of these tasks and their relation to one another." (Thompson 1967:58).

This attitude, which is doubtlessly integral to nonindustrial economies (cf. Chapter Six), is incompatible with a complex division of labor, especially a labor process in which labor is bought and sold. This latter relationship imparts a social and economic dimension to time. "Those who are employed experience a distinction between their employer's time and their 'own' time. And the employer must *use* the time of his labour, and see it is not wasted: not the task but the value of time when reduced to money is dominant. Time is now currency: it is not passed but spent" (ibid.: 61).

Thus, if it was the Puritans who gave Western Europe its future orientation, it was the factory owners and managers of early industrial capitalism who mediated the transformation of time into a commodity by buying labor in units of days, hours, and minutes.

The disciplining, by management, of workers to the exigencies of industrial manufacturing was at heart the instilling of what might be called a "clock-oriented" as contrasted to the above-mentioned task-oriented image

leisurely and routine character. There are no autonomous points of reference to which activities have to conform with precision. (Evans-Pritchard 1939:208).

INTEGRATION OF UNIVERSALS

Throughout this discussion of world-view universals I have attempted to indicate how they are in different ways and to varying degrees interpendent. As we saw, the backbone of a world view is the opposition and integration of the Self and the Other. From this most primary structure we were able, using both genetic and structural arguments, to identify other universals as necessarily deriving from the presence of Self and Other. The first of these was Relationship. The existence of Self and Other as well as further necessary major discriminations within the Other are also tantamount to the origin and structure of the Classification dimension. Whereas Classification is a static structure, Relationship is dynamic in that it deals with interaction between, first of all, Self and Other, and later with interaction among elements both within the Self and within the Other. It is thus from this dynamic aspect of the Relationship universal that we derive the general category of Causality. And as we saw, the cognition of causality is dependent not only upon Relationship, but also upon the cognition of space and time.

We can diagrammatically summarize these interconnections (Figure 6) by using lines to indicate the main logico-structural linkages. In one sense these lines represent the genetic development of the various universals as discussed in this chapter and summarized just above. But they also represent the main influences at any given point in the life of a world view.

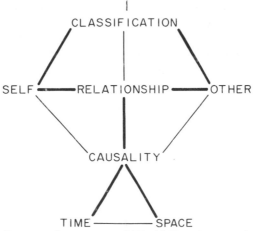

Figure 6. Integration of World-View Universals.

This scheme can be compared with Redfield's (Figure 1). In both, the opposition of Self and Other is the primary axis of world view. But in Redfield's model each dimension is in effect an isolated category which presumably can vary independently of the others. To the contrary, the lines of Figure 6 represent dynamic interconnections in which the presence of assumptions in any one has logico-structural implications for all the others. I have argued that those relationships indicated by heavy lines are the most direct, but that nevertheless all dimensions are directly or indirectly connected one with another.

Chapter 4

A CROSS-CULTURAL MODEL OF WORLD VIEW

The previous chapter dealt with the first of the three main problems in world-view theory: What are some world-view universals that will serve as a basis for cross-cultural description and comparison? Now that we have established such a set of categories we can turn to the other two problems. One is, what are the forces that shape world views (viz., the contents of these universals)? The other is, What influence does world view have on behavior? As will become clear, it is impossible to answer one of these questions without paying attention to the other, but let us start by looking at the first.

WHY THERE ARE DIFFERENT WORLD VIEWS

In surveying different cosmologies and folk philosophies of the world, and the underlying world views upon which they are based, we are faced with the problem of explaining why differences exist among them. The world-view universals we outlined in Chapter 3 are the categories of thought that together are the skeleton of all human world views. The differences among world views are, for the most part, differences in the contents of these categories. That is, although every world view must contain assumptions about the nature of Self, Time, Causality, etc., these assumptions may differ a great deal from one world view to another.

It is convenient in analyzing these differences to speak of *external* versus *internal* causes. External here refers to noncognitive environmental forces which, when perceived, influence the content and shape of thought. Internal causes result from world-view assumptions jostling each other, attempting, as it were, to achieve logico-structural integration among themselves and between themselves and the external environment. External and internal thus correspond roughly to environmental causes (in a very general sense) versus psychological causes, respectively. It is necessary here to distinguish between these external causes in the local social and geographic environment and what, for lack of a better term, I call "outside sources of change" (Figure 7). This refers to economic, political, social and cultural forces that impinge on the local community from outside of it. These sorts of changes are illustrated in Chapter 7, which shows that Mexican peasant world view is to a large extent a result of the rural village's unequal relationship with centers of power and wealth that dominate the local community. These outside sources of change plus the local communities' overt response to them and to their environment in general (action) result in history. History thus alters the physical, social, and mental landscapes, and must therefore be taken into account (again see Figure 7).

External Causes

In our previous discussion of perception and concept formation (Chapter 2), we examined the way in which it is possible for different individuals to form different images of reality. But the question behind this is, Why is this capacity present, and how do such specific contents, rather than others, come into a world view? The seemingly most appropriate theoretical framework for seeking an explanation is that of general evolutionary theory (see for example Simpson 1964). According to the tenets of Darwinian evolutionism, upon which modern thinking of biological and cultural evolutionism is based, the selection of morphological and behavioral traits is by virtue of the adaptive advantage that they confer to the species in question. Following from this principle we would assume that the development within the genus *Homo* of the capacity for seeing reality in markedly different ways enhanced survival by allowing local groups to develop world views appropriate to their particular habitats.

But here we immediately confront a basic conceptual problem: What are we to consider as "environment"? In some sense, the concepts, symbols, and social organization of a society are part of the environment. We must deal with this problem below, but as a first approximation in seeking the reasons for the shape of particular world views, let us look to the physical environment. And to pursue this idea, let us continue to look at the Time universal and inquire into additional possible physical environmental influences on it.

First of all, there are obvious astronomical phenomena that have qualities of periodicity and duration. There is the regular sequence of day and night, the phases of the moon, and the apparent north-south migration of the sun which is associated with the changes of the seasons. One of the most notable features of these astronomical phenomena is their regularity. Another is their pervasiveness in that they have undoubtedly been of concern to all peoples of all times. They do, however, intrude into the thinking of some peoples more than others. Geographic location accounts in part for this. Near the equator, for example, celestial phenomena are minimal in their range of daily and annual variation. In the tropics days do not vary greatly in length throughout the year, and accordingly, as the path of the sun is always relatively high, the annual average temperature does not fluctuate widely. Violent tropical storms may come and go, but the main characteristic of the climate is its monotony. But even here in the tropics with their characteristic narrow annual temperature ranges, there are other annual cyclical phenomena, most notably a more or less widespread annual distribution of rainfall that marks each year into wet and dry seasons.

In the higher latitudes seasonal changes become generally more extreme, and consequently of greater concern to people. For societies whose economies are adapted to seasonal variations in resources, these annual rhythms are one of the main forces directing their activities. This is true both for agriculturalists (who must closely correlate preparation of the soil, sowing, and harvesting with the seasons) and for hunters and gatherers (who must regulate their activities to the movements of game and the seasonal availability of plant resources). One instance of such extreme dependence on seasonal conditions is the traditional Eskimo (Mauss and Beuchat 1906), who practiced what amounted to a double economy. Winters were devoted to living in coastal villages and hunting sea mammals. In summer these communities broke up into smaller groups that moved inland to hunt land animals and gather plant foods. One indication of the extent of this regular annual rhythm of Eskimo thought and religion is that winter and summer activities are also conceptually separated by an elaborate set of taboos that proscribe mixing them.

This sort of dependence on and attention to the annual seasonal round appears to shape oscillating images of time, such as those discussed in Chapter 3, in which time is conceived at one level of abstraction as a virtually endless repetition of events. In such orientations the historical past is characteristically shallow and assumed to not have been much different from the present. Similarly, it is assumed that each succeeding generation will be a rather close replication of the previous.

Evans-Pritchard (1940) gives perhaps the best ethnographic account of such a society, the Nuer of the Sudan. A horticultural and pastoral people, the Nuer's economic and social activities are strongly determined by an annual cycle of rains and droughts which leads Evans-Pritchard to speak of ecological time, which is based on this seemingly eternal sequence of annual seasonal rounds.

This oscillating image of time appears to be the Nuer way of regarding the passing of perennial natural and social events that conform to the same rhythm from year to year. But superimposed on this annual rhythm are transformations that endure across years, such as the life span of individuals or of kin groups. For such longer-period phenomena the Nuer have another temporal orientation, and one that is also based on an environmental frame of reference, although it is taken from the social environment. As Evans-Pritchard says,

> There is, however, a point at which we can say that time concepts cease to be determined by oecological factors and become more determined by structural interrelations, being no longer a reflection of man's dependence on nature, but a reflection of the interaction of social groups. (Evans-Pritchard 1940:104)

One way in which this other method of time reckoning works is that social events—weddings, raids, a camp location of a particular year, etc.— are used as points of reference. An alternative means of doing this, and one that has more potential time depth, is provided by the social structure. In this second social method, "distance between events ceases to be reckoned in time concepts as we understand them and is reckoned in terms of structural distance, being the relation between groups of persons" (ibid.: 105). The sequence of male age sets in Nuer society provides one such reference system, and the kinship and lineage system another. In this latter system of reckoning, reference to times in the past may be made by referring to the kinship or lineage distance between living persons or groups. Given the patrilineal descent system of the Nuer, social distance between relatives or between social segments such as clans and lineages is a direct function of the remoteness of their first common ancestor. Thus, a reference to social distance between groups indicates some point in the past. In this system, contrary to ours, the temporal depth is conceived not in terms of temporal units such as years, but in degrees of agnatic relationship among living people.

Notions of oscillating time appear most typical not only of societies that live close to the earth, so to speak, such as hunters and gatherers and tribal agriculturalists, but also of preindustrial civilizations such as the Babylonian and Aztec. In their notions of cosmic time, such people often have a belief in recurrent cycles of creation and destruction of the world which appear to be symbolic replications of the diurnal, lunar, and annual solar cycles that figure so prominently in their concepts of time as experienced within one's own lifetime.

A fundamentally different notion of time seems to occur among technologically sophisticated peoples. In industrial societies people are insulated from the annual changes of nature. The lives of shopkeepers, factory workers, and bureaucrats are remote from the rhythms of plants and animals, and are in this sense more monotonous. Affluent urban dwellers may live in air-conditioned homes, travel to work in air-conditioned cars, and pass most of their remaining working hours in other artificially controlled environments. Tall buildings and indoor living make it less likely that they will be aware of the annual north and south migrations of the sun's rising and setting. And street lamps and polluted air blot out view of the night skies, thus reducing awareness of annual changes in celestial phenomena. For hunters and gatherers and for peasant farmers these natural rhythms are dramatically conspicuous and of great importance in being associated with the rhythms of subsistence activities and adaptation to seasonal changes. By contrast, modern urbanites are apt to work year-round at jobs little affected by the seasons. And in their homes, their diet and living patterns are similarly relatively unaffected by the rhythms of nature.

The images of time held by inhabitants of industrial urban societies are not, however, unaffected by environmental influences. These influences are now just different. For one thing, historians tell them of past times that were quite different, and perhaps anthropologists describe to them the life and times of peoples in the distant past. And beyond that, geologists provide evidence for a time depth of the earth in a much greater scale. Furthermore, social and environmental changes tend to be rapid in industrial societies. Within their own lifetimes individuals in them are able to recognize extreme changes, and today science-fiction writers and futurologists attempt to depict changes yet to come. In such societies change from year to year is seen as the norm, rather than a seemingly endless repetition of annual cycles. This urban datum is of course the linear image of time (Chapter 3), which consists of three major and distinct segments—past, present, and future, with the notion of some sort of progressive or cumulative change running through them. Time in urban societies also takes on more meaning as an abstract concept. It is measured and apportioned in much more discrete units and with much greater concern. In some sense it is as a container, something to fill with activities. It can be "wasted" and "saved," and it is often equated with money.

There are of course many other sorts of environmental influences on world view, and on dimensions of world view other than time; examples of such appear throughout this book. Human society with its institutions, customs, and roles is also a major part of the environment, and has paramount importance in shaping the world view of the individual. We will discuss at length this social component of the environment and its influence on world view in Chapters 5, 6, and 7.

Internal Causes

Except for the dog, no other mammal has moved into such a wide variety of the world's geographic areas as have humans. But although dogs have followed humans over virtually the entire land surface of the earth, their actual adaptive radiation can be said to be much less extensive than that of humans. The cause is the ability of humans to significantly alter and actually create ecological niches that are more suitable for their habitation. The ability to do this is dependent on the above-mentioned relative independence of humans from instinctually determined behavior. In other words, man's ability to adjust to different environments is far greater because of this plasticity of response. As human beings migrated around the world they profoundly altered the physical environments into which they moved. Among other ways, they did this by using fire to clear brush lands and woods (thereby to promote the growth of grass-eating animals and other game), through agriculture, by building shelters and communities, and by making clothes that protected them from adverse weather. Most study of human evolution and such adaptations as these has focused on their physical and geographic aspects, since they are relatively well-preserved in archaeological and historical records.

Similarly, when looking at idea systems, there is a general tendency in the social sciences to see them as reflections of technology and as adaptations to physical environments or the resultant social structures. To regard human behavior and idea systems solely in such terms is to commit what can be called the "materialist fallacy." The main feature of this fallacy is that it seeks causes of human behavior and thinking entirely or primarily in conditions that are external to the mind. The vulgar materialist position thus does not recognize that ideas and symbols may also have major influences on behavior. But it is also possible to achieve excess in this direction and impute an unreal independence and determinacy to ideas by overemphasizing their power to shape material and social conditions. An attempt to explain social and cultural phenomena solely in terms of world view would be to commit a variant of this idealist fallacy. And yet, ideas—world views—are in some degree independent of material and social forces, and it is to this problem that we must now turn.

It is in the dynamic aspect of ideas and images that we find this second force shaping world views, and accordingly, a second basis for analysis. (The reader will remember that the first basis results from the adaptive necessity of a world view having to fit its environment in some way, and that these two types of forces—we are calling them internal and external—always interact in the shaping of a particular world view.) Since we are talking about a particular cause of world view, we must examine what we mean by *causality* in this particular sense. We can perhaps best do so briefly by comparing this type of causality with that primarily recognized and used in the natural sciences. In the natural sciences causality is dealt with in terms of directly measurable energy and physical force. Events are accordingly explained in terms of the interaction and transformation of energy and force as they conform to mechanical and statistical laws. But when we deal with world view we leave the realm of physical phenomena and enter the realm of mental events, and in doing so leave behind physical causality and its particular kind of regularities.

The most significant difference is that mental events are not directly subject to the principle of conservation of mass and energy that pertains in all types of physical action. A mechanical, chemical, electronic, or any other physical "cause" can never provoke a direct effect greater than itself. Matter and energy are always constant in cause-and-effect relationships. But this principle is not at work when we are dealing with images, ideas, or information of any kind. When, for example, one person reads a book he acquires information, but the knowledge in the book or in its author is not diminished. In the act of learning, imagining, or inventing, one does not expend information. To the contrary, at the completion of the act, the person possesses more information and additional images. These new images may then effect new behavior.

Although ideas, attitudes, sentiments and the assumptions that lie behind them fundamentally differ from physical phenomena, they are not without their own type of order and causal relationships. The difference is that whereas physical causality has as its parameters the regularities of matter and energy, the parameter of mental phenomena is *meaning*. The failure to clearly recognize this distinction has resulted in great confusion in the social sciences. This confusion has, in part, an historical origin. The modern physical sciences for the most part preceded the social sciences. Accordingly, as the social sciences developed they looked, intentionally and unintentionally, to their predecessors for usable models. The problem is, of course, that human behavior has this added dimension of mental activity, which is not a physical phenomenon and not subject to physical causality.[1]

Now it might be argued, as behaviorists do, that mental phenomena—ideas, images, etc.—are no more than shadowy reflections of the physical world, and that therefore physical causality is the only type of causality operative in the social sciences. According to this position the way in which ideas and images are actually formed is due to conditioning, which is a complex physical event. There are several effective antibehavioral arguments, but perhaps the most telling is the one which rests on the existence of truly creative activity. Creativity, from this view, results from the spontaneous recombining of images, ideas, and symbols, apart from any direct conditioning influence. This argument is usually made within the psychological context of individual creativity, and to my knowledge has not been extended to cultural phenomena. Briefly, the outline of this argument would be as follows: While it is possible to trace many physical (environmental) influences on cultural forms (particular beliefs and world-view assumptions), there are large areas of culture that lead, as it were, a life of their own, or one that is at least partially detached from the constraints of the physical world. Yet these mental phenomena are not chaotic; they do have a certain order and consistency, both synchronically and diachronically. The crucial point here is that this order is not due to physical causality, but rather to what we can ambiguously refer to as meaning.

The essential function of thought—world view—is to establish meaning, of which there are two, now familiar, dimensions: an adaptive or external one and an internal one. To illustrate, we can take linguistic meaning as an example. One way meaning is established in language is by denoting certain things and events with words which correspond to them. The other is by internal relationships among words, as determined by the syntax and overall structure of the language, plus linguistic and nonlinguistic frames and contexts. Similarly, thought in general proceeds by relating to things external to it, and also by virtue of its inherent structure, which also shapes thoughts and permutations of them. Again, it must be emphasized that these two aspects of thought are not independent but mutually influence one another. We find such mutual interaction whenever thought confronts the external world. Thought itself is structured by certain logical and structural principles, which may or may not be culturally specific. Take for example syllogistic relationships. In the syllogism "All trees are plants; this is a tree; therefore it is a plant," there is a direct correspondence between the form and content of the syllogism and aspects of external reality (trees and plants and a presumed genetic relationship among them). But the abstract syllogism "All Xs are Ys; this is an X; therefore it is a Y," is also possible. The fact that this case is also meaningful is due entirely to an internal logical relationship. External reality is irrelevant. It is in this general sense that we may speak of meaning as deriving from both external (environmental) and internal (mental) conditions. And it is in this sense that we can speak of external and internal influences on ideas and images.

But as I shall illustrate in the following chapters, formal logical relationships such as the syllogism are only one type of internal ordering of thought, and one which is no doubt relatively insignificant. And yet, one of the main characteristics of thought is its internal consistency and structuring. Granted that many world views and systems of thought in general often appear bizarre and irrational when first encountered, nevertheless, when examined in terms of their underlying images and assumptions, they usually are found to be coherent and internally consistent. Thus, we can say that a world view is ordered by certain *logical* and *structural* principles. I refer to this internal force shaping world views as *logico-structural integration*. Our concern will be to show some of the kinds of such interrelationships that pertain among the various world-view universals, or more accurately said, among the images and assumptions of these universals.

Projection and Reification

Any world view is at best a partial and necessarily inaccurate image of reality. Especially in technologically simple societies, accurate understanding of nature and humanity is lacking. Celestial and meteorological phenomena, physical principles, and so forth are poorly understood. Knowledge of germ-caused ailments and of mental illness as a social process may be totally absent. And even emong more sophisticated peoples large areas of existence remain mysterious. Humans seem to be uncomfortable not having answers to basic concerns such as life, death, illness, cosmology, and their own destinies in general. Consequently humans tend unconsciously to supply satisfying answers that often have little direct bearing on the things they purport to explain. In supplying answers, people draw on their experiences and understanding in other areas of life, and fashion the answers out of this material. This process is referred to as *projection* and the ideas, the symbols, the false knowledge so created are uncritically assumed to be "out there" in the real world. These images are thus *reified*, made things, assumed to be aspects of the environment, when in fact they are reflections of that environment, especially of social structure, as more or less accurately perceived and organized in the world view.

Projections are in a sense metaphors of reality. Like metaphors, they make that which is relatively intangible, abstract, or poorly apprehended appear more concrete by likening it to something that is more directly experienced or otherwise more salient, e.g., time *flows*, love is *sweet*, fascism *stinks*. Projection, to be projection, must however be done naively, that is with no conscious awareness that this process is at work. When a naive projection occurs, one then attributes to the projection the same ontological status as say to a rock or to a cousin. In other words, rather than regarding the symbolic creations for what they are, the people who are doing this projecting assume that the projections belong to the "real world," which is represented in Figure 7 by the box labeled *Social and Geographic Environment*. By means of projection and reification a people thus provide themselves with the content and structure of their religion, myths—their spirits, ghosts, gods—and other forms of folklore. Among anthropologists of a psychoanalytic bent, these symbolic elaborations are known as "projective systems." The concept of projective systems is basically good. But as generally developed in anthropology it has been trivialized by a narrow individualistic psychoanalytic orientation that attempts to reduce projective systems to childhood experiences, as shaped by childrearing practices. The concept has much more relevance for the modern world if instead of thinking from child training we start with the general economic and social conditions of life and in particular with the class relations within a society. For example, the projective systems of the poor and the rich have more to do with their standards of living, the quality of their lives and their control over them than they do with childhood experiences, which in any event are more likely than not largely shaped by these more basic conditions.

If projection be thought of as the head side of a coin, then *reification* is the tail side. Discussion of it in a similar sense to the one used here begins in volume 1 of Marx's *Capital*. Its first appearance is in the section on "The Metamorphosis of Commodities" (1967, p. 209), where Marx, analyzing circulation of money and commodities, speaks of the "personification of things and reification of persons," i.e., "the conversion of things into persons and the conversion of persons into things." Lukács, discussing this reification of commodity exchange, notes, "Its basis is that a relation between people takes on the character of a thing and thus acquires a 'phantom objectivity,' an autonomy that seems so strictly rational and all-embracing as to conceal every trace of its fundamental nature: The relation between people" (Lukács 1971:83). The other mention by Marx is in the Appendix to Volume I in the section on "Mystification of Capital, etc." where the same sort of analysis that is applied to circulation of commodities and money is applied to the process of production. Here, "just as in the case of money, the creative power of labor [seems] to possess the qualities of a thing" (Marx 1976:1052)—a thing that belongs not to the laborer but to the capitalist. Reification of labor power is thus an aspect of its alienation from him to whom it belongs. I am here using "reification" in a much more general sense, but within the same general spirit in that irrational folk beliefs and ideas which (like labor power) belong to individuals in whom they originate are assumed by those individuals to exist apart from them.

Marx himself suggests—unintentionally perhaps—how it is possible to see reification at work elsewhere than in the false objectification of commodities and labor whereby "a definite social relation between men . . . assumes, in their eyes, the fantastic form of a relation between things" (1967:72). He finds an analogy in the "mist-enshrouded regions of the religious world." Here, by means of reification, "the productions of the human brain appear as independent beings endowed with life, and entering into relation with both one another and with the human race" (ibid.). In this way, I would argue (see Chapter 7) that just as the capitalist alienates the product of labor from the laborer, so do the elite of organized religion often alienate attitudes and sentiments generated by common people struggling for existence in relative states of ignorance. And just as the capitalist converts the workers' labor power into wages less in value than the value of the labor power expended, so does religion reify these sentiments into spiritual personages and relations that are assumed to be real by those whose sentiments made this process possible. The heavens become filled with phantasmal spirits and ghosts who are assumed to intervene in human affairs as do events of natural and human origin. "The religious world is but the reflex of the real world" (ibid.: 79).[2]

The degrees to which projective symbols are created and reified differ considerably cross-culturally. One of the tasks of a world-view analysis is to determine what the projections of a people are, what it is that shapes them, and the degree to which they are reified. We will return to this issue, with examples and analysis, in Chapter 7.

THE MODEL

We can discuss the world-view model by referring to Figure 7, which represents the dynamic interrelationship between the material environment, world view, sociocultural behavior, and cultural symbol systems.

In the diagram the arrows represent shaping forces or influences among the phenomena indicated in the boxes, with the direction of the arrows indicating the direction of the forces or influences. Human existence must occur within particular social and geographic environments that include modes of production, customs, social organization, and a landscape. Assuming that the inhabitants of an environment (in the general sense used here) have occupied it for some time—several generations or more—they will have come to perceive it and relate to it in a "traditional" way. This way of perceiving the environment is nothing more nor less than their world view, or from an analytic point of view, the propositions that we derive to summarize it. The environment thus shapes world view; in other words, the way in which the

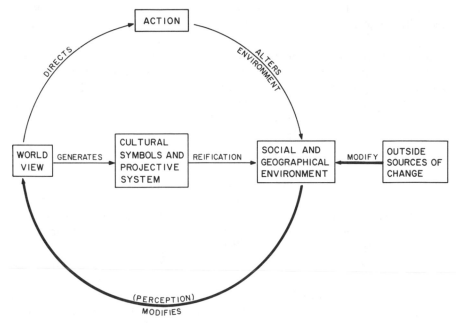

Figure 7. The World-View Model.

environment is perceived is largely dependent on the nature of the environment itself, as defined above.

A world view is in turn, as we have also discussed above, the mental basis for acting within the total environment. Before action can occur the perception of this environment must occur at some level of consciousness or unconsciousness. Invariably there are alternative possible means, modes, and ends of action, and choice among them depends on whether and how they are perceived and on existing values. The values affecting choice-making are themselves dependent not only upon perception of alternatives present, but also upon underlying world-view attitudes about such things as the good life and ways to achieve it, i.e., attitudes about the best ways to maximize security and happiness, as well as notions about security and happiness themselves. In this way, world view shapes more or less regularly patterned sociocultural behavior. In a similar manner, as touched on above, these underlying cognitive orientations also affect the production of cultural symbols and the shape and content of projective systems. As for the social behavior, as it is acted out it becomes embodied in social structure, customs, and institutions and thus becomes part of the total environment. Similarly, cultural symbols and projective systems, as they are generated from underlying world view, become part of this total environment.

The dynamics of this model are thus dialectic: Perception of the total environment occurs, and is in part determined by the nature of that environment. These perceptions are organized systematically into a set of assumptions about the nature of that total perceived reality—into a world view. This world view in turn becomes the basis for socially and physically relating to that environment, and in this way alters the environment; the altered environment in turn will affect the way in which it is perceived.

It is possible to conceive of such a model as remaining in equilibrium, such that the intervention of human action on the environment does not alter it through generations. In actual human societies such equilibrium is no doubt improbable, and most likely there are only slow versus rapid rates of human impact on the environment, and resultant perturbations in world view.

There is an additional source of disequilibrium in such a system—any influence from outside of the environment that intrudes into it and alters it to the point that it results in the inhabitants perceiving it in a new way. In Figure 7 these outside sources of change are represented by the box so labeled. These include such things as climate shifts that alter the landscape, invasions, wars, and epidemics.[3] Such dynamic relationships between world view, behavior, and environment are illustrated in Chapters 5, 6, and 7.

Chapter 5

LOGICO-STRUCTURAL ASPECTS OF WORLD VIEW

To recapitulate, we have so far isolated two major influences on world view. One is the shaping force of the environment and history—or *external* forces. Thus, the simplest and least powerful explanatory statement that we can make is that certain general types of world views are associated with certain social and geographic environments, or that change in the environment will effect changes in the world view. If it were possible to control completely these external (or what we might also call historical) influences, then we might ask if world view and environment are dynamically interrelated in such a way that together they constitute a coherent system that would maintain itself in equilibrium or undergo predictable transformations. The answer is a qualified No. The reason, as I have already indicated, is that a world view as a system has some independence of material and social influences because of its own *internal* dynamics. In other words, within the overall world-view-environment system, world view may itself be considered a subsystem, the parameter of which is the environment in the broadest sense. As a system, a world view is itself ordered by the dynamic interrelationships among its elements, which are the images and assumptions that form the contents of the various world-view universals. These interrelationships are what I have been calling a logico-structural integration.

In constructing a model of a world view, we expect to replicate these logico-structural relations in the derived basic propositions that represent assumptions in the various world-view universals. Therefore, we can say that certain propositions about some of the various universals of a world view tend to imply compatible and preclude incompatible propositions in both the same and other dimensions. Thus at any given time in its history a world view is to some degree a more-or-less logically consistent and structurally integrated set of assumptions. Now that we have available the necessary terms and concepts, we can apply them to specific analyses of logico-structural integration.

CLASSIC GREEK COSMOLOGY

Let us take as an example the logical integration of major features of ancient Greek cosmology. For the sake of simplicity I shall deal only with what I have called second-order assumptions and images, that is, ones which are overtly expressed in native cosmology and ethnoscience. With this in mind, then, we can find no better single body of data for such an analysis than the writings of Aristotle (384–322 B.C.). Although virtually no feature of Aristotle's cosmology is acceptable to modern science, it nevertheless presents what is perhaps the most unified and extensive view of man and the universe ever written. Many of Aristotle's ideas were of course original, and there is therefore the problem of how representative they were of Greek world view in general. This is, however, not of concern here since we are merely taking him as an example to demonstrate the logical coherence of certain aspects of one cosmology. The material that follows is extracted mainly from two of Aristotle's books, one called *Physics*, the other *On the Heavens*. Both were extremely influential and dominated physical science, especially astronomy, until Galileo. The particular world-view universals of this cosmology that I wish to examine are certain aspects of Space and Causality.

Aristotle's universe is contained within an immense sphere on the surface of which the stars are located. Within this major sphere and concentric with it are nested a number of spherical shells. The innermost of these carries the moon, and outward from this shell are progressively larger ones, some of which carry the various other "planets" that are visible to the naked eye. Although there are only seven visible planets including the moon, there are 55 shells. The region between the innermost shell (of the moon) and the outermost (of the stars) is filled with ether, a transparent, weightless, crystalline substance which unlike the components of the earth is pure and unalterable. In apparent contradiction to his own assumptions Aristotle maintained that the planets, stars, and shells are made of the ether. These shells are arranged so that adjacent ones are in contact. The outermost one is in motion and by friction transmits its motion to the next innermost one, which in turn transmits it to its other neighboring shell. In this way this motion is transmitted inward in varying rates to all the shells, thus maintaining the celestial layers in motion. At the center of the universe is the earth, which is itself a sphere concentric with the celestial shells. The area between the surface of the earth and the inner surface of the lunar shell contains air, and lesser amounts of fire and water, which along with earth are the elements of the sublunary region of the universe. These elements of the sublunary world are, in contrast to the ether, subject to change, and are involved in growth and decay.

This universe is finite and unique; absolutely nothing exists beyond the outer surface of the sphere of the stars. And at every point within this surface, i.e., within the universe, there is some form of matter—either the four sublunary elements or the quintessential element ether in the celestial region. In other words, Aristotle maintains that in principle there can be no voids, no vacuums anywhere in the universe, since nature always acts to prevent their formation. This assumption was quite consistent with the technological development of Greek mechanics, which lacked anything resembling vacuum pumps. It was also supported by observations of the working of siphons and the refusal of water to flow from a small-necked bottles unless there is a second opening to prevent formation of a vacuum. Thus, for Aristotle, space and matter are in a sense coterminous in that there can be no space without matter. And since the spherical universe is finite and unique, there is no matter outside it, and therefore no space. If matter and space existed elsewhere, then so might other worlds, and that possibility would contravene the finiteness and uniqueness of the universe as Aristotle conceived it; we will return to this point below.

These assumptions taken alone seem quite conjectural and arbitrary, since there was no way that Aristotle could demonstrate them all. But the force of these arguments was based on common-sense terrestrial observations which did support the arguments when the observations were interpreted in terms of the very cosmology that they were used to validate. This is but one instance of the inevitable interdependence of fact and theory; observations can be considered facts only when they are set within some implicit or explicit conceptual framework.

The main conceptual underpinning that established observed terrestrial and celestial "facts" as facts within Aristotle's cosmology was his theory of motion. Movement is but one particular aspect of causality, and therefore to understand Aristotle's theory it is necessary to review his ideas of causality in general. These are most developed not in his books *Physics* and *On the Heavens*, but in a separate one dealing with theology and later titled by others *Metaphysics*. Were space available here we could trace many logical ramifications into this area, but we must limit our discussion to those ideas that have to do with Aristotle's theory of motion. The analysis of causality in *Metaphysics* has to do with the book's main argument, which demonstrates that God, as Aristotle thinks of Him, is the First Cause: motion must have something that produces it and this something must itself be motionless; there must be some unmoved mover. The argument proceeds by analogy to ideas and emotions that while not moving themselves are capable of causing bodily movement. Thus God, who is pure thought, is the original source of motion. Aristotle is ambiguous about how this motion gets transmitted to observable things such as the stars, and at one point says that God is not definable as "the unmoved mover," but nevertheless the unmoved mover is responsible for the movement of the celestial shells. This type of causality is, in modern terms, reductionistic and animistic. The will or desire of the unmoved mover is the source of celestial motion; in Aristotle's terms it is therefore a "final cause" because it provides a purpose for motion and for change in general. The argument in *Metaphysics* is thus an argument based on final causes. This seems to be a return, in sophisticated dressing, of the common Greek animistic belief that the sun and planets were gods. Given these attitudes in popular Greek cosmology, "It was natural that a philosopher who could no longer regard the heavenly bodies themselves as divine should think of them as moved by the will of a Divine Being who had a Hellenic love of order and geometric simplicity. Thus the ultimate source of all movement is Will: on earth the capricious Will of human beings and animals, but in heaven the unchanging Will of the Supreme Artificer" (Russell 1945:204).

In *On the Heavens* Aristotle is concerned not with the first (viz., final) cause of motion but with the actual movements of bodies. Here the circular motion of celestial bodies is distinguished from the motions of falling bodies, projectiles, and other inert terrestrial objects. Another type of change, which we will not deal with here, is the generation and corruption that earthly bodies undergo. In Aristotle's terms such change in living things proceeds from efficient causes (which most nearly approximate our notion of mechanical causality) as influenced by final causes (their ends) and formal causes (their inherent forms). Similar alteration in the simple nonliving things is accounted for by material causes, that is, by properties inherent in their matter. With this outline of Aristotle's ideas of causality in mind we can examine his theory of motion of inert terrestrial bodies which is such a central part of his cosmology.

To begin, we may ask why in Aristotle's universe some things fall to the surface of the earth, while others such as flames and clouds move away from it. His answer is that things in the sublunary world constantly attempt to seek their proper resting places. Thus fire being the lightest element seeks the periphery of the sublunary sphere, and air and water seek their proper places in lower levels but above the surface of the earth. They would be neatly stratified in their respective levels were it not for the motion of the lunar shell, which constantly mixes them. As fire and water obey their natures, so objects composed primarily of the fourth element, earth, also seek their proper resting place, which is the center of the earth, attempting to do so by the shortest possible path. This is quite observable whenever we pick up a solid object and feel it striving to return to the earth. This is then an explanation in terms of causes.

As was mentioned above, some of Aristotle's main spatial assumptions are that the earth is at the center of the universe, that it is stable and spherical, and that the universe is unique and finite. Let us take these assumptions one by one to see how they articulate with his ideas of motions.

As to the earth's *centrality* in the universe: Aristotle explains, "The natural motion of the earth as a whole, like that of its parts, is towards the center of the Universe: that is the reason why it is now lying at the center" (quoted from Kuhn 1957:84). He maintains that earthly matter actually seeks the center of the universe, and that as a result of this the centers of the earth and universe coincide. Earthly matter thus in effect seeks the center of the earth.

Now from this chain of reasoning, which is based on the observation of the weight and falling of objects, it is a short step to the assumption that the earth is *immobile*. Thus Aristotle argues, "If it is inherent in the nature of earth to move from all sides to the center (as observation shows) . . . it is impossible for any portion of earth to move from the center except under constraint" (ibid.). In other words, "If then any particular portion is incapable of moving from the center, it is clear that the earth itself as a whole is still more incapable, since it is natural for the whole to be in the place towards which the part has a natural motion. . . ." (ibid.). The earth therefore does not move. But if it were moved it would, if unrestrained, return to the center.

Other more abstract notions of space articulate to the assumptions about motion, the earth's stability, centrality, and sphericity, Space is something absolute with its own intrinsic geometry. It is this absolute space that defines the natural positions of bodies and the lines along which they move to these positions. What this means then is that the natural motion of a stone, for example, is influenced by space alone rather than by other bodies or forces. Motion in the sublunary world is thus different from that in the celestial. And it is also more sophisticated by comparison with modern mechanics and Piaget's hierarchy of causal concepts (Chapter 3). Whereas celestial motion is in part animistic, terrestrial objects are subject to the geometric coordinates of the sublunary world. They are, in other words, subject to external rather than purely internal causes. This theory is not completely mechanistic, though, for the inherent nature of the sublunary elements is what determines how they react in this space. The causality operative here is mechanistic in that the four sublunary elements are comparable to charged particles (if we can imagine four distinct electrical charges rather than just two) that are sorted out to various regions of a magnetic field. But there is no explicit theory of force, such as gravity, acting on the elements, and the language used is all in terms of how elements, by virtue of their natures, *seek* their proper resting places. Although Aristotle speaks here in terms of material causes, there remain underlying animistic assumptions. These become more obvious if we compare Aristotle's theory with Newton's First Law of Motion, with which it is incompatible. In Newton's universe, bodies at rest remain at rest unless acted upon by an external force; they do not move about because it is their nature not to move.

Aristotle demonstrates that the earth is *spherical* by applying the laws of motion to a reconstruction of the earth's formation. The earthly particles which were to coalesce into the earth must have in the beginning been swarming about, each seeking the center of the universe. As they moved to it, the first to arrive would have gone right to it. Successively later-arriving particles would not be able to displace them and would thus build up on the surface in areas closest to the center. A sphere being the only shape whose surface is everywhere equidistant from its center, then in this manner an expanding sphere would form until all earthly matter had accreted to it and the earth assumed its present size and shape. Aristotle also buttresses this argument for the earth's sphericity with empirical observations: he notes that the shape of eclipses of the moon appear as though cast by a round object, and the apparent position of the heavens changes as one moves north or south on the surface of the earth. Thus his model is not only woven together by an internal logic but is also a model that incorporates a number of common-sense observations.

Another such common-sense argument for the earth's *stability* was current in classical Greece and was used to refute the possibility that the apparent diurnal motion of the stars and planets was due to a revolving of the earth on its north-south axis. The argument is based on the principle of motion by which earthly objects seek the center of the earth. This being accepted, should an object be thrown into the air with a trajectory that began perpendicular to the surface of the earth, it would seek to return to the earth's surface by the most direct path. Therefore, if the surface of the earth were moving from west to east—which would account for the movement of the stars—the object would arrive back on the surface west of the point whence it was launched. And by similar reasoning, clouds, which naturally seek their proper position in the sublunar region, would be seen to always move westward relative to the earth's surface as it revolved to the east under them.

Now the major problem in any geocentric cosmology that deals with astronomic phenomena is to explain the motions of the planets, which appear erratic compared to the comparatively much greater regularity of the motions of the stars. The word "planet" in Greek means wanderer, and the planets were so denominated because of their movements through the constellations of the zodiac. Accounting for and predicting the positions of the planets using a geocentric model such as Aristotle's is most difficult. Recasting the problem in a heliocentric model would seem to have been an intriguing alternative for Greek astronomers to experiment with. Some, such as Aristarchus, Heraclides, and others did construct heliocentric models, but the idea did not become popular because even "though difficulty in solving the problem of the planets might have provided an astronomer with a motive for experimenting *in astronomy* with the conception of a moving earth, he could not do so without upsetting the accepted basis of terrestrial physics in the process. The very notion of a moving earth would be unlikely to occur to him, because, for reasons drawn from his nonastronomical knowledge, the conception seemed so implausible" (Kuhn 1957:85).

From the premise of the earth's centrality, which as we can now see is embedded in a number of interlocking assumptions, it is possible to trace Aristotle's connection to the premise that the universe is *finite*. It must be finite because an infinite universe can have no center, and without a center there can be no natural positions defined in reference to it. And without natural positions the law of motion has no basis.

Other internal connections also exist. Earlier we touched on the premise that the universe is everywhere filled with space-matter: nature "abhors a vacuum." This concept too is mutually dependent upon the law of motion. Since it is space that determines motion, and objects are everywhere subject to motion, space-matter is everywhere present in the universe. This is accepted on principle.

The premise of the universe's *uniqueness* does not have any strict logical basis in the other premises. There is one feeble argument that if the universe were infinite, then there would exist no special central point at which the earth could have formed. Obviously this reasoning totally neglects the possibility that there could conceivably be multiple such centers of formation, as contemporary cosmologists recognize multiple centers for the coalescence of nebulae into stars. Furthermore, one might have asked Aristotle, why could not a void exist beyond the sphere of stars of this universe, and other self-contained "universes" exist within it? Such a possibility would not violate the workings of this universe since their space-matter, should they be so constructed, could not affect this universe across the intervening void. The insistence of the uniqueness of the universe thus seems to be born chiefly out of a desire for completeness of explanation and consistency in not allowing for voids beyond this universe when they do not exist within it.

In this brief examination of Aristotelian cosmology we have teased out only a few of the logical threads that weave it together. Even though there are apparent superficial contradictions, it is basically of tight construction. In comparison to our modern world view—which has been informed by telescopes, Galileos, and Newtons—Aristotle's cosmology seems patently nonsensical unless we realize, as we have discussed, that it was highly consistent with observations of nature. As in all viable world views, there was a definite interplay between the construction of this cosmology and the way the world was perceived. The logical coherence of this cosmology no doubt accounts for its resistance to piecemeal changes. A change in any of the major assumptions necessitates changes in others. Although modified by church scholars to make it conform more exactly to Catholic theology, the basic outline of this cosmology persisted in Western Europe through the Middle Ages. It is only within this overall intellectual framework that the late acceptance of heliocentrism is understandable. For the immobile earth to begin revolving around the sun the very image of nature had to change.

The above example reveals two fundamental kinds of logico-structural relationships that exist within a world-view model. The first of these kinds comprises the relationships among the various basic propositions, like the consistency between the propositions about space and causality. The relationships of the second kind exist between the basic propositions and corollary concepts, behavior, institutions, and symbols that are shaped by the basic assumptions. It is this second kind of logico-structural relationship that allows us to explain and predict social and cultural forms once the relevant basic propositions have been established.

To further illustrate this sort of internal patterning of world views let us examine some of the assumptions inherent in several other world views and see how they more or less cohere into patterns that orchestrate beliefs and behavior. Let us take first what I shall loosely refer to as the modern scientific and biblical world views, and examine their images of Time and see how they tend to imply particular assumptions in other universals.

SCIENTIFIC AND BIBLICAL WORLD VIEWS

As was noted earlier, men and women who have been highly trained in the natural sciences other than theoretical physics tend to think of time as linear and as running at a constant rate. Their image of time's depth and range is, in the conduct of their daily lives, often consistent with the prevalent shallow and future time prevalent in modern industrial culture. But as scientists they have an image of the countless years of geologic and astro-nomic time. This image of time is, as we have also already discussed, con-sistent with their cosmologic theories. Now a cosmology has inherent within it a notion of causality, and scientific causality is for the most part a genetic theory: the essence of such ideas is that things are presently the way they are because of all the events which preceded them. Explanation of why things are the way they are thus involves showing how they developed. Accordingly, some philosophers and historians of science have argued that this basic premise of modern science had to await the emergence of a linear image of time before it could appear. The important components here are regularity and irreversibility.

This image of time associated with current scientific cosmology is com-patible with the idea of "uniformitarianism," the notion that natural pro-cesses are everywhere and at all times the same: physical, chemical, and biologic phenomena are deemed the same today as when life began. When this idea of immutability of natural laws was proposed by Descartes and others, it was strongly opposed by Christian theologians. In a universe run according to invariable mechanical processes, God would also have to obey them, and therefore be incapable of exercising divine authority and will. Such a god would therefore be incapable of performing miracles and mak-ing revelations. The spread of this single image of natural processes con-siderably eroded the foundation of the prevalent Christian image of the universe. Insofar as Christian thinkers held this new image of natural processes, they necessarily had to create a new image of God's relation to them. One answer, as we have already seen, was to relegate God to the role of prime mover. As men of science now came to think of the universe as an analog to the clockworks that ran their own lives, God in effect became the clockmaker who built it and set it in motion, but, once having done so, left it alone to tick on through eternity.

A necessary corollary of a genetic temporal image is that biologic and geologic changes proceed slowly and without abrupt alternations. Within biology, natural selection as a process shaping the morphology and behavior of organisms proceeds by the accumulation of billions of minute changes. Similarly, the formation of a landscape is the end result of physical process-es barely perceptible within the lifetime of a human. A necessary requisite for such causal ideas is thus an image of virtually illimitable time depth within which changes can occur.

Now let us take a much briefer temporal image, one like that held by people who believe in a literal interpretation of the Bible. What are the implications of such an image of time for other dimensions of their world view? For one thing, this temporal image of necessity implies a very differ-ent notion of causality. Some editions of the King James version of the Bible have marginal notations indicating that God created the world 4004 years before the birth of Christ. This date was determined by James Ussher, archbishop of Armagh, who based his calculations on genealogies mentioned elsewhere in the Bible. This means that the world as we know it today is a little less than 6000 years old. (The traditional Jewish date of Creation is 3761 B.C., and the Byzantine is ca. 6509.) Compared to the geologic time of geologists and biologists, this is hardly time enough for any significant change to have occurred by natural processes. Accordingly, in the biblical view of causality, natural processes cannot conform to uniformitarian principles. Instead a god is assumed to exist who can perform instantaneous miracles and cause worldwide catastrophes. This is an image of what a nonconcurrer might call erratic causality, as opposed to genetic causality. Contemporary conditions are not so much the end result of slowly accumulating changes that can be understood by study of their history as they are the result of an omnipotent, unfathomable, and somewhat unpredictable divine will that can create an entire world *de novo*. This biblical image of time and causality is also consistent with its image of the future. The world is to end in a catastrophe, and perhaps not too long from now.

Images of cosmic space in these two world views are also logico-structurally compatible with their respective temporal images. The biblical universe is geocentric, whereas the scientific universe is no longer even heliocentric. Instead our solar system is now seen as existing in the periphery of a rather mediocre galaxy, in a universe that has no readily identifiable center. In the biblical image of the universe, the world and the Self on the world are located in a finite space and time of human proportions. Likewise, in the scientific world view there is also an internal correspondence between cosmic space and time in that both are immeasurably great.

It is also possible to speculate on the images of Self one would expect to be associated with these two world views. The biblical Self appears to have been terrified of the insignificance it would have in a Copernican universe, and from so having to admit that there might exist other inhabitable worlds. For most of the readers of this book it is no doubt difficult to imagine the consternations and fear that the idea of a heliocentric universe poses to people who regard the earth as the center of the cosmos. One of the first books to popularize heliocentrism was Fontenelle's *Conversations on the Plurality of Worlds* (1686). In it a savant explains to a French lady that it is the earth which revolves around the sun, and not vice versa. She expresses her shock by saying, "In such a large universe I would be lost, no longer knowing where I am; I would be nothing. Such an earth is so terribly small" (from Bury 1932:115; my translation).

Nikos Kazantzakis describes similar feelings that he experienced upon first learning of the modern views of astronomy and evolution, which were so different from the images he had acquired from previous religious instruction.

The first secret, the truly terrible one, was that the earth, contrary to our belief, is not the center of the universe. The sun and the star-filled heavens do not submissively revolve in circles around the earth. Our planet is nothing but a small and insignificant star indifferently tossed into the galaxy, and it slavishly circles the sun. . . . The royal crown had tumbled from the head of Earth, our mother.

I was overcome with bitterness and indignation. Together with our mother, we too had fallen from our place of precedence in heaven. In other words, our earth does not stand as a motionless lady in the middle of the heavens, the stars revolving respectfully about her; instead, she wanders among great flames in chaos, humiliated and eternally pursued. Where does she go? Wherever she is led. Tied to her master, the sun, she follows. We too are tied, we too are slaves, and we follow. So does the sun; it is tied also, and it follows. . . . Follows whom?

In short, what was this fairy tale our teachers had shamelessly prated about until now — that God supposedly created the sun and moon as ornaments for the earth, and hung the starry heavens above us as a chandelier to give us light!

This was the first wound. The second was that man is not God's darling, His privileged creature. The Lord God did not breathe into his nostrils the breath of life, did not give him an immortal soul. Like all other creatures, he is a rung in the infinite chain of animals, a grandson or great-grandson of the ape. (Kazantzakis 1965:144–155)

Such a feeling makes more understandable the zeal with which the Inquisition tried Giordano Bruno and burned him at the stake, and made Galileo recant. The inhabitants of a Ptolemaic universe were terrified with the insignificance they would have in a Copernican universe, with the new sense of Self it implied. What meaning is there to being one of God's people if you exist on a mote of dust in an illimitable expanse of space filled with far more impressive celestial bodies? And similarly, the image of Self, given meaning by being seen as located in *the* historic period, was threatened with insignificance when perceived in a geologic time scale.

What about the sense of Self in the scientific world view? Just above we saw the biblical man's sense of self-identity was tied to his belief in an omnipotent and more or less benevolent deity who among all things in the universe took a special interest in man, and thus elevated him to a special place among God's creatures. The scientific response to the vanishing of God's power amounted to a shift from an image of Self as subject under God to an image of Self as having mastery over nature through understanding of her laws.

Taking into account these logico-structurally interrelated images, it is more clearly understandable why there is such a lack of understanding between people imbued with a modern scientific world view and those with a biblical world view. In arguments between such people each adversary attempts to compel the other to accept his statements by logical demonstration of evidence or by appeal to authority. But even the most elegant logic and the most profound authority must rest upon some prior premises or legitimacy. This bedrock of perception and belief is world view.

WORLD VIEW AND SOCIETY

One of the most intriguing problems in world-view theory is the nature of the relationship between thought and social organization. In some of the more simplistic theories, social forms are seen as somehow real objective phenomena of which ideas are mere shadows that change as society changes because of material or economic forces. Conversely, ideas may be seen as the origins of actions in social life and therefore as shaping society. Considered in terms of this simple dichotomy, the world-view theory presented herein might appear to be idealistic in that primary emphasis is given to the analysis of ideas in human life. But in fact, this world-view theory does not argue that ideas are in any causal sense primary to the material or social conditions of the society in question. This concern with ideas represents, instead, a preference to give most attention to the analysis of a people's thought on the assumption that it, if not the cause, is at least the single most pervasive and consistent structure by which we can conceptually bridge across various domains of life.

Implied in the above statement about "bridging" is the notion that the various areas of thought and society —both within and among themselves— of a people are integrated. This notion invites the question, To what degree might they be integrated by presumed logical and structural interconnections? An enthusiastic but naive reply would be "entirely." Were this true, we would not then need to bother with problems of logico-structural inconsistencies. But these do exist, no doubt in every society and culture, and so we must accept the fact that the edifices which house thoughts and behaviors are less than perfectly constructed. Here walls are off plumb, some of the rooms lack doors, and segments of the foundation may be misaligned or missing altogether. In all probability we are apt to find, continuing within this architectural metaphor, that our subject of study is most haphazardly constructed, with all sorts of loose boards left hanging out, holes in the roof, and so forth. But yet, it is a lived-in structure whose overall form does shape the lives of those living within it. Therefore, rather than expecting to find complete neatness and symmetry in the plan, we should be content to apprehend its fundamental features. Thus a Victorian mansion, no matter how imprecisely constructed, is still a Victorian mansion compared to an Indian wickiup. And the conduct of life and the content of thought is apt to be quite different in both.

This is a roundabout way of arguing that although world views are in varying degrees internally inconsistent and contradictory, nevertheless it is often possible to discover fundamental and far-reaching relationships between the thinking and the social organization of a given people. In the various examples of logico-structural integration offered in preceding pages, the main concern has been to demonstrate integration among ideas—images and assumptions. Let us now, therefore, examine the potential for analyzing the logico-structural integration existing between major world-view images and their respective social structures in one particular society.

Self, Time, and Society in Bali

"At base, thinking is a public activity—its natural habitat is the houseyard, the marketplace, and the town square. The implications of this fact for the anthropological analysis of culture . . . are enormous, subtle, and insufficiently appreciated." With these words Clifford Geertz (1973:360) begins an essay which is an excellent analysis of the logico-structural integration of Self, Time, and social structure on the island of Bali.[3] Geertz begins by adopting a notion from the social phenomenology of Alfred Schutz.

An integral part of Schutz's concept of "the paramount reality" in human experience is that of personhood or personal identity, which is comparable to the world-view universal of Self. To this end he breaks down the notion of "fellowmen" (what we here would refer to as "fellowselves") into predecessors, contemporaries, consociates, and successors. Briefly, consociates "are individuals who actually meet, persons who encounter one another somewhere in the course of daily life" (ibid.: 365). Contemporaries, like consociates, live in the same period, but not the same place. Although participating in the same general cultural milieu, they do not normally meet. Whereas consociates share both time and space, and contemporaries share a common time, one shares neither space nor time with one's predecessors and successors; there is no possibility of interacting with them at all. Predecessors have already lived; they can be known of, and their acts affect the lives of those they precede, viz., their successors, whereas the reverse is not possible. Similarly, although one cannot know of his successors, his actions can influence them, and again, the reverse is impossible.

DEFINITION OF SELF

Now putting aside for a moment this category of personhood/persons, let us look at the more common labels used in Bali to identify individuals.

Geertz notes six different types: (1) personal names, (2) birth-order names, (3) kinship terms, (4) teknonyms, (5) status titles (or "caste names") and, (6) public titles of chiefs, rulers, priests, and gods. Again, as with the notion of personhood, Geertz examines these terms for what they, as "symbolic orders of person-definition," reveal about the underlying notions of person, Self, and Time, and the forms of social conduct that are predicated upon them and that reciprocally condition their form.

Personal Names. All Balinese have personal names, which almost invariably are arbitrary nonsense words ritually bestowed after birth, and which are retained for life. They are, however, rarely used either to address or refer to someone. The Balinese hamlet, which is a politically organized endogamous and strongly corporate community, is in effect a world of Balinese consociates. Within each hamlet duplication of personal names is avoided. Personal names are also monomials in that they connote no familiar connection or other sort of membership. They are seldom spoken and are unimportant in public life. Furthermore, there are moral proscriptions against using those of one's forebears, including one's parents. Personal names are thus significant by virtue of their public insignificance. They are an "intensely private matter," and as symbols they represent all that remains when the other socially more significant labels of one's person are removed. During one's life, this social designation which is most specifically his own is minimized, and at death only a man and perhaps a few close friends know his personal name, which then disappears with him. With this minimizing of personal names there is also the muting of "the more idiosyncratic, merely biographical, and, consequently, transient aspects of his existence as a human being . . . in favor of some rather more typical, highly conventionalized, and, consequently, enduring ones" (ibid.: 370).

Birth-Order Names. At birth each Balinese child is given one of four standard birth-order names, depending on whether it is the first, second, third, or fourth born; these names are *Wayan, Njoman, Made,* and *Ktut,* respectively. Upon the birth of fifth and successive children the names are again bestowed in the same order. These terms are used mainly within the hamlet for children and for young adults without children.

Upon the birth of a couple's first child, use of their birth-order names is discontinued, and they are then referred to by the now possible teknonyms (see below). What we are calling birth-order names, however, do not necessarily indicate the birth order of living siblings, since high infant mortality rates may make a Ktut the oldest and a Wayan the youngest of a set of living siblings. But what "they do suggest is that, for all procreating couples, births form a circular succession of Wayans, Njomans, Mades, Ktuts, and once again Wayans, an endless four-stage replication of an imperishable form. Physically men come and go as the ephemerae they are, but socially *dramatis personae* remain eternally the same as new Wayans and Ktuts emerge from the timeless world of gods (for infants, too, are but a step away from divinity) to replace those who dissolve once more into it" (ibid.: 371–372). Leaving aside for a moment this suggestion of a certain temporality implied in this institution of birth-order names, let us go on to other Balinese labels of persons.

Kinship Terms. Balinese kinship terms, like personal names, are rarely used as terms of address. Their main social use is instead referential, and then only to indicate some specific point about kinship relations; they are virtually never employed as a general means of identifying people. Thus, like the system of personal naming, this system of labels is minimal in the ordering of common interactions with the hamlet. But in this attenuated form it also reflects the Balinese notion of Self in that it "defines individuals in a primarily taxonomic, not a face-to-face idiom, as occupants of regions in a social field, not partners in social interaction" (ibid.: 373).

Although, like the personal-naming system, the kinship terminological system is unimportant as a device for ordering day-to-day social interaction, it is nevertheless structurally consistent with the Balinese notion of Self. "For, as a system of significant symbols, it too embodies a conceptual structure under whose agency individuals, one's self as well as others, are apprehended; a conceptual structure which is, moreover, in striking congruence with those embodied in the other, differently constructed and variantly oriented, orders of person-definition. Here, also, the leading motif is the immobilization of time through the iteration of form" (ibid.: 373–374). This repetition of form occurs in the reciprocal use of the same term in the third generations both above and below the generation of an individual taken as a point of reference. In order words, one refers to both his great-grandchild and great-grandparent by a single term, *kumpi*.[1]

This practice suggests an underlying equivalence of "great-grandparent" and "great-grandchild," between whom the genealogical span of four generations constitutes a fundamental unit. This equivalence is also apparent, for example, in funerary obligations: although a man's children, grandchildren, and great-great-grandchildren, if he has any, are expected to pay homage to his spirit, his great-grandchildren have no such obligation. The reason—they are *kumpi* to him and therefore not his junior; within the Balinese metaphor, they are the same age. "As such, they are not only not required to show homage to his spirit, but they are expressly forbidden to do so. A man prays only to the gods and, what is the same thing, his seniors, not to his equals or juniors" (ibid.: 374).

Geertz's interpretation of this practice is as follows: The Balinese have, as is indicated in other institutions, a proclivity to minimize the social distinctiveness of individual personalities and to attempt to immobilize time. They are, however, faced willy-nilly with the fact of generational differences. Thus, within the sequence of seven generations with which one must relate in their own life, distinctions must be made that go against this tendency to immobilize diachrony. But terminologically the ends of this sequence fold back into the middle in that one's great-grandparent and great-grandchild are both equated with oneself. Therefore, rather than generations being represented as a linear extension through time, they are seen as two articulated cycles of three elements each, with a total of five due to the identity of those elements equated in the *kumpi* relationship (See Figure 8, in which arrows indicate descent).[2]

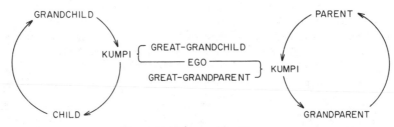

Figure 8. Balinese Kin Terms.

Teknonyms. Since personal names, birth-order names, and kinship terms are of minor importance, another convention must be employed for addressing and referring to people. The Balinese accomplish this by using teknonyms in a system that works as follows: Say a couple has their first child, whom they name Joe (Geertz uses this American name for illustration). Immediately upon naming Joe they both become known as Mother-of-Joe and Father-of-Joe. Not only that, Joe's grandparents and great-grandparents are similarly known as Grandmother-of-Joe, Grandfather-of-Joe, etc. "Thus, over the 'natural' four-generation *kumpi*-to-*kumpi* life span, the term by which an individual is known will change three times, as first he, then at least one of his children, and finally at least one of his grandchildren produce offspring" (ibid.: 376).

As with the other naming conventions, this one also is structurally consistent with perceptions of one's Self and of others. First of all it serves to define the husband-wife pair in terms of a father-mother pair, which is the basic social unit in Balinese society. It also underscores "the enormous value which is placed upon procreation" (ibid.: 377). Considering this convention not just in terms of single pairs of fathers-mothers, grandfathers-grandmothers, etc., but within the context of the entire hamlet, it serves to classify individuals into "procreational strata," i.e., childless people, people with children, people with grandchildren, and people with great-grandchildren.

For the individual, his (or her) procreative status "is a major element in his social identity, both in his own eyes and those of everyone else. In Bali, the stages of human life are not conceived in terms of the processes of biological aging, to which little cultural attention is given, but of those of social regenesis" (ibid.: 377).

This is an interesting practice. Whereas most peoples of the world tend in some way to define a person in terms of who produced them, the Balinese do the opposite and define themselves in terms of whom they produce. Geertz sums up the implications of this practice for notions of Self and Time as follows:

> What links "Great-grandfather-of-Joe," "Grandfather-of-Joe," and "Father-of-Joe" is the fact that, in a sense, they have cooperated to produce Joe — that is, to sustain the social metabolism of the Balinese people in general and their hamlet in particular. Again, what looks like a celebration of a temporal process is in fact a celebration of the maintenance of what, borrowing a term from physics, Gregory Bateson has aptly called a "steady state." In this sort of teknonymous regime, the entire population is classified in terms of its relation to and representation in that subclass of the population in whose hands social regenesis now most instantly lies — the oncoming cohort of prospective parents. Under its aspect even that most time-saturated of human conditions, great-grandparenthood, appears as but an ingredient in an unperishing present. (ibid.: 379)

Status Titles. In Bali virtually everyone has an inherited title, one of many, all of which are ranked into a more or less fixed prestige hierarchy. These titles are markers whereby, taking into account one's own title, one knows the proper demeanor to display to others, and vice versa. The legitimation of this hierarchy is rooted in Balinese mythology, and roughly it corresponds with the actual realities of personal power, influence, wealth, and reputation. There are, however, many discrepancies between actual social status and what the titles of individuals ideally indicate of their status. Geertz asks how these common inconsistencies are handled within the overall system. In effect, they are damped out by submerging the entire status hierarchy system within a much more general hierarchical classification — the Hindu *varna* system, borrowed from India. This "caste" hierarchy consists of four ranked main categories — *brahmana, satria, weisa,* and *sudra,* going from highest to lowest. Village Balinese do not actually consider each other in terms of the *varna* categories in day-to-day interaction, but instead employ them for making general correlations among the holders of different status titles.

Status titles of individuals thus bear no implication of inherent personal, moral, or spiritual value. And, moreover, insofar as they are markers of individuals, these individual titles are greatly minimized by the lumping of the many status identities they denote into the four far more anonymous *varna* categories. This convention thus mutes the diversity of individual differences and unique historic occurrences by locating people in a set of impersonal, immortal status categories.

Public Titles. As in perhaps all societies, in Bali there are public titles for individuals depending on their occupation or other official position. Whereas these are important components of personal identity for Westerners — people are what they do — they are not so to any great extent in Bali.

There is a strong conceptual and actual boundary between public and private life, at all levels of society. The public sector comprises a number of corporate bodies, such as hamlets, irrigation societies, congregations of local temples, and so forth. Each of these bodies has officers responsible for its administration, each of whom bears a specific title by which he is addressed. Thus at the lower levels there are various village chiefs, priests, etc., and at the higher such officers as kings, princes, lords, and high priests. But whereas Westerners would speak of an official as occupying such roles, it is more appropriate to say that the Balinese *become* that role in that other aspects of their personhood are subordinated, symbolically at least, to this identity. Personal identity is not defined by biographical traits such as age, sex, or achievements, but by one's typological location in this impersonal, unchanging spiritual hierarchy.

As kinship terms and teknonyms indicate an ascendancy toward divinity (insofar as they indicate passage through the life cycle that culminates upon death with return to the world of the gods), so do public titles in that the higher ones merge into those of the gods. At this level "there is literally nothing left of identity but the title itself" (ibid.: 388). In this regard Geertz contrasts Balinese gods with those of the Greeks, which had quite distinct, elaborated personalities and activities that were of great interest to their devotees. But unlike the Greeks, Balinese have little interest in the biographies, personalities, or motivations of their gods. In this regard, images of divine beings appear to be projections of the ideal mode of fulfilling public office, the holders of which are "without features, individuals with respect to whom the usual indices of perishing humanity have no significance" (ibid.: 388). In worshipping their gods the Balinese confront "the image of what they consider themselves at bottom to be: an image which the biological, psychological, and sociological concomitants of being alive, the mere materialities of historical time, tend only to obscure from sight" (ibid.: 389).

The main theme that emerges from this examination of naming conventions is a consistent tendency to "depict virtually everyone—friends, relatives, neighbors, and strangers; elders and youths; superiors and inferiors; men and women; chiefs, kings, priests, and gods; even the dead and the unborn—as stereotyped contemporaries, abstract and anonymous fellowmen" (ibid.: 389). Geertz, citing Schutz, notes that the progress of the life cycles of oneself and one's consociates is a most visible indicator of the passage of time. So also is the awareness of the past existence of predecessors and the future existence of successors. But as naming conventions demonstrate, these differences are muted by in effect immobilizing the life cycles of consociates into a constant present, into which are also collapsed predecessors and successors. This is achieved at the expense of the idiosyncratic and biographic aspects of individuals, or in a word by depersonalizing them. And implicit within this depersonalization of individuals, then, is a detemporalization of time. If this image of simultaneity is necessary to maintain the Balinese notion of Self, we would expect it to also be reflected in other cultural conventions as well as naming.

CALENDARS

As we saw in Chapter 3, the time-reckoning conventions of a people may offer insight into their images of time. Geertz's description and analysis of Balinese calendrics is a good case in point.[3]

The first notable feature of Balinese time reckoning for units greater than the day is its apparent complexity. There are two types of calendars, one of which is lunar and solar, and the other based on the articulation of cycles of named days. Geertz refers to this second calendar as "permutational." It is comparable to the way in which the seven Western named week days cycle independently of the numbered days of the month. The Balinese permutational calendar consists of ten different such cycles, which range from one of 10 days down to the shortest, which consists of only one day—"the ultimate of a 'contemporized' view of time" (ibid.: 392). Of these ten cycles, those with 5, 6, and 7 named days are most significant. The articulation of combinations of these three cycles thus gives supercycles of 30, 35, 42, and 210 days (the products of 5×6, 5×7, 6×7, and $5 \times 6 \times 7$, respectively). Specific days are identified within any of these four supercycles by the combination of day names of the appropriate component cycles, and in this way are analogous to our Friday the thirteenth. Nationwide, within this 210-day calendar there are some 32 major celebrations and other special events falling on specific days indicated in this manner. In addition, there are many local temple celebrations, also specified by the articulation of five-, six- and seven-named day cycles. Since most Balinese belong to six or more temples, they lead a most active ritual life.

Such an elaborate calendar might lead one to suspect that the Balinese

are most concerned to mark the passage of time, that they have a strongly developed linear sense of time. But Geertz argues for a different
interpretation.

> Details aside, the nature of time-reckoning this sort of calendar facilitates
> is clearly not durational but punctual. That is, it is not used (and could only
> with much awkwardness and the addition of some ancillary devices be used) to
> measure the rate at which time passes, the amount which has passed since the
> occurrence of some event, or the amount which remains within which to com-
> plete some project: it is adapted to and used for distinguishing and classifying
> discrete, self-subsistent particles of time—"days." The cycles and supercycles
> are endless, unanchored, uncountable, and, as their internal order has no signi-
> ficance, without climax. They do not accumulate, they do not build, and they
> are not consumed. They don't tell you what time it is; they tell you what kind
> of time it is. (ibid.: 393)

The permutational calendar is free-floating in that it is not anchored to
any external reference point, such as the Christian calendar. As such it is
consistent with this detemporalized image of time. But what about the
lunar-solar calendar? It is anchored to the periodicity of the moon and sun,
and as such serves as a frame of reference for such things as events in the
agricultural cycle that must be located in time. But Geertz argues that its use
also reflects this punctuated sense of time. "In general, the lunar-solar calendar is more a supplement to the permutational than an alternative to it. It
makes possible the employment of a classificatory . . . 'detemporalized'
conception of time in contexts where the fact that natural conditions vary
periodically has to be at least minimally acknowledged" (ibid.: 398).

Above, we have seen how naming conventions are one aspect of
Balinese culture that support the fiction that fellowmen are contemporaries
rather than consociates, successors, or predecessors. This is achieved symbolically by minimizing that which is unique and changing in individuals
and by emphasizing qualities of the Self that are seen as common to all,
changeless, and therefore of greater value. And as we also saw, inherent in
this definition of Self is a static view of time that is also apparent in calen-
drical conventions. Balinese images of Self and Time are therefore in this
way compatible. Aside from the question of which—Self or Time—is
primary in the sense of shaping the other, the point here is that one is the
logical and structural concomitant of the other.

In the ethnographic material concerning naming and calendrics summarized above there are occasional data concerning social action. Since we
are exploring the relationships between world view and social structure, let
us further examine the social context in which these images of Self and Time
exist.

CEREMONY AND ABSENCE OF CLIMAX

If we take as a given the image of Self depicted above, from it we should be able to predict somethings about the style of social interaction in Bali. In other words, if we assume that the way in which Balinese perceive others and attempt to present themselves to these others is predicated on the same image of Self that underlies naming conventions, then we would expect to find that in their social interactions the Balinese in effect conspire to maintain this same image of Self. Geertz unfolds the logic of the relationship between image and action as follows. "A sheer contemporary needs an absolute present in which to live; an absolute present can be inhabited only by a contemporized man. Yet, there is a third side to this same process which transforms it from a pair of complementary prepossessions into a triangle of mutually reinforcing cultural forces: the ceremonialization of social intercourse" (ibid.: 399).

What Geertz is referring to by "ceremonialization" is one of the most ethnographically noteworthy aspects of Balinese society, which has attracted the attention of anthropologists and other observers. This is the high degree to which social interaction is formalized, such that daily life has many qualities of a ritualized performance. Balinese social life is an interlocking set of highly specified roles that people play out with great intent on performing them in close accord to an agreed upon and highly valued script. This style of interaction is a necessary behavioral correlate of the image of Self.

> To maintain the (relative) anonymization of individuals with whom one is in daily contact, to dampen the intimacy implicit in face-to-face relationships —in a word, to render consociates contemporaries—it is necessary to formalize relations with them to a fairly high degree, to confront them in a sociological middle distance where they are close enough to be identified but not so close as to be grasped: quasi strangers, quasi friends. The ceremoniousness of so much of Balinese daily life, the extent (and the intensity) to which interpersonal relations are controlled by a developed system of conventions and proprieties, is thus a logical correlate of a thoroughgoing attempt to block the more creatural aspects of the human condition—individuality, spontaneity, perishability, emotionality, vulnerability—from sight. (ibid.: 399)

This sense of proper "performance" is expressed in part in the folk concept of *lek*, which Geertz renders in English as "stage fright." By this he refers to "a diffuse, usually mild, though in certain situations virtually paralyzing, nervousness before the prospect (and the fact) of social interaction, a chronic, mostly low-grade worry that one will not be able to bring it off with the required finesse" (ibid.: 402). Should and when this happens the illusion (which of course is never more than partial) of anonymity is shattered the individual's personality is revealed. "When this occurs, as it sometimes does, our triangle falls apart: ceremony evaporates, the immediacy of the moment is felt with an excruciating intensity, and men become unwilling consociates locked in mutual embarrassment, as though they had inadvertently intruded upon one another's privacy" (ibid.: 402).

Another quality of Balinese social behavior that has intrigued anthropologists is that social events rarely seem to follow a trajectory that attains a peak of intensity. Thus, just as Balinese theatrical productions, which are the focus of community ceremonies, have no denouements, nor the music any crescendos or finales, neither does day-to-day social interaction typically arrive at any appreciable consummation. This absence of climax is difficult to substantiate without marshalling extensive enthnographic materials. Here I can but mention additional variations of this cultural style, such as quarrels rarely coming to a head, an avoidance of abrupt decisions in favor of a slow evolution of events and transitions, and how rituals lack any strong focal point, but seem "to consist largely of getting ready and cleaning up" (ibid.: 403).

> Social activities are separate performances; they do not march toward some destination, gather toward some denouement. As time is punctual, so life is. Not orderless, but qualitatively ordered, like the days themselves, into a limited number of established kinds. Balinese social life lacks climax because it takes place in a motionless present, a vectorless now. Or, equally true, Balinese time lacks motion because Balinese social life lacks climax. The two imply one another, and both together imply and are implied by the Balinese contemporization of persons. The perception of fellowmen, the experience of history, and the temper of collective life—what has sometimes been called ethos—are hooked together by a definable logic. But the logic is not syllogistic; it is social. (ibid.: 404)

In his demonstration of the integration of features of Balinese world view and behavioral style Geertz does not argue that all aspects of Balinese culture and society are completely and harmoniously articulated. His position is less ambitious, but more realistic. What he does say is simply that once having identified this "triangle of forces" consisting of images of Self and Time, and their corresponding behavioral style, a number of important institutions, which are mutually compatible and sustaining, fall into place.

> A penchant for "contemporizing" fellowmen blunts the sense of biological aging; a blunted sense of biological aging removes one of the main sources of a sense of temporal flow; a reduced sense of temporal flow gives to interpersonal events an episodic quality. Ceremonialized interaction supports standardized

perceptions of others; standardized perceptions of others support a "steady-state" conception of society; a steady-state conception of society supports a taxonomic perception of time. And so on: one could begin with conceptions of time and go around, in either direction, the same circle. The circle, though continuous, is not in a strict sense closed, because none of these modes of experience is more than a dominant tendency, a cultural emphasis. . . . Yet, they *are* dominant; they *do* reinforce one another; and they *are* persisting. And it is to this state of affairs, neither permanent nor perfect, that the concept "cultural integration"—what Weber called *"Sinnzusammenhang"*—can be legitimately applied. (ibid.: 406)

So far we have reviewed Geertz's analysis of the synchronic integration of Balinese world view. But he also considers what sort of changes this integration might be subject to. The importance of the Balinese perception of Self, the experiencing of Time, and standards of propriety having been demonstrated, it is a reasonable assumption that anything which attacks them would effect transformations that would reverberate throughout Balinese culture.

If the Balinese develop a less anonymized view of one another, or a more dynamic sense of time, or a more informal style of social interaction, a very great deal indeed—not everything, but a very great deal—would have to change in Balinese life, if only because any one of these changes would imply, immediately and directly, the others, and all three of them play, in different ways and in different contexts, a crucial role in shaping that life. (ibid.: 409)

As an ongoing self-regulating system these features of Balinese culture appear to be quite stable, and subject to no great internal tensions. Any major changes affecting them are therefore most likely to come from outside of it.

The point of this long discussion of Balinese world view and social structure has been to suggest that thought and society in general are inextricably constituted, one within the other. We can now proceed to explore, in the next two chapters, yet more comprehensive instances of world view and its relationship to reality.

Chapter 6

CALIFORNIA INDIAN WORLD VIEW

To illustrate how the world-view universals articulate I should like to present an analysis of the world view of the Indians of California as they existed before contact with Europeans. This analysis deals mainly with the internal logico-structural integration of the world-view universals. Less attention is given to the ways in which this world view is a result of a certain general type of social organization, which in turn is associated with the level of technological development present in aboriginal California. The applicability of historical materialism to prestate classless societies such as those we are dealing with here is currently being hotly debated. We will deal specifically with the relationship among history, economy, social structure, and world view in Chapter 7, where the issues are clear-cut. But although we shall not here discuss at length the uneven feedback relations between world view and the social and geographic environment, the general nature of this relationship should be apparent.[1]

Aboriginal California was culturally quite diverse. Of the 12 major language families in native North America, 7 of them are represented in this area, and within these there were some 104 distinct languages and dialects spoken by the local populations, which were typically distinct cultural groupings. For the most part, these were not organized political units, such as those of say the Southwest or the Great Plains. Instead, local California populations are best thought of as "tribelets," which consisted of the people living in a particular valley, along the banks of a certain stream or stretch of coast, or associated with some other natural geographic zone. Generally the people of a local area were related by kinship ties and spoke a certain dialect. The cultural diversity was a reflection of the tremendous geographic diversity of California, which ranges from the deep fog-enshrouded forests of the northwest ranges to the arid deserts of the southeastern part of the state, from hundreds of miles of seashore to the alpine mountains of the Sierra Nevada, from groves of oak trees with abundant crops of acorns to extensive rich marshlands in the Central Valley, and so on.

But within this wide diversity there were common ethnographic traits that unite the entire region into a recognizable cultural area. Thus, at a higher level of generality there are features of native thought, society, and economy that stand out in marked contrast with their counterparts in European civilization. It is certain such general characteristics of native California world-view that I wish to discuss in terms of the world-view universals that we now have at our disposal: Self, Other, Relationship, Classification, Causality, Space, and Time. We are also concerned to see how these world-view concepts are logically and structurally integrated among themselves, and how they relate to concepts, practices, and social structure of aboriginal California.

CAUSALITY

Let us begin by examining what is undoubtedly the most fundamental concept in California Indian thought and is also the key to all the others. It is best translated as *power*. Power is essentially an inherent aspect of creation; it is a vital force, an energy that pervades the world and is responsible for virtually everything that happens. It is like electricity in that it too is ubiquitous, occurring in some degree in all things, but unevenly. That is, it tends to be concentrated in certain special objects, places, or persons, perhaps only at certain times or under special conditions. And like electricity, power is inherently amoral, something that may be put to any number of uses, either good or bad. Also like electricity, it is inherently dangerous if not properly handled.

Since power is so all-pervasive and important, and since its functioning tends to be consistent, one can, through knowledge of it, come to understand it and thus utilize it to advantage. A basic concern in life is therefore to gain knowledge of power, and in this sense such knowledge is virtually synonymous with power.

Because power was seen as omnipresent and completely malleable, all phenomena were potentially useful as sources of power. The fact that potential power residing in an object was not immediately obvious could simply signify a failure on the part of an observer to have the requisite knowledge to recognize and use it. Thus, it was important to preserve an empirical attitude toward all new phenomena or ideas and cautiously test them against the framework of cultural realities which were already known . . . . Because it was understood that the sources of power were so diversified, an eclectic and experimental attitude toward power existed in California. Man was not dependent upon one source of power, but attempted to acquire power from as many sources as possible. (Bean 1975:28)

The ways in which individuals acquired power varied from group to group. In central California special dream helpers appeared to individuals while dreaming or in induced trance states and taught them special formulae or other knowledge. In Southern California the aboriginal presence of such personal helpers who bestow power is in doubt. Certainly this complex was absent among the Yuman tribes along the Colorado River. Here, instead, there was a means of power acquisition most unusual for the rest of California. These people also obtained power while dreaming—not from the visitations of a guardian spirit, but rather by themselves visiting, while dreaming, one of their culture heroes at the beginning of the world. Kroeber, speaking of the Mohave who are of the Yuman tribes, notes that they "adhere to a belief in dreams as the basis of everything in life" (Kroeber 1925:754). Alternatively, an individual's power might have come to him prior to his birth from having associated with cultural heroes or divine animals at the beginning of the world. The acquisition of power was quite different in northeastern California. Here it appears that only shamans were visited in dreams by guardian spirits, who placed within the shaman's body special disease objects or "pains" that would be fatal to ordinary people. With instruction and training by older shamans, a novice who acquired such "pains" came to control them. Elsewhere in Northern California there is the notion that a shaman is one who controls spirit familiars whom he entices or commands to do his bidding: it is they who actually diagnose and cure diseases and attack selected victims. A shaman here is thus one who controls a greater number of spirits and pains than ordinary people, say six of them as opposed to four. For some people the acquisition of personal power appears to have become an obsession, but generally a certain moderate amount was considered optimal, the reason for this being that power itself is as potentially harmful as beneficial, and also, as discussed below, an inordinate concern with power was likely to provoke accusations of seeking it for antisocial ends, most specifically witchcraft.

Since this basic concept of power ultimately influences the other world-view universals, we will in examining them have ample opportunity to further discuss it as we proceed.

SELF AND OTHER

Some of our best information on the concept of Self in California comes from Dorothy Lee, who investigated it among the Wintu of Northern California (Lee 1950). The Wintu concept of self differs markedly from Self in United States culture in that it is not nearly so separate from the Other. Whereas the Self and the Other of native English speakers are sharply distinguished, the Wintu Self and Other are more continuous. This is not to say that the Wintu Self is the same as the Other. Instead, whereas the English speaker's Self is a kernel, conceptually walled off from the Other, the Wintu Self may be thought of as radiating out from some point within the individual. Reality, rather than being cleaved into two mutually exclusive categories—Self and Other—is a continuum with an unspecified Self at one end which merges by degrees with the Other. As we would expect of such a diffuse, unlocalized Self, there is no Wintu word for it.

The Anglo Self (i.e., the concept of Self typical of native white English speakers in the United States) is not only sharply bounded from the Other, it also seems to be relatively small. It certainly is not coterminous with the physical body, which we refer to as "my body," or "her body," just as we refer to parts of the body as belonging to the Self: my arm, her face, etc. "Unlike us, a Wintu self is identical with the parts of his body and is not related to them as other, so long as they are physically part of him" (ibid.: 540). The English Self is also a small part of the noncorporeal personality, and appears to be localized mainly in the conscious mind, which is the most valued realm of the personality as indicated by its superior position in spatial metaphors. Thus an English speaker "falls" asleep, and "falls" into unconsciousness when the "higher" faculties are impaired. The Self is also distinct from the emotions, which reside in the basement of the personality; thus one's Self may be "overcome" by a rage or "sink" into "depression."

The Self in United States culture not only is typically small and relatively well-bounded, but it also tends to be associated with "normal" waking consciousness. This state of mind is but a small segment of the entire spectrum humans are capable of experiencing. Any experience (other than sleep) that departs markedly from this usual mode is defined as insanity and is most often terrifying or painful. The native Californians, however, regularly sought by a number of practices to induce what most modern people would consider abnormal states of mind. The reason for doing so was inevitably to come closer to, to somehow acquire, personal power. By fasting, by use of narcotic plants such as Datura or native tobacco, or by prolonged dancing and solitary vigils, visions were induced in which the individual directly encountered personifications or embodiments of power.

For example, dream helpers might transcend ordinary time and space to appear to supplicants (see below). Such experiences and the positive value placed upon them were predicated on a sense of Self seen as essentially unbounded and continuous with the Other.

One's sense of Self is preeminently a social phenomenon in that it is formed mainly through one's relationship with others. It is these others with whom we regularly interact or who act upon us who in effect give us our sense of Self. We should therefore find that this diffuse, relatively noncentered Self corresponds with aspects of social relations and organization. For example, in United States society there is much concern with "individuals" —individual rights, privacy, and private property. The basic units here are individuals, or more specifically, the Selves which reside in them. The sharp boundary between Self and Other predisposes us to take the Self as the basic point of reference. Oswald Spengler traces the development of this attitude in Western culture and how it culminated in an "existence which *is led* with a deep consciousness and introspection of the ego, and a resolutely personal culture evidenced in memoirs, reflections, retrospects, and prospects and conscience" (Barnouw 1963:33 quoting Spengler). As has already been noted in Chapter 1, this attitude is also reflected in language; for example, the Latin *sum* is replaced by *ich bin, je suis, I am,* viz., a word for "I" is introduced (ibid.: 34). Whereas we would say *I go,* the Wintu use one unanalyzed word, *harada* (I-go or we-go) and use *ni* (I) or *niterum* (we) only for clarification or denotation (Lee 1950:540). Consistent with the diffuse Wintu image of Self, a lack of concern with the individual as a point of reference is expressed here.

In Chapter 6 we discussed how the European Self, this "I," is seen as existing at the center of the universe, so to speak. In contrast to this, there is linguistic evidence that suggests the Wintu Self is not so centrally located.

> Take, for example, the term which we used for the individual about whom we are going to speak; *ego: I.* If the anthropologist wants to make a kinship chart, he starts with *ego.* If I conjugate, I start with *I run,* and I call this the first person as a matter of course; and rightly so, since, in present day English, the third person with its *-s* suffix is derivative. In Wintu, on the other hand, the third person is primary, and the first is derived. (Lee 1950:542).

Thus, in United States culture our attention is on our individual *selves* in contrast to society and nature. But the Wintu, with their diffuse boundary between Self and Other, see things quite differently. When speaking about Wintu culture it is therefore appropriate to speak of Self *in* society, rather than self *and* society. Lee illustrates this through her experience in recording the biography of Sadie Marsh, a Wintu woman.

When I asked Sadie Marsh for her autobiography, she told me a story about her first husband, based on hearsay. When I insisted on her own life history, she told me a story which she called, "my story." The first three quarters of this, approximately, are occupied with the lives of her grandfather, her uncle and her mother before her birth; finally, she reaches the point where she was "that which was in my mother's womb," and from then on she speaks of herself, also. (Lee 1950:543)

Elsewhere Lee notes, "To us, in the words of Ralph Linton, 'society has as its foundation an aggregate of individuals.' For the Wintu, the individual is a delimited part of society; it is society that is basic, not a plurality of individuals" (Lee 1944b:185). This distinction is also apparent in the way group decisions are made in Indian versus white society. The whites are content to do things by voting, that is, by counting the individuals for and against an issue. This idea is foreign to Indian politics. It is not individuals within the group that make a decision; it is the group that decides. Thus rather than seeking a majority or plurality of like-minded people, the ideal solution is complete group consensus.

The Wintu Self corresponds with the general Californian concept of power. Power is diffuse, more or less pervasive, flowing, radiating from one area or object to others. It is the grand unifying principle. Accordingly, the Self — the force that animates the individual — is but one local transitory form of power. It would be inconsistent with all assumptions about power to conceive of some quantum of it in the individual as unique and separate from the power residing in the Other.

In cultures around the world, belief in the "soul" is widespread. We can look at the modifications that a people have given to this general concept as a projection of their assumptions about the Self. In United States culture, for example, this concept is relatively unimportant, and many people deny the existence of personal souls. This is consistent with a materialistic attitude toward reality and high values on things that are tangible. But among the Californians, the concept of soul, although taking many different forms in different groups, was inevitably well developed and, as suggested above, was a personalized manifestation of power. Throughout the area the belief that the soul could become detached from the person was pervasive. This could happen because of some trauma or through capture by nefarious forces. A common treatment in such cases was for a shaman specializing in such things to send his own soul or his familiars to find or recapture the errant soul. This complex of beliefs about soul loss thus well illustrates underlying assumptions about the way in which the Self is seen as participating in the Other.

RELATIONSHIP WITH THE OTHER

Given the propositions about the Self, the Other, and Causality, certain propositions logically follow about the Relationship between Self and Other.

First of all, one of the main characteristics of the diffuse implicit Wintu Self is that it is not, as with the Anglo Self, a fixed entity that acts upon the Other. The English-language Self owes its existence largely to the assumption that it is or potentially is, or should be, in control of aspects of the Other. This is apparent in the frequent use in modern English language of such phrases as "I hit the ball" (i.e., *I act on the Other*). This is but one main instance of a more general subject-verb-object construction common in modern English, which is consistent with the linear causality discussed in Chapter 3. This linguistic usage is clearly consistent with a distinct Self that must be present as the source of such action which is directed at a distinct Other, so as to control it. Going from within out, the English-speaking Self is first of all—when functioning *properly—in control* of *its* emotions, just as it is in control of its body parts and their functions. Maintenance of control is highly valued, and one who becomes flooded with emotions has "lost control," and is suspected of weakness or insanity, as are those given to mysticism or ecstatic states. There is considerable evidence that the Self in the United States seeks not only mastery over its body and mind, but over all other aspects of the Other, and is epitomized in such phrases as "the struggle against nature." The Wintu attitude toward the Other contrasts with this: whereas the English-speaker's concern with control is possible only because the Self is distinct from the Other and therefore able to act on it, the Wintu inclusion of Self within the Other implies a different relationship altogether. Here, rather than a concern with *control over*, there is concern to balance the many *inter*-relationships between Self and Other. This attitude can be summed up as seeking *harmony with*—or perhaps better said, *between*—Self and Other. Lee refers to this as an

> attitude of humility and respect toward reality, toward nature and society. I cannot find an adequate English term to apply to a habit of thought which is so alien to our culture. We are aggressive toward reality. . . . Our attitude toward nature is colored by a desire to control and exploit. The Wintu relationship with nature is one of intimacy and mutual courtesy. (Lee 1944b:187)

To illustrate these two differing attitudes Lee quotes Cora DuBois's account of an old Wintu woman speaking in sorrow about the coming of the white people.

. . . the white people never cared for land or deer or bear. When we Indians kill meat, we eat it all up. When we dig roots, we make little holes. . . . We don't chop down the trees. We only use dead wood. But the white people plow up the ground, pull up the trees, kill everything. . . . The spirit of the land hates them. They blast out trees and stir it up to its depth. They saw up the trees. That hurts them. The Indians never hurt anything. . . . (DuBois 1935:75–76)

This strong sense of identification with the Other is consistent with the way in which the Self and Other are conceived. If the Self is seen as continuous with the Other, then an attitude, a relationship of respect and maintenance toward the Other is a product of enlightened self-interest.

The key to understanding how this harmony is promoted and maintained is again the concept of power. Since power tends to function consistently, and since one can through knowledge of it come to understand it and utilize it to one's advantage, a basic strategy in life is therefore to seek to understand and relate to power in life-supporting ways. Thus, the individual can directly interact with power to maintain a harmonious relationship with his surroundings. Should he fall ill owing to some oversight of his own, or owing to the malevolent manipulation of power by an enemy, there are immediate actions he can take to counteract these events and return to a normal state of harmony.

Thus, through the use of knowledge in the broadest sense, it is possible for humans to directly participate in maintaining harmonious relationships between themselves and their environment. But this intervention is not merely a direct physical intervention in the manner of Westerners; rather, it is through the application of the rules governing the manipulation of power. Especially in dangerous and ambiguous situations a prudent Wintu did not attempt to deal with them directly, but attempted to determine the underlying power relationships. In uncertain situations there was always the danger of being harmed by power and certain ritual precautions were therefore necessary when interacting with it. Much of the extensive ritualism in California was at bottom an attempt to insure that humans, individually and collectively, when in uncertain or precarious situations, related to power in the most life-supporting way.

For the individual, then, possession of some minimal quantity of power was essential. For just as social, economic, and amorous success are attributed to power, misfortune and illness are due to a deficiency or excess of power. Thus, in California, one's sense of Self was intimately associated with ideas about personal power, and there was a concern to acquire and maintain at least some minimal quantity of it—power either in a pure abstract form, or in some other form such as dream helpers, special power objects, or "pains." Indeed, death—the end of one's normal human existence —was essentially the loss of all of one's personal power.

Since power is ubiquitous, its presence may strongly color one's general outlook on the world. There are two possibilities here: one may either see the presence of power as a valuable asset for attaining desired things —health, success in hunting, trading, love, etc.—or one may feel threatened by its negative potential, especially as it might be maliciously directed toward one's Self by malevolent people or spirit beings. In this latter case it becomes the central feature of a paranoid view of one's relationship to one's world and is not unlike the delusions of modern paranoids who imagine that they are subject to the insidious influences of invisible death rays, radiations, or electric fields. There is some reason to believe that this latter type of attitude became more prevalent after the disastrous effects of white contact, i.e., that the power concept served as a generalized projection of the intolerable conditions imposed on the Indians by the invaders. The Indians often interpreted this catastrophe as due to a loss of or lack of the knowledge necessary for dealing with power in these new conditions. Without such knowledge, one was unable to predict how power would behave and the world became even more erratic and uncontrollable.

CLASSIFICATION

There is in California world view a general style of classification that contrasts with modern thought. In modern world view there is a strong tendency to focus on the particular rather than the generic, whereas among California Indians the trend is just the opposite (see Lee 1944a). This concern with the generic aspect of reality rather than the particular is apparent in the widespread type of California creation myth, which has the following basic outline. At the beginning of creation the matter and power of the world were essentially undifferentiated. It was from these that "the first people" were formed. Usually these were animals with such human characteristics as the ability to talk. These creatures, such as Coyote, Fox, Hummingbird, and Bear, who existed in the mythic time at creation, later became differentiated into the many individual animals and people present today. *Coyote* is embodied in all the particular coyotes, but *Coyote* himself still exists in mythic time. This is quite in contrast with the white view, which sees each particular animal as distinct and unique. When a white hunter kills a deer he kills *a* deer; the white hunter assumes that his encounter with any particular deer has no effect on encounters with other deer. But for the Indian, each encounter with a deer is an encounter with *Deer*. It is because of this relationship that a hunter is enjoined not to indiscriminately kill deer, and to completely utilize one when he does, lest he offend *Deer*, who will not send more deer to this disrespectful hunter. By the same reasoning, a man who has a totemic relationship with some generic entity, such as some animal, may be required to observe certain taboos in respect to that animal. Thus, a member of an Antelope clan may be prohibited from killing antelopes because of his spiritual kinship with *Antelope.*

This focus on the generic rather than the particular is consistent with the paradigm of Self and Other, which we discussed above, in that the primary focus is on the whole rather than on the individual. The Californians cognized reality, as we do, as particularized into discreet units, but these particulars were but secondary aspects of underlying unities. Just as the Self saw itself as essentially continuous with the Other, so it saw an inherent genetic unity among many things of the Other.

The matrix of this unity is power, the force energizing all of creation. Since it is a neutral force, with only its effects being helpful or harmful, we should be able to anticipate certain moral assumptions, which we can also discuss in terms of Classification. In Christian societies, one's spiritual condition and fate are determined to some extent by one's moral actions. Christians, ideally, attempt to control their destinies by good acts as judged by some standards given to them by their master principle, God. But in California, since power—which is the counterpart to the Christian god—is amoral, one does not conceive of one's relationship to it in terms of good and evil and corollary notions such as innocence, guilt, atonement, and damnation; rather, one is simply either successful or unsuccessful in the acquisition and use of power. Consistent with the notion of a fundamental, neutral power is an absence of a strict dichotomy between good and evil such as cleaved the Medieval Christian world into two largely distinct realms, personified in God and the Devil. The moral unity of the Indian world is expressed in some California groups by the notion of a unitary Great Spirit, who, unlike the Christian God and Devil is imbued with neither good nor evil. He is rather the supreme personification of neutral power. In other California societies, such as the Achumawi, there is no such personification of power, no single God-like principle. For them, the "whole universe is full of immanent life, and this life is capable of transforming itself at every moment into *tinihowis*" (Angulo 1928:162). These *tinihowis* are diffuse, amorphous nonindividualized beings rather than discrete entities; they are immanent forces (ibid.: 36f.).

Another distinction between white American and California Indian world views arises from the ubiquity of power. Since power is immanent in all things, and all events are "caused" by it, there is no fundamental distinction between "natural" and "supernatural" phenomena, as we discussed in Chapter 3. It is possible to say that some things, places, or people are imbued with more power than others and are therefore more sacred. Thus, in this sense, a continuum of sacred to profane exists as in all societies, but something is sacred or profane only by virtue of the amount of power inherent in it. In either case, whatever happens is due to power. This view is fundamentally different from the European, which recognizes "natural" events and phenomena that are amenable to scientific study versus "supernatural" events and phenomena that are miraculous. A miracle, as defined in one dictionary, is "An event or effect in the physical world deviating from the known laws of nature or transcending our knowledge of these laws; an extraordinary, anomalous, or abnormal event brought about by superhuman agency." In Indian thought, with its unitary concept of power, this concept of miracles could not exist.

Just as aspects of the world are imbued with power, so are people. And just as differing amounts of power explained differences among nonhuman things, power differences were also the main cause for the differences among humans. In United States culture the differences between individuals and groups are explained in terms of the wealth, influence, reputation, or political power that they possess. But in aboriginal California these qualities were merely the outward indications of a quantity of more fundamental personal spiritual power.

In the wealthier and more socially differentiated California societies there were well delineated social hierarchies with so-called "big men" and powerful shamans at the top and "slaves" at the bottom. One's position in this hierarchy was explained in terms of his or her power. And similarly, differences in wealth and military strength among groups were accounted for by their respective power (Bean 1975:30–32).

The human life cycle was also explained in terms of personal power. Some South Central and Southern California groups believed that one acquired knowledge of power as one grew older. Thus, if not senile, very advanced age was taken as an indication of greater power. But in North Central California the decrease in physical strength in old age indicated a loss of power (ibid.: 28).

Another aspect of power as the basic causal principle is that proper manipulation of it allows those who are so skilled to transform themselves into other human or animal forms. Accordingly, in terms of the Classification dimension, identities tend to be more fluid. "Is this a bear, or is it a shaman in the form of a bear?" Much discussion has been devoted to this so-called "prelogical" tendency of "primitive thought." The gist of this argument is that such notions demonstrate the lack of a well-developed principle of identity, which is one of the foundations of Western formal logic. Thus, although there is no good evidence that people of traditional societies such as California Indians lack the identity principle, we might suspect that since some of these basic cosmological categories are ordered so differently from those of Western peoples the world must have a very different quality for them. A similar attitude is common in peasant Mexico, where things are not necessarily what they appear to be according to their external, superficially observable qualities (See Chapter 7 and Kearney 1972:59–69). A prudent person therefore pays attention to the deeper meaning of things. He does not deal lightly with the unknown, and even seemingly familiar things may not be what they appear to be. This attitude is reflected in Wintu speech forms. The Wintu never assert something as absolutely true as we do when we say *it is*. In every predicative utterance the Wintu speaker must indicate by the use of suffixes how he has come to know or infer the truth of his statement. Thus, just as the English speaker must indicate number and tense in each of his sentences, the Wintu speaker is obligated by his grammar to indicate his source of knowledge, of which there are five distinct types.

> In one of the common stories about the German, the Frenchman, and the Englishman, the first two, pointing to bread, say, "I call it *Brot*," and "I call it *pain*"; but the Englishman says, "I call it bread and it *is* bread." The Wintu never say "it *is* bread." They say, "It looks-to-me bread" or "It-feels-to-me bread" or "I-have-heard-it-to-be bread" or "I-infer-from-the-evidence-that-it-is bread" or "I-think-it-to-be bread," or, vaguely and timelessly, "according-to-my-experience-be bread." (Lee 1950:542)

Classification of the phenomenal world is consistent with this attitude of qualifying and reserving final judgment as to the nature of things. In the modern Western world view, one of the main divisions of things is that between living and nonliving things—animals and plants versus all other physical objects. In the California universe there is a similar categorization of physical things into animals, plants, and other things, but there is not a corresponding strict distinction between "living" and "nonliving" things. To the contrary, as described above, animating power is an inherent potential attribute of all things. As the Achumawi say, "life is the same thing as power" (Angulo 1975:62). Thus, whereas for white people the "natural" world is mostly inert and lifeless, for the Indian the world is all imbued with the life-force of power—the entire world is in this sense animated. An Achumawi man expresses his view of Indian versus modern thinking on this point by saying, "Everything is alive. That's what we Indians believe. White people think everything is dead . . . ." (Angulo 1973:81).

TIME

Time in aboriginal California seems to have been similar to Time among the Nuer whom we discussed earlier, in that there was no explicit notion of time per se. Events did not take place at some specific point on a clock or calendar. Insofar as specified dates were fixed they were so many days, moons, or years from some other event. But for the most part the timing of events was determined by their actual occurrence rather than some point in an artificial scale. Months, viz., moons, were often named, but rather than having what for us have become meaningless labels, they tended to take their name from natural events with which they coincided: "ice on streams," "growth begins," "bulbs mature," "manzanita appears," etc. "Reckonings often differed and there was no standard but nature's by which to settle disputes. When the acorns actually fell, argument as to the acorn moon was decided" (Kroeber 1925:209). There seems to have been little concern or need for exact precision with time units of less than a day. And in general people were unconcerned with their age or the time since an event which had occurred several years previously; the elapsed time simply was not important.

The concern with the generic aspect of creation discussed above is reflected in the image of time and in the various means of power acquisition. Among those peoples in which individuals were visited by dream helpers, these helpers, whether animals, plants, or personified natural phenomena such as Thunder or Fire, were the generic aspect of the helper, rather than a particular manifestation of it. Similarly, among those peoples who acquired power by visiting their culture heroes, it was the generic aspect of the hero that they encountered. To do this is was deemed necessary to travel into mythic time (we would say "back into," but I wonder if that is correct) when they were not yet particularized. Here at the creation, one could encounter the undifferentiated beings who control the world. And also, it was here that one was closer to the full undiminished source of power.

Necessary for this nexus of ideas about Time, Classification, and Causality is a conception of dreaming quite alien to white thinking. In dreams it was possible to enter into the mythic landscapes and time, and meet with the characters who reside there.

> It is always in dreams that historical time is abolished and the mythical time regained—which allows the future shaman to witness the beginnings of the world and hence to become contemporary not only with the cosmogony but also with the primordial mythical revelations. (Eliade 1964:103)

The Mohave shamans therefore insisted that in their dreams they received their powers from their cultural hero at the beginning of the world (Kroeber 1925:754). "I was there, I saw him," a myth teller may say of his hero. Among the Mohave and other groups myth and dream are thus equated, and result in an image of mutable time completely alien to our own uniform, onward march of time.

There is a definite positive value on this primordial mythic time. Special effort was made to "go" to this more perfect time that existed before the appearance of death, sickness, conflict, and suffering. One reason conditions have deteriorated is a progressive loss of power since the time of creation (Bean 1972:161). The nonmythic time of ordinary existence in which the years come and go is thus essentially "entropic" (Blackburn 1975: 70–71). In contrast to the scientific evolutionary view of time in which the world and its creatures are evolving to "higher," presumed better forms, the Indian view sees all change as a departure from the perfect conditions of the mythic time of creation, which, almost paradoxically, exists parallel to what whites would call the present. The barrier between these two eras is ruptured by shamans who penetrate it from this side, and by dream helpers who travel from it into the "present."

To a large extent, then, historic change also was viewed as further unfortunate departure from creation. This was explained as due to loss of knowledge of how to manipulate and relate to power properly, according to rules laid down at the creation. The most catastrophic series of all historic events was of course the calamitous arrival of non-Indians. The California peoples responded to the white invasion in various ways which were consistent with their own temporal images. Foremost here was their predisposition to prevent and correct events by seeking to abolish history. One of the most dramatic instances of this was a revivalistic religion known as the Ghost Dance. This movement, which originated among the Northern Paiute of Nevada in 1870, spread widely throughout northern California. The core of its ritual and ideology was concerned with effecting the removal of the whites and a reinstitution of the precontact existence, which by all comparisons was preferable to the devastation brought about by the invaders. Other peoples, who apparently have future time orientations, when in similar desperate situations are prone to utopian movements that seek not a return to a more desirable past existence, but the inauguration of some new glorious period in the future.

Aside from this degenerationism, or entropic view of time, there is good reason to believe that the California Indian image of midrange periods of time was basically oscillating. We know from the archaeological record that culture and environmental changes in California were remarkably slow over the past 4000 years. Such constant conditions would have promoted an image of time in which each year within a person's life span would be seen as essentially a repetition of previous ones. This endless annual repetition was also apparently a desired condition. In Northwestern California, the major ceremonies and dances were referred to as "world making." Generally, these were associated with important annual subsistence events such as the autumn acorn harvest and the summer salmon runs, and were concerned with renewing the world, that is, insuring that it would once more cycle through its proper phases and maintain life. The man who recited the formula for this rite was referred to as "world maker." Among the Yurok this formula narrated "the establishment of the ceremony by spirits of prehuman race and its immediate beneficial effect" (Kroeber 1925:53). These ceremonies can be seen as intended to offset the inherent degradation of the world and to insure as well as possible the regular passing of the years. The implicit assumption here seems to be that departure from the primordial plan could only be degenerative. The strategy in these rites was therefore to replicate ritually and symbolically the actions the prehuman beings performed when they created the world.

Thus, in California, whether we are talking of the Ghost Dance, the dream helper, Yuman dream-myth time, or the World Renewal complex of the northwestern part of the state, fundamentally similar temporal images prevail: there is a value on the past, epitomized in the time of creation, and a concern to annul history and insure the continuation of the present, or to actually reverse time and, as whites would say, regain the past.

SPACE

Since spatial concepts are much affected by environment, and since there was such great geographic variation throughout aboriginal California, we would expect variations in cosmologies, and especially in directional terms and conventions. Indeed there was variation in spatial concepts among the peoples of California, yet they held certain concepts in common that contrast sharply with prevalent modern images of space.

In general, in modern world, along with greater technological control of nature, there has been a trend away from the influence of natural conditions on directional conventions and also presumably therefore on spatial concepts as well. This situation is thus similar to the changes that have occurred in the development of modern versus traditional images of time. Another major difference between spatial attitudes of aboriginal Californians and modern whites is visible in the way they respectively divide land up into recognized territories. Whites frequently survey boundaries in straight lines and also use natural geographic features such as watersheds or streams as boundaries that arbitrarily cut through environmental zones.

But the [Wintu] Indian knew the land with the soles of his feet; he thought of it in terms of its actual surface, of its varying plant and animal population, not as a surveyed chart on which certain great structural traits stand out. The valley offered him one mode of progress, food, occupation, and materials to work with, the hills another; and the same differences existed between the long, reedy marsh and the solid plains. Thus it was almost inevitable that different nations should come to occupy each tract. (Kroeber 1925:352)

And DuBois (1935:4), also speaking of the Wintu, notes that they do not think of different territories as separated by sharp lines, such as are represented on maps of these areas made by whites. Wintu boundaries tend to be vague, one area phasing into another. Here again is apparent the basic difference in classificatory style discussed above: an awareness of continuity and gradation versus an either-or exclusiveness.

Differences in Yurok and Wintu directional terms and spatial concepts correspond to differences in their habitats. The Yurok are pre-eminently a river people who inhabited the banks of the lower Klamath River and stretches of ocean shore north and south of the river's mouth. The Klamath River winds through Yurok territory and is the main geographic feature in their world, and it serves as the major spatial referent. In lieu of the use of the cardinal directions, the basic Yurok directional concepts are *pets* (upstream) and *pul* (downstream). "The river is rather crooked, and hence *pets* may stand for almost anything in our terminology" (Waterman 1920: 193). This convention applies also to Yurok territory along the coast; the river comes into the ocean after running in a northwest course, and thus by extension, direction northward along the coast is "upstream" and southward is "downstream." Other directional terms also are in reference to the river: *hiko* means across the stream, *won* means up hill, i.e., away from the stream on one's own side, and so on.

> If a Yurok says "east" he regards this as an English word for upstream, or whatever may be the run of the water where he is. The name Yurok itself—which in its origin is anything but an ethnic designation—means "downstream" in the adjacent Karok language. The degree to which native speech is affected by this manner of thought is remarkable. A house has its door not at its "western" but its "downstream" corner. A man is told to pick up a thing that lies "upstream" from him, not on his "left." (Kroeber 1925:15)

Now the Wintu, living in the northern Central Valley and in the hilly country to the west of it which were dominated by no single major geographic feature such as the Klamath River of the Yurok, instead avail themselves more of cardinal directions, and do so in a manner consistent with what we have already discussed regarding their concept of Self. In examining the Wintu concept of Self, taken as typical of other California Indians, we found several ways in which "the universe is not centered in the self, as it is with us" (Lee 1950:542).

> The Wintu use of *left* and *right*, as compared with ours, shows again this difference in orientation. When we go for a walk, the hills are to our right, the river to our left; when we return, the hills change and the river, while we remain the same, since we are the pivot, the focus. Now the hills [so to speak] have pivoted to the left of me. This has been English practice for many years,

since at least the fourteenth century. To the Wintu, the terms left and right refer to inextricable aspects of his body, and are very rarely used. . . . When the Wintu goes up the river, the hills are to the west, the river to the east; and a mosquito bites him on the west arm. When he returns, the hills are still to the west, but, when he scratches his mosquito bite, he scratches his east arm. The geography has remained unchanged, and the self has had to be reoriented in relation to it. (Lee 1950:543).

Although their directional conventions were not so completely dominated by waterways as among the Yurok, stream direction was still an important orientation for the Wintu and other North and Central California peoples. It is only in Southern California, where streams are far apart and flow intermittently, and where the ceremonial symbolism of the Southwest is a near influence, that purely solar directional conventions occur (Kroeber 1925:16). An exception to this possibly occurred among groups living on the southern coast, since it is common for coastal peoples to use the distinction between "oceanward" versus "inland."

The placing of humanity, and especially one's own group, at the center of the universe is a common theme in California cosmologies, as it is in many pre-Copernican societies. At first glance this principle seems to go against what I have said above about the noncenteredness of the Self. This theme, however, seems to be more a result of a limited geographic knowledge of regions beyond the tribal territory. Although there are many variations, in general California cosmologies describe a tripartite universe consisting of upper, middle, and under worlds. The upper is often the abode of creator gods or other culture heroes, while the under is often the land of the dead and of monstrous mythic beasts. The world in which humans live, the middle world, is a large, flat, more or less disk-shaped island floating on a sea, or perhaps existing in a void.

Yurok mythology is typical here: the Yurok territory is at the center of this great disk. And at approximately the geographic center of their territory is a special location, a town called Genek, on the bank of the Klamath River, which is recognized as the exact center of the world. The Yurok cultural hero came into existence and lived here with a number of other generic mythological figures such as Thunder, Earthquake, and the Porpoises; the depressions left by their house pits are said to be still visible. From an ethnological point of view it would be satisfying to find that the world renewal ceremonies mentioned above took place at this "center of the world," but it appears that the larger size of other hamlets and the economic significance of certain places, such as special salmon-fishing sites on the river, determined their location.

Power is pervasive throughout the universe, but humans by virtue of their location in the middle world are ideally located "for bringing power from the upper and lower universes into play in the middle world" (Bean

1975:27). Also, it is by virtue of power that the souls of shamans may journey to distant places in any of the three worlds. This travel might also be accomplished by using power to transform the shaman into some fast-traveling creature—a bird, an insect, or whatever. And, as we discussed above concerning Time, such feats may also involve travel into different times, especially into the mythic time of creation. Conversely, such manipulation of time and space by the shaman may result in bringing the inhabitants of mythic time into the present, or in a drawing near of distant places. This image of space is therefore unlike the absolute space prevalent in modern world view; like time and the form of particular objects, Indian space is fluid and alterable.

A common theme in traditional cosmologies is an elaboration of symbols of centers versus peripheries (Eliade 1954:12–16). The structure of this symbolism is most apparent in the common California cosmologic plan in which the people in question live at the center of a large disk-shaped world which itself is between two or more upper and lower worlds. Ptolemaic geocentric cosmology is of course another similar example. A parallel theme has to do with an opposition between areas where "humans" predominate versus areas where often dwell "barbarians" who are not considered truly human. Speaking of the Chumash, Blackburn (1975:73–74) refers to these oppositions as an "assumption of Centricity." Thus, for example, the village or hamlet is pre-eminently a human place. Just as the entire tribal territory was an area of relative familiarity and security compared to foreign places, so was one's own village, or hamlet, or camp an island of even greater security. As one goes out in any direction from such a center, it is as if one goes through concentric areas of progressively more unknown and therefore dangerous areas where there are ambiguous creatures and people who use power malevolently. A structural implication of this image is that the center—whether it be of the cosmos, the middle world, the tribal territory, or the village—is the antithesis of the periphery. At the center, humans with knowledge are ideally placed to control power for positive purposes. And in some cases we find that this plan is replicated again in house construction and symbolism. Among many groups the dwelling and ceremonial houses were semisubterranean circular structures. Typically there was a sacred center post, often equated with the center of the cosmos, an *axis mundi* that symbolically extended above and below to the upper and lower worlds. The shaman might climb this post to magically send his soul through the smoke hole in the center of the roof so that it could travel to the other worlds.

POWER AND SOCIAL CONTROL

From our brief description of social structure it is apparent that most groups of California Indians had no elaborate legal codes, courts, or police forces. An interesting question then is, How did they govern themselves, make group decisions, and deal with disputes and feuds? We know that social life flowed on for the most part rather smoothly. How was this possible in the absence of a legal machinery such as we seem to need to hold our society together?

All societies must have some underlying moral assumptions that regulate and legitimize proper, normal ways of living. As Durkheim maintains, without such common moral assumptions, individuals will start to act in individualistic ways; there will be no common expectations and the group will decay into a state of anomie, or normlessness. Although not in written laws or commandments, the Californians did have such precepts. Anna Gayton provides a typical example among the Yokuts and Mono, and comments that social life was generally harmonious because of certain values and attitudes:

> The sense of right and wrong, of duty to one's relatives and neighbors, was instilled in children as they grew up. Truthfulness, industry, a modest opinion of oneself, and above all, generosity, were regarded not so much as positive virtues as essential qualities. Informants today condemn those who are greedy, jealous, or egotistical. It was largely upon the personal character of individuals that the peace of a community depended. (Gayton 1930:408)

We might ask, what forces preserved these attitudes in the absence of formal law enforcement? An obvious answer is that the kind of behavior they produced was conducive to group survival, and this is no doubt true. But still, there were, as in perhaps all societies, temptations to take unfair advantage of the weaker, to steal from one's neighbors, to cheat them, and take reprisals for emotional slights. Without appearing cynical, we might look to a more fundamental basis for the attitudes which kept such unsocial actions within tolerable bounds.

This problem is all the more interesting since anyone could potentially avail himself or herself of power to secretly attack others. The most common method of doing this was to magically inject some "poison" or foreign object into the victim's body. The attacker might do this himself by performing the necessary rituals, or he might send a spirit familiar to do it. Another method was to hire a shaman to do the dirty work. The attack was usually made directly on the victim, but sometimes a close relative of the victim was attacked instead, thus indirectly causing the intended victim to suffer in this way and possibly pay great sums for a cure.

Sickness in general was assumed to be due to such attacks. Therefore when someone fell ill, one of the first concerns was to attempt to determine what human or nonhuman agent was responsible. The usual treatment was related to the presumed cause, that is, removal of the "poison" or foreign object. The victim, or his or her family, most likely would seek the services of a healing shaman who had the ability to remove the injurious substance. The most common method of doing this was by sucking it out, and such shamans were therefore referred to as "sucking doctors." Sometimes they would first make a small incision in the skin over the affected part to aid removal of the material. And likely as not they would demonstrate its removal by spitting it from their mouth and displaying it. This latter practice seems most often to have been a bit of showmanship for the benefit of the patients and their families. Thus, although the shaman may have been sincere in his tasks, he himself often assumed that the poison was invisible, and simply displayed something tangible—a pebble, some mountain-lion whiskers, whatever—for positive psychological effect.

After this essential and more immediate treatment, the next task of the shaman was to ascertain what or who was responsible for the attack. If it was some nonhuman thing such as an enchanted spring, an offended spirit or animal, there were appropriate ways to placate them. But if the shaman determined that a human was to blame then the appropriate action was most often deemed to be a counterattack. An immediate implication of this is that one thought twice before deciding to attack someone in the first place. If an attacker was detected he was then open to counterattack by the same means that he had initially employed. Anna Gayton put forth an analysis of this situation which anthropologists have since come to observe in many other stateless societies. In answer to the question of what maintained peace and social harmony she answers as follows:

> . . . largely by means of an influence which had no legal basis, the fear of sorcery. This factor in civil life worked for public good; it was an awe-inspiring force itself, and served as a tool for chiefs when used by them through their shamans. The fear of sorcery operated between any one individual and another. If, as we have said, the peace of a community depended largely upon the personal character of each person, the personal character in turn was determined or molded by belief in supernatural powers which could be turned against one. A man dared not cheat another at gambling or trading, commit adultery, or neglect any civil or ceremonial duty toward his neighbor, lest the offended person visit sickness or death upon him or some member of his family, either by his own power or that of a shaman hired for the purpose. On the other hand, a man could not take offense for no reason, and retaliate by this means unless completely justified, for the matter would eventually be aired before the chief. Thus sorcery as a deterrent of crime kept a balance of peace in everyday life. (Gayton 1930:409)

Certain signs revealed those who were using power malevolently. Generally they tended to be "mean" people, who were aloof, bitter, and possibly stingy. That is, they acted contrary to the ideal norms of being truthful, modest, and especially—generous. Because of this, the threat of malevolent shamanism cut two ways: not only was there concern lest one provoke an attack in consequence of unsociable behavior, but such behavior might also mark one as a person "who threw poison around." Such a person was also subject to reprisal and thus the fear of being accused of being a malevolent shaman was counterpoised against the temptation to engage in such nefarious actions. A shaman's victims would in all likelihood not feel capable of directly counterattacking their aggressor. One option open to them was to seek the aid of another shaman who was equal to the task and might be commissioned for a price. Another possibility was that several victims might conspire to direct their combined powers against their common enemy. There was yet another possibility. When a malevolent shaman became widely feared, a general consensus might be reached that community action had to be taken. Thus at some point, a spokesman might formalize this sentiment into plans to execute the undesirable shaman.

The temptation to misuse power was greatest for shamans, since they had greater control of it. For this reason ordinary people had much ambivalence toward them. On one hand, shamans and their skills were necessary for the general well-being of the group—to heal the sick, to treat rattlesnake bites, to maintain the fertility of the game, to control the weather, and to magically combat enemies. But the shamans' presence created much anxiety and suspicion that they might succumb to the temptation to use their power malevolently.

Shaman's Song

What do I remove from my mouth?
The disease I remove from my mouth.
What do I take out?
The disease I take out.
What do I suck out?
The disease I suck out.
What do I blow about?
The disease I blow about.
As a head only, I roll around.
I stand on the rim of my nest.
I am enveloped in flames.
What am I? What am I?
I, the song, I walk here.
I, the dog, stray,
In the north wind I stray.
An arrowpoint I am about to shoot.
A bad song I am.
The earth I sing of.   (from Kroeber 1925:321)

CONCLUSION

Some aspects of native California world view and associated beliefs appear irrational to modern white Americans who are apt to disregard concepts such as power and magical poisoning as useless superstitions. But considered within their own intellectual and social contexts, such beliefs are by no means irrational. In daily life, in societies where these beliefs existed, they did have real effects. Above we saw how the concept of power was an integral element in the "legal" system. Similarly, if space here permitted, we would find that people actually did die from magical poisoning, or more accurately said, from believing that they were being magically poisoned.[2] Also, belief in other shamanistic powers made it possible for healing shamans to often effect cures through symbolic mediation on their patients' minds and bodies in what could be called psychosomatic therapy, which was often supplemented by the use of medicinal plants and surgery. The point here is that even though beliefs in power, magical poisoning, and other aspects of California world view were false in a literal sense, they nevertheless were "real" in that they effected results. Some of these results were, as we have seen in the case of social control and healing, mainly adaptive. In a less positive sense they were, as we have also seen, conducive to an unrealistic paranoid view of reality.

Any world view is at best an approximation of reality, rather than an accurate image of it. Many bearers of the general modern world view take pride in assuming that theirs is the most accurate and presumably adaptive world view in the history of humanity, and in many important ways, such as understanding physical, psychological, and social phenomena, it perhaps is. And yet, it is ironic that this world view may in fact be quite maladaptive. Compared to the many thousands of years in which the general features of California thought and society existed, the modern world view is but a brief experiment. Modern economic attitudes and practices are a case in point, and are explainable in terms of the underlying world-view images in the Relationship and Time universals. Modern industrial peoples tend to have an aggressive, exploitive attitude towards nature and society. It is supported by a linear-future image of time in which change and "development" are actively sought. Here is an attitude that seeks to alter dramatically the social and physical environment in which it exists, and in doing so creates an inherently unstable situation, especially in a finite world whose physical limitations must inevitably constrict the kind of economic expansion on which industrial society thrives.

Thus from some far-distant historical perspective it might be revealed that that particular combination of thought and social forms which constituted native California culture and society was in terms of length of existence much more adaptive than its present modern counterparts. In other words, it is just possible that the native California images of Relationship between Self and environment, of Causality, and of the other universals formed a world view that was more consistent and more viable than our own.

Chapter 7

MEXICAN PEASANT WORLD VIEW

This chapter is one final application of the world-view model. Because I am familiar with Mexican peasantry I shall apply the model to this type of society. As in the case of the California Indians discussed in the previous chapter, there is considerable variation among Mexican peasant communities and among individuals in these communities. But at the level of generality with which we are dealing here, the common feature of social structure, economics, and thought stand out in clear contrast to say middle-class urban North American or aboriginal California Indian society and culture.

The main theme of the following pages is the relationship between living conditions in the broadest sense and world view. The argument developed is that the most basic feature of life in the Mexican countryside is poverty. Economic scarcity and the conditions that cause it are the main forces shaping this world view. Therefore, to explain Mexican peasant world view we must examine rural poverty in historical perspective. In doing so we will give primary attention to the past and present position of Mexican peasants in national and international economy and society. That is, we again recognize the primary role of external forces and infrastructure as shapers of world view.

In Mexican history the main key to the analysis of infrastructure is land, or more specifically, land tenure and use. For it is control of land that has historically conveyed access to the main sources of wealth: agriculture, mines, and tribute. And, since land without human labor is useless as a source of wealth, he who would command large or small amounts of land

171

must command labor—that of others or his own. This simple fact requires us to examine social relationships, and in particular the relationships of production in the countryside. These lead us directly to an analysis of peasants as a social class vis-à-vis other classes with whom they articulate socially and economically. These relationships are local, national, and international in scope. Of special interest is the development of these relationships in the Colonial and post-Colonial periods, the influence of foreign powers, especially the United States, and at all times the relationships between the peasantry and the city. We will see how these historic outside forces (see Figure 7) affect village economy, social structure, interpersonal relations, and the family, which compose the immediate environment in which world view is formed, and in which it in turn shapes people's actions in daily life. But first, who are Mexican peasants?

One distinctive characteristic of peasants is that they usually produce primarily for their own consumption. In this way they are unlike "farmers," who raise crops mainly for sale for a profit, often employing workers to do so. A second distinctive characteristic of peasants is that throughout history they have been forced to yield portions of their harvest, labor, or other resources to nonpeasant, nonagrarian segments of their nation states. This fundamental relationship between peasant and nonpeasant has endured throughout the major transformations from feudal to capitalist—and in some cases to socialist—societies. "What changed with these transformations was not the peasant's mode of struggle for survival, but the methods used for extracting a surplus from him: compulsory labour services, tithes, rents, taxes, sharecropping, interest on loans, production norms, etc." (Berger 1978:346). For our purposes these general structural features are of greater importance than other standard criteria used in typologies of rural Mexican agrarian communities and individuals, e.g., Indian versus mestizo, so-called communal versus collective (ejido) versus private land tenure, or level of income.[1]

Although assault on their land is the main threat to peasants, peasant communities are constantly defending themselves against attempts of outsiders to capture several of their other most valuable possessions. Peasants have historically provided two things that cities and landed elites need in order to grow and operate: food and labor. The historian McNeill (1976) has compared this relationship between nonpeasants and peasants to that which exists between a successful biological parasite—say body lice, leeches, or the virus that causes measles—and its host. The parasite must strike an evolutionary balance between two contradictory tendencies. First of all, it must parasitize aggressively enough so that the host does not repel it. But at the same time it must not extract too great a "tax" and kill off its host population. Similarly, elites in extracting labor, food, and other commodities from peasants must strike a balance. On one hand they must not exceed limits beyond which the peasantry will be unable to reproduce itself and its economy. On the other hand, the state—which is the instrument by which elites perpetrate this exploitation—must not allow peasants to become economically and politically strong enough to revolt and smash the power of the elites. The significance of this class relationship in peasant societies is of such basic importance in the formation of world view that we must explore it at some length.

The following sections of this chapter correspond to the components of the world-view model (Figure 7). The best place to enter the model is the box labeled Outside Sources of Change. This refers to the social, economic, and political forces which through time have impinged on Mexican peasant communities, and to which they have responded with characteristic life ways and ideology.

HISTORIC DETERMINANTS OF MEXICAN PEASANT WORLD VIEW

Precolumbian Mexico

Mexican peasantry arose with the first Mesoamerican civilizations about 2000 B.C. As are many modern civilizations, these ancient ones were built on an agrarian base provided by rural villages. The present inequitable relationship between countryside and city in Mexico thus has roots in Precolumbian society. Other roots go back to the sixteenth-century Spain, where comparable relationships had also developed. In Mexico we have most knowledge of this situation in the Central Highlands for the period immediately preceding the Spanish Conquest. The Aztecs, following a general Mesoamerican practice, extracted tribute and labor from subjugated peoples within the areas they dominated. In this arrangement communities of each area were required to deliver to their Aztec lords set amounts of agricultural produce, other goods, and labor. The greater part of these values were delivered to the Aztecs by the local nobility, who accumulated the required wealth from their own "serfs" and slaves. A large class of agrarian freemen of commoner status *(macehualtin)* paid taxes in goods and labor directly to the Aztec state. Well-developed markets and interregional trade also served to channel commodities from the countryside into the cities.

Conquest and Colony

When the Spanish conquistadores arrived in the early sixteenth century they found this system of tribute and taxation to their liking and themselves collected the wealth so accumulated. The first colonial institution established for this purpose was the *encomienda*. This legal and social arrangement was first used over conquered Moors in Spain and later over Indians in the West Indies. As transplanted to Mexico the encomienda was a "trust" whereby the Spanish Crown granted individual conquistadores the right to collect tribute in the form of goods or labor from Indian communities. In return the *encomenderos* (those who had been granted these trusts) were obligated to bring the presumed benefits of Christian civilization to those Indians assigned to them. In a few cases the Spanish *encomenderos* continued to extract from Indian communities the same goods and labor that the Aztecs had demanded. But almost without exception the Spanish were more rapacious than their Aztec predecessors.

In the Valley of Mexico and elsewhere Indian town officials were made responsible for collection of tribute in their own communities, and they often overassessed tributaries for their own profit. The tribute system underwent many modifications until its abolishment in 1810. Until then it was the largest expense of the Indian communities. Unable to bear this constant burden, many towns were in chronic arrears. After the late 1500s Indian town officials became personally responsible for unpaid tributes and those unable to pay were treated as criminals. When these obligations were unpaid in the debtor's lifetime they were inherited by his descendants.

> The record of the first encomienda generation, in the Valley [of Mexico] as elsewhere, is one of generalized abuse and particular atrocities. Encomenderos used their Indians in all forms of manual labor, in building, farming, and mining, and for the supply of whatever the country yielded. They overtaxed and overworked them. They jailed them, killed them, beat them, and set dogs on them. They seized their goods, destroyed their agriculture, and took their women. They used them as beasts of burden. They took tribute from them and sold it back under compulsion at exorbitant profits. Coercion and ill-treatment were the daily practices of their overseers, calpixque [local tyrants], and labor bosses. The first encomenderos, without known exception, understood Spanish authority as provision for unlimited personal opportunism. (Gibson 1964:78)

Primarily as a way of checking the potential power that the *conquistadores* stood to acquire by virtue of this new wealth and distance from royal surveillance, the Spanish Crown developed another colonial policy designed to further its control over the most valuable commodity in New Spain—Indian labor. This involved the formation of *congregaciones*, literally the congregating of Indian people into hundreds of new settlements. Most of these appear to have been established on the sites of existing Indian towns and villages, while others were newly established. In either case, dispersed populations were herded together into these planned communities.

There were three purposes of these settlements. One was to facilitate the governing and conversion of the Indians. Another was to make them less accessible to the predations of the conquistadores, who desired to acquire feudal fiefs in News Spain and were thus a threat to the Spanish monarchy. Royal directives granted these new Indian communities considerable degrees of internal autonomy and at least ideally the means for economic self-sufficiency. These settlements were intended to serve as sources of labor and tribute for the Colonial government, the recipients of Spanish grants and the Church; and finally, as Gibson (1964:283) observes, ". . . Spaniards could hardly consider congregación without realizing that the proposed regroupings would make new tracts of land available for Spanish use."

These communities, once formed, provided islandlike refuges for the devasted Indian population. In these enclaves Indian culture and society were reconstituted in ways that would allow them to survive under the new masters. Those that were successful have persisted into the present as contemporary rural peasant communities. The history of these communities is one of constant outside assault on their economic and political integrity, and of the defensive strategies they have devised to protect themselves.

Beginning in the late 1500s and continuing into the early twentieth century, one type of institution more than any other assailed these rural corporate communities. This was the *hacienda*. In its various forms the hacienda was a large corporate land holding which usually originated from royal land grants. The owners of haciendas were either individuals, family lineages, the Catholic Church, or ecclesistical orders. As an economic and social type the hacienda is ambiguous. Haciendas were somewhat capitalistic in that they often raised livestock and crops and mined silver and gold for profit. But *hacendados* (masters of nonchurch haciendas) were feudal throwbacks insofar as they aspired to establish a rural landed aristocracy based on Iberian models. Many haciendas, especially the early ones, were in effect feudal manors of which the hacendado was the autocratic master, often the general of his own private army. The rise of the hacienda coincides with decline of centralized Colonial government power and of its ability to protect the communal Indian villages.

In addition to land, the other main resource that hacendados wished to control was labor — labor to run the herds, work the land and mines, and provide services for the hacendado and his family. In their hunger for land and labor the hacienda inevitably descended on the other main corporate entity in the countryside, where these two values were located — the rural peasant villages. By expropriating land, the hacienda inevitably acquired labor in the bargain. Deprived of their land, peasants were forced to either seek their destinies within the interstices of the greater colonial society — mainly in the cities — or become sharecroppers or fieldhands working on hacienda lands. The former delivered up a percentage of their harvest to nonproductive landlords, while the latter worked hacienda lands, in effect as serfs. In both cases they often as not worked land that had formerly belonged to their village. Once attached to haciendas, peasants often became bound to them by cycles of perpetual debt on credit extended by the hacienda's *tienda de raya*, which was a company store.

The greatest single blow to the communal villages was a series of "reforms" in the late 1800s. Desirous to develop agriculture and in general promote progress in Mexico, liberal forces, beginning in 1856, were able to enact legislation that eliminated communal corporate land holdings. They assumed that this creation of private property in land would promote the rise of a prosperous middle class of capitalist farmers as in the United States. The main targets of these reform laws were the communal villages and religious corporations, which had extensive properties. With village lands now subject to the forces of the market, concentration of land by large owners accelerated. Peasants, who for the most part had no concept of private property, often found that they had exchanged their lands for pieces of paper. Thus was completed the first major cycle in Mexican history in which the peasant was dispossessed of land. As we will see below, comparable developments are again taking place in the Mexican countryside today, resulting in the creation of a large landless rural proletariat.

After the Revolution

This wholesale assault on the villages and on peasants in general finally provoked the outbreak of the Mexican Revolution in 1910. By this time the haciendas had swallowed up virtually all of the productive land in the Mexican countryside, dispossessing the peasantry in the process. In this year 1 percent of the population possessed 95 percent of the national territory while 96 percent of the population possessed only 2 percent of the land (Stavenhagen 1976:13). The main issue of the Revolution was, understandably, agrarian reform: return of alienated lands to the peasant villages. The battle cry of the Revolution, *Tierra y Libertad* (Land and Freedom), bespeaks the order of priorities. The holocaust that ensued, in which 1 million people lost their lives out of a population of 6 million, is the most dramatic expression of the importance of land to the peasantry. The entire colonial and postcolonial experience offers one fundamental lesson: land is the most valuable of possessions that the rural poor can hope to possess. Without it one is susceptible to the most predatory of forces in society. With it one can at least be assured of "something to eat." The history of the Mexican peasantry more than anything else is the history of its attempts to acquire and defend possession of land.

The Present as History

The 1910 Mexican Revolution, the resultant constitution of 1917, and subsequent agrarian reform essentially eliminated the hacienda as a major form of exploitation of the rural populace. But one of the most notable characteristics of peasantry throughout history is its persistence as a social and economic type. This is certainly true in contemporary Mexico. Today the structural relationships between the rural poor and concentrations of wealth and power in the city are more subtle but hardly less pernicious for the welfare of the Mexican peasantry. Let us now examine the contemporary social, economic, and geographic conditions in the Mexican countryside. We shall begin by focusing on agricultural economics.

Mexico, like other underdeveloped capitalist countries and the Soviet Union, has given primary importance to urban industrialization as a way of promoting economic growth. This development has been in large part financed by agriculture, that is, by transfer of wealth from the countryside to cities. This transfer of wealth occurs by a number of mechanisms. Two important ones on which economic data exist are banking and price differences between agriculture and other sectors of the national economy. The money chaneled out of agriculture by banking and price differences is more than that expended on agricultural development by the federal government. In sum, there is a net flow of wealth from the countryside to the city. Other mechanisms that also transfer wealth in this direction are discussed below.[2]

How do peasants fit into this situation? Within the agricultural sector there are two distinct but interrelated modes of production: a commercial capitalist one and a peasant one. Of the two, capitalist agriculture is in a preferential position and peasant agriculture is to a great degree dependent on it. Many fortunes are made in the former and perpetual poverty is prevalent in the latter. To understand the dynamics of peasant economy, society, and thought we must examine the way in which these two types of agriculture articulate with each other, and with the national and international economies.[3]

Commercial agriculture in Mexico, as in the United States, is a rural capitalist industry that has several defining traits. First, the main productive entity—land—is privately owned by the individual or corporation which uses it or by a landlord who rents it out. In both cases the means of production—land, machinery and other inputs—are controlled variously by landowners, growers, or financier capitalists who together constitute an agricultural elite. Second, these individuals and firms engage in agricultural production for the market in order to gain profit. And third, just as is the case with urban industries, capitalist agriculturalists hire labor that does the actual work of production.

Peasant agriculturalists are like capitalist farmers in that they may either individually or collectively "own" or rent land, but they are unlike capitalist farmers in that typically peasants engage little or no labor. Mexican peasants are also unlike commercial agriculturalists in that they produce primarily for their own consumption rather than for a market. In other words, they are more concerned with subsistence and survival than with profit. They are not uninterested in the idea of profit, but given their meager productive capacities production for profit is not possible for most peasants. A number of conditions account for this essential difference between peasant and commercial agriculture. One of the more important has to do with the economics of size. Commercial agriculture is associated with large operations. A characteristic of capitalist and other forms of commercial agriculture is a tendency toward consolidation of land and financial resources. This results from stronger capitalists acquiring the land of weaker ones and also from the penetration of capitalist agriculture into peasant areas.

Peasant land tenure is plagued by the opposite tendency—to fragmentation and the formation of minifundia. Fragmentation of peasant holdings is a result, on the one hand, of population increase such that each generation available amounts of land must be portioned out among more individuals, and, on the other hand, of loss of peasant land to commercial producers and soil erosion. There are also distinct differences in the quality of peasant and commercial agricultural lands. Commercial operations occupy the better bottom lands while peasant agriculture persists in mountainous areas and areas lacking a potential for large-scale irrigation and mechanization. At this time in history it appears that capitalist agriculture in Mexico has occupied and developed virtually all of the land for which it is politically and economically feasible.[4]

Peasants, who have been dispossesed from the better lands and denied access to them, now scratch out less than subsistence incomes on lands which for the most part are agriculturally marginal, given the environmental conditions and economic resources available to them. Were peasants to pay themselves the minimum wage for their own labor they would operate at a deficit—which in effect they do (Bartra 1975a:131-135). Capitalist agriculture, dependent as it is on wage labor, is thus unable to penetrate into such areas of low fertility where production returns would not exceed labor and other costs. In other words, in peasant areas there is little or no possibility for the direct extraction of profits in the form of surplus value created by the labor or workers. As a result the peasant mode of production persists peripheral to the capitalist agriculture to which value is transferred by all the other mechanisms discussed herein.

Another major difference between peasant and capitalist agriculture is that the latter is strongly supported by the federal government. Since the 1940s Mexico has invested heavily in technological research and development, which has been designed to promote large-scale commercial agriculture. This strategy, referred to commonly as the Green Revolution, was initiated by the simultaneous development of high-yielding wheats and hybrid corns sponsored by the Rockefeller Foundation and by the construction of large-scale irrigation projects that opened to intensive cultivation lands that were formerly nonarable or suitable only for rain-fed agriculture. The Green Revolution was promoted as a way of feeding the Mexican masses. But most of the grain produced from the "miracle seeds" was exported from Mexico—directly, or indirectly by being used as feed for animals (poultry and cattle) raised for export. The effect of this policy was to cause a deficiency of staples for the domestic market which, beginning in 1971, had to be made up by food imports from shrinking quantities in the world market. Although Green Revolution exports became significant in Mexico's balance of payments, the income received from these exports was not allocated to improving the diet or general lot of the rural poor. During this period of intense agricultural development the federal government essentially neglected peasant agriculture, which is carried out under different environmental, social, and economic conditions toward which Green Revolution research and development were not directed. As was noted above, peasant agriculture is for the most part confined to areas dependent on rainfall and generally lacks the potential for large-scale irrigation. It also tends to be in mountainous terrain and therefore unsuited for mechanized cultivation. The new seed varieties developed by the Rockefeller technicians produce their spectacular yields only under optimal conditions that include not only irrigation but also application of fertilizer, herbicides, and pesticides. Even if the necessary irrigation were available to small-scale peasant cultivators, the additional necessary inputs are priced beyond their reach. They are, however, available to the commercial growers to whom the federal government and financial agencies readily extend credit. Such formal credit sources are not adequately available to peasant cultivators. Furthermore, since these high-yielding corns are hybrids, credit must be available to buy seed for each season's planting; again the peasant cultivator is excluded here and forced to sow local indigenous varieties from seed corn held over from the preceding harvest.[5]

That peasant cultivators have not been totally eliminated by the spread of capitalist production is due in large measure to the agriculturally marginal lands they occupy, which would not yield a profit for market-oriented production. Peasants are able to survive here only by an economic intensification that is unprofitable in capitalist terms and by seeking income outside the peasant sector. Recent surveys classify 84 percent of Mexican farm units as infrasubsistence or subfamily holdings (Stavenhagen 1978:33), meaning that they are too small and unproductive to support the families which work them. Survival therefore is possible only by seeking additional income from outside the peasant sector. Seasonal migratory wage labor on commercial agricultural lands and urban employment are the two main sources of supplemental income. This situation is advantageous for commercial agriculture because it assures a steady supply of cheap labor when and where needed.

Furthermore, because of the dual nature of peasant livelihood, in which peasant production, primarily for autoconsumption, supplements wage income, peasants are not totally dependent on wages for their subsistence. Capitalist farmers can therefore pay these workers less than subsistence wages (Esteva 1976:5). In other words, rather than the costs of reproduction of the work force coming entirely from wages, as in the case of a completely proletarianized work force, a substantial part of this cost is borne by the peasant mode of production, which in this way subsidizes capitalist agricultural production. In other words, by not being entirely dependent on paid employment, peasant workers are able to accept lower wages than full-time workers. For this and other reasons the minimum rural wage differs from the urban on the average about 15 to 25 percent (Reyes Osorio, et al. 1974: 142).

As producers and consumers, peasants also live in a situation in which prices for agricultural commodities they may occasionally sell rise more slowly than the prices for manufactured commodities they must buy. The reason for these differences in prices is the lower wages paid for agricultural work—both for fieldhands and self-employed peasant producers. Lower wages also mean higher profits for commercial growers.[6] The profits made in commercial agriculture are for the most part expended by those who receive them in ways that do not circulate back into the village economy. This situation is another instance of the many ways in which value is transferred from the peasant economy to other sectors.

Small producers also operate at a disadvantage in the market because of other reasons in addition to the inequity in price differences mentioned above. A common situation in many peasant households is for peasants to be out of money and in debt at harvest time and thus forced to sell part of their crop when prices are lowest. As Eric Wolf says, they have little "withholding power." Similarly, small cash resources result in limited purchasing power in general. The same peasant who sells part of his crop when prices are low may later in the year be out of food and forced to buy grain when prices are highest. Likely as not they will be buying from speculators who had the capital to buy when prices were low.

Peasants often find themselves out of cash to buy food or other necessities. Not having easy access to institutional sources of credit, they must turn to money lenders who charge usurious rates, typically about 10 percent per month. This heavy expense is a major drain on many household incomes and dissipates income before it is earned. Village money lenders typically reinvest part of their earnings in grain speculation and merchandise. For the most part their expenditures, whether the buying of a truck, building materials, stock for a store, or luxuries for personal use, are made outside the local community. Village entrepreneur-money-lenders are thus another conduit that siphons wealth from the countryside to the city.

These inequities between countryside and city are increasing because of population growth. At present the Mexican population is increasing at about 3 percent per year. Technological improvements and productivity are not increasing at anywhere near this rate. The result is increasing pressure on the life-support capacities of peasant agriculture. As a further result, every year more and more peasants are permanently or temporarily forced out of their local communities to seek work elsewhere to make ends meet.

LOCAL SOCIAL AND GEOGRAPHIC ENVIRONMENT

The preceding section deals on a large scale with conditions affecting the rural peasantry. Having established this macro context, we can now turn to the way peasants perceive these conditions and respond to them. The main theoretical problem here is to demonstrate the causal relationship between these greater external structural conditions and local social and ideological responses to them. Few peasant-workers are able to explain explicitly how the dual and dependent nature of their income makes possible a high rate of profit for commercial agriculturalists and their allied interests. But they are all acutely aware of the differences in wealth, privilege, and general well-being that distinguish them from their employers. Lacking education and access to relevant sources of information as they do, few peasants are aware of all the economic and social relationships whereby wealth is drained from the countryside and from them. Yet they are acutely aware of their situation, though in different terms. It is not the functionings of regional, national, and international economics, markets, and politics of which they are most cognizant. What most interests them and most influences their thought and actions is the quality and conditions of day-to-day life. As we have already suggested and as we will further discuss below, these local conditions are largely results and extensions of the macro conditions. To examine the influences of the macro context on the micro we need an appropriate unit of analysis. The most useful is the local agrarian community, the peasant village. There is not space here to discuss at length the various types of such villages, but we can spell out prevalent characteristics that delineate this general social type. In 1977 the rural population (defined as those living in communities of less than 2,500 inhabitants) was estimated at 23 million, which was about 41 percent of the entire nation. Of these, 15.9 million live in communities under 1,000 (1979 estimates); this figure is expected to grow to 17.4 million in 1982 and to 23 million by the year 2000 (*Comercio Exterior de México* 1979:243). The general quality of life in these communities is suggested by the nutritional status in the countryside, where

> 96% of the pre-school population suffers from malnutrition. . . . While 15% in the high-income sector enjoys 50% of the country's agricultural production, 30% in the poorest range has access to a mere 10% of such production. The average campesino's diet—made up [primarily] of corn, beans and chili—, contains less than 2,000 calories and only 54 grammes of protein per day. This, which is insufficient in itself, grows even less at certain times of year and in certain regions, to such an extent that it may be compared with the lowest consumption levels in the world. (ibid.: 244)

In terms of social scale the agrarian community is intermediate between the family on the one hand and the city and nation on the other. It is the main setting in which peasants for the most part live and with which they identify. It is the main mold that shapes their images of themselves and of the world. Much of the society and culture of such communities is integrated in such a way that they are mutually re-enforcing.[7]

To better illustrate these conditions and the kind of world view that results from them, let us now turn to two particular peasant communities in Mexico with which I am familiar. One, Ixtepeji, is a strongly mestizo-Zapotec town in the Sierra Juárez of central Oaxaca (Kearney 1972). The other I shall call Los Cedros (Stuart and Kearney 1981). It is also in the state of Oaxaca, but near the Guerrero border. All native residents of Los Cedros speak Mixtec as their first language and most of the women and small children speak virtually no Spanish.

Los Cedros is literally and figuratively at the end of a long road, the other end of which goes to nearby provincial centers and eventually to other cities in Mexico and to the United States over 2000 miles away. People, goods, labor, money, and services flow in both directions along this road in such a way that the net flow of wealth is in the direction of the cities of Mexico and the United States. We have already examined how this flow of people and food tends to impoverish peasant communities in general. Los Cedros is also typical of most Mexican peasant communities in that because of lack of land and other reasons discussed above households are unable to grow enough corn and beans—the two main staples—to get them through more than about six months of the year. The town as a whole thus buys more corn and beans than it sells. Local small merchants buy corn cheaply in the village and at distant markets when prices are low after harvest time and then store it in the village. Then when local people deplete their family granaries, the merchants sell them corn at a considerable markup. These same merchants also buy manufactured goods from retail and wholesale outlets in provincial cities and mark up prices in the village for resale to an essentially capitve clientele that is least able to afford these high prices. The small peasant's immediate problem is to acquire the cash to buy these commodities. There is little wage labor in the local area and wages for what there is are low. Men must therefore leave the community from time to time to seek work. Their main destinations are large tomato and cotton fields in northwestern Mexico and the orchards and fields of California. These journeys involve great physical hardship and much homesickness and anguish for the families that are separated in this manner. Those men who attempt to enter the United States illegally are especially at risk of being robbed and otherwise exploited. For example, $200 is the usual fee charged by smugglers for a ride from the border area near San Diego, California, to points about 80 miles north where work may be available. The migrant worker is most likely paying for such "services" with borrowed money. To avoid paying these "coyotes," the men of Los Cedros frequently cross the international border on foot east of San Diego and walk through the mountains for anywhere from three to ten days.

These migrant workers, whether in Mexico or the United States, are the bottom stratum of the working class. They often work for less than the minimum wage, lack legal protection, benefits, medical attention, and schools for their children (who often accompany them in Mexico but seldom in the United States). Their living conditions are typically abysmal, their diets inadequate.[8]

The people of Los Cedros are acutely aware that they relate to the greater society from positions of relative powerlessness, and this awareness is a major component of their general world view. But it is in the context of day-to-day life within the community that world view is primarily formed and perpetuated. Let us now turn from these general economic and structural relationships that articulate Los Cedros to the greater world and look to the crucible of village life, which is, as I shall show, both a result of and an adaptation to the social, economic, political, and environmental consequences of dependency and poverty.

WORLD VIEW AND ACTION

Throughout the preceding our main argument has been that poverty —a curse from the historic past and from contemporary forces mostly from outside the local community—is the most crucial feature of Mexican peasant existence. In terms of world-view theory, then, the first problem is to analyze and describe how this poverty is conceptualized by those who live in it. We can do this using several of the world-view universals, showing how they are logico-structurally integrated. As we describe the basic assumptions and images of each universal we will see how they influence the way people as individuals lead their daily lives and how their individual behavior collectively creates part of the social and physical environment these individuals perceive. In other words, the strategies individuals follow in their own lives become, in the aggregate, a large part of the economic and social matrix which they perceive and respond to. The circle (Figure 7) closes.

Other

The most appropriate universal with which to begin an examination of poverty is the Other. The question here is, how do the rural poor see their situation? A useful point of departure is the theoretical model developed by George Foster (1965a) which he calls the Image of Limited Good. Although Foster does not mention poverty per se, this model is nevertheless concerned with how Mexican peasants perceive the scarcity of basic resources. Foster's model was developed from field work in the village of Tzintzuntzan in the western Mexican state of Michoacan. Theoretically it is consistent with the general model of world view in the present work, in that it assumes that world view is formed mainly by economic, material, and social conditions of the community. In brief, the argument is that the people of Tzintzuntzan (and members of other similar peasant communities) realize that given their present means of production they have insufficient sources of income "to fill even minimal needs" of all members of the community.[9]

The economy of Tzintzuntzan is based on agriculture, pottery, and fishing. Foster notes that none of these sources of wealth can be significantly expanded. In the case of farming, the primary resource, land, is completely apportioned. The pottery market is saturated. And the fishery, Lake Patzcuaro, has a finite number of fish in it. The people do not hold out any hope of significant technological developments or outside assistance that would alter this situation. For purposes of analysis Foster assumes that the community is a closed system in the sense that with few exceptions its members have access to only the local finite resources. From this there follows a corollary assumption to the Image of Limited Good: "if Good exists in finite quantities, and if the system is closed, it follows that *an individual or a family can improve its position only at the expense of others*. Hence, an apparent improvement in someone's position with respect to good—especially economic good—is viewed as a threat to the entire community" (Foster 1967:124). According to this logic, if someone gains Good, then someone else must lose it. If the source of the good fortune is unclear, then one has

. .

reason to suspect it comes from him or her. Thus, anyone's good fortune or improvement is seen as a threat to all others. "That someone's advantage implies someone else's disadvantage seems to me to be the key to understanding the Image of Limited Good" (ibid.). Foster shows how this essentially realistic perception of the material-economic conditions of the local community shapes much of village social structure and also influences assumptions about the nonmaterial world. I will note some of these below in discussing the Self and projective systems, respectively.[10]

The Image of Limited Good was worked out in the relatively stable and prosperous area known as the Sierra Tarasca. There is good reason to believe that in a village such as Los Cedros the bases of wealth are more meager. Indeed, in Los Cedros it seems appropriate to speak of an Image of Diminishing Good. Let us develop this argument by first looking at the main economic resource in the village: land. All other things being equal two main considerations determine wealth derived from land available to the members of an agrarian community. One is the absolute amount of land available; the other is the number of people competing for access to it. In Los Cedros the amount of land suitable for agriculture is shrinking, mainly owing to soil erosion caused by overuse of the land and deleterious agricultural practices which in turn are due to lack of capital for investment in better methods. At the same time that the absolute amount of usable land is shrinking there is an imbalance between births and deaths such that each year more people are born than die. As a result, in the long run more people are competing for less and less land.[11] And as was noted earlier, at present agriculture provides less than half of the community's nutritional requirements, the difference being made up by economic intensification within the community (see below) and by wage labor out of the community. Given the primary importance of land to agrarian peasants, here certainly is a basis for an Image of Diminishing Good.

For many generations the people of Los Cedros have had to squeeze as much income out of their local land and economy as possible. All but a small minority of families in the town have had to do this without the benefit of sufficient capital to invest in profit-making enterprises. Therefore, aside from migrating in search of wage labor, the only other recourse is to intensify work to achieve increasingly diminishing returns. In Los Cedros this is most obvious in the economics of households, households being the basic units of production and consumption. All the available labor resources of the family must be mobilized if it is to survive economically. This means that the work day is long and unrelenting, and that the children and the elderly are of necessity forced to work. Much of this work of children is invisible in that it never appears in official labor statistics. It consists of running errands, caring for smaller children, tending animals, gathering cooking fuel, and dozens of other household chores. Such work is nevertheless of utmost importance in the marginal economics of households, in that it frees adults to devote more time and energy to productive agricultural and craft work. One pernicious result of this situation is that it prevents many children from attending school regularly.[12] For children who do go to school, responsibilities at home are often a major drain on their time and energy, and are given higher priority than school work. Such obstacles to education perpetuate "backward" attitudes and generally inhibit the spread of progressive thought, and thus affect world view.

Another example of this labor intensification: the main marginal source of income in Los Cedros is the weaving of palm hats and baskets. Several species of local palms provide raw material that anyone in the village may gather and use. In the case of hats the villagers do not produce a finished product; instead they leave them untrimmed and unbleached for eventual finishing in hat factories. Virtually all women in the village weave palm and also a majority of the men. It takes about four hours to make one hat and by using all her "free" time an average weaver can make one hat a day. Most of these unfinished hats are bought by local merchants who resell them to other middle men in the provincial city, who eventually sell them to hat factories in more distant cities. The price the weaver receives is two and a half pesos, or less than four cents in United States currency in August 1982. These same weavers, when they buy a finished hat in a local regional market or possibly from the same merchant to whom they sell their unfinished hats, will pay eight or ten times this amount.

This sort of intensification of household economic activities is endemic in the community in general. Here, as also among the urban poor, it is a response to pervasive underemployment. All conceivable economic niches are carved out and filled, regardless of how marginal they may be. For the most part these are small-scale secondary occupations whereby people work harder and harder at marginal jobs and earn less and less. A fundamental result of this intensification is that from early childhood virtually all of one's waking hours in Los Cedros are devoted to economic activities, to making a living, within an environment of material and financial scarcity. In the pages that follow I shall describe how this experience is one of the major immediate forces shaping world view in Los Cedros, and in peasant communities in general.

Now the question arises, what about those who leave the community temporarily? As was noted above, most of them seek work as day laborers in agriculture. Are their experiences such that they shape their perceptions differently? To answer this we must shift our focus back to the macro level and examine the social and economic conditions they encounter. The single most telling statistics here are those describing the population growth rate in Mexico. At present Mexico doubles its population in about twenty years.

As was noted above, the development of peasant agriculture is lagging considerably behind this trend, thus forcing more peasants to seek wage labor outside the community.[13] The population pressure within Los Cedros is a microversion of national demography. The result is that whereas within the village peasants compete primarily for land, outside the village they compete primarily for jobs. Whether they look for jobs in factories, in agribusiness, or as dishwashers or sweepers, their numbers and lack of organization give them virtually no bargaining power. Consequently they must sell their labor for the low wages noted above. And like the land-per-person ratio in the village, the jobs-per-worker ratio in the country at large is very low and shrinking. Most current estimates place unemployment in Mexico at around 40 percent. Thus, even as peasants are being proletarianized (though they may be increasing in absolute numbers) by the spread of capitalist agriculture, population increase, and soil erosion, fewer jobs are available in commercial production. This condition is due, again, to population increase and also to increased mechanization in commercial agriculture. At the same time, overall agricultural productivity is increasing more slowly than the rural population. All of these conditions are, from the point of view of the peasant trying to get or to hang onto land or a job, conditions of diminishing good, increasing competition, and poverty.[14]

Thus both in the community, as agriculturalists, and outside it, as wage laborers, peasants rightly see themselves as in direct competition among themselves for scarce economic resources. That they are also in unequal competition with nonpeasant sectors of the national and international economy is less apparent to them. We will return to perceptions of these aspects of the Other below.

Self, Relationship

Given the images of Other we have just outlined, we can turn to the Self and Relationship universals. How does this sort of perceived environment shape people's concept of themselves and of their relationship to their environment and to other humans?

I have already discussed how the people of Los Cedros are thrown into economic competition with each other for the means to make a living. Said differently, there is little group cooperation. Part of the reasoning behind this reluctance to enter into cooperative enterprises seems to be the assumption that, in an economy of scarcity, there simply is no potential for many people to improve their situation. At best it can be done only by individuals. The logic of the situation implies that one person's gain is another's loss. Only a few select individuals may get ahead. But for most, not falling behind is the main goal.

This strongly developed tradition of individualism is not just a feature of social behavior. At bottom it is an image of Self. The way the people of Los Cedros see it, the more one enters into relationships with others, the more one opens oneself to being taken advantage of by them. To my repeated queries about why the people of Los Cedros do not form buying and selling cooperatives, the standard reply is, "And who is going to hold the money?" An economy of intensification and marginal return is an economy of extreme competition. Each individual is quite conscious of how ready he or she is to exploit reasonable chance for gain, and realizes that one's neighbors are just as desperate and aggressive. Life in an economy of scarcity is precarious. One is in constant danger of falling behind, of losing out to those who are able to compete more sucessfully. To enter into relationships is to let down defenses and make oneself vulnerable. The best strategy is to limit involvement to what is essential. Rather than opening oneself to others, one therefore falls back on one's resources as much as is possible. Doing so, one realizes that he is to a very great extent alone in a hostile world. In a community of like-minded individuals these perceptions are of course realistic.

Historically, Mexican peasant individualism has origins in the decline of pre-Columbian corporate kin groups during the Spanish Conquest and their replacement by bilateral kinship. Whereas aboriginal patri-clans were collective and served to organize large numbers of relatives into more or less cohesive groups, post-Conquest society was fragmented. The pre-Conquest corporate collectives devolved into individuals thrown on their own resources. The atomistic nuclear family became and still is the basic unit of production and consumption.

Today in most of rural Mexico the preferred living arrangement is for a couple and their children to have their own household. This preference for living in nuclear families is re-enforced by several economic conditions noted by Eric Wolf (1966a:70–71). One is the fragmentation of land holdings through inheritance. Another is a prevalence of wage labor where, as in Los Cedros, workers are hired as individuals rather than as groups of relatives. These conditions re-enforce the tendency for one to turn inward and minimize involvement with others.

The fabric of village social structure is woven out of this individualism and is understandable only in terms of it. One of its most notable features is the relative absence of social groupings greater than the nuclear family. Rather than voluntary corporate associations such as cooperatives, village social structure is a seamless network of individuals, each of whom judiciously forms economic and social bonds with other individuals. This individualism contrasts markedly with the images of Self and Relationship prevalent in aboriginal California (Chapter 6).

Given the type of society and economy, with whom does it make sense to form relationships? The thinking here can be phrased in terms of propositions concerning the Self, Other, and Relationship: *The Self is poor and powerless. The Other comprises two kinds of people, those who are also poor and powerless and those who are not.* Therefore the best economic and social strategy is to form relationships with others who are wealthy and powerful, since more is to be gained with them than in relationships with others who are equally poor and powerless. This strategy is made possible in a community such as Los Cedros by the existence of considerable wealth differences whereby there are a few families of "rich people" *(ricos)*, and a few families of "poor people" *(pobres)* who are abysmally destitute even by local standards. Most of the rest of the town ranges between these two extremes. The *ricos* have large land holdings and own local stores and cargo trucks. They are the main patrons in town because they are in a position to extend credit, lend money, offer a few cents more for handicrafts, and do any number of other "favors." They are also the main local employers of wage labor. In a word, they control scarce resources for which potential clients must compete. One competes by striving to deliver what the patron wants, whether it be business, regular payments, votes, or a hard day's work.

The word *patron* is interesting. It comes from the Latin *patronus,* meaning protector or defender, and was derived from the word for father, *pater.* The Spanish cognate of patron is *patrón*, and is a word frequently heard in villages such as Los Cedros. As the etymology of this word suggests, it is in the Mexican peasant family that this institution—pyramidal client-patron relationships—has one of its roots, especially in the relationship between fathers (patrons) and sons (clients), and among these sons as brothers (competing clients). Within the family the father is *the* patron. It is he who dispenses and withholds scarce favors, of which there are not enough to satisfy all of his sons who are thus thrown into competition (see Kearney 1972:119–120).

This strategy results in a vertical ordering of society between clients and patrons rather than the formation of horizontal strata of equals.[15] This vertical grain of village social structure is but a small segment and replication of Mexican society. Virtually absent in Mexico are the special interest groups so common in the United States which can bring powerful pressure on Congress to affect legislation in their favor. Political power is not coalesced in Mexico in this manner. Instead it is channeled through the national patronage system controlled by the ruling political party (PRI), of which the presidency is the pinnacle.[16]

These patron-client relationships are like the pre-Columbian pyramids with staircases running up the sides for carrying offerings up and handing largesse down: wealth and power accumulate at the top and favors flow down. At each step an individual who is a patron to many below him may be client to a few above him. At bottom this system extends into communities such as Los Cedros. The village is linked to the outside world by individuals who have found commercial and political patrons outside of it. This pyramidal structure thus not only organizes vertical relationships within the town, but is also the main funnel whereby wealth leaves the town as we described earlier. As such, the structure and the world-view assumptions that perpetuate it are a fundamental aspect of the relationship of dependency we discussed above.

In this society one is conditioned, as it were, to look up and down for associates rather than sideways to one's equals. One's equals are in fact seen not as potential allies, but as competitors. One looks down to see who can be controlled and dominated. And one looks up for patrons. Surviving, if not getting ahead, is thought to depend not so much on what you know, but who you know. Sometimes it is necessary to approach someone above you, some patron whose favor you need, but whom you do not know. Here a *palanca*, literally a lever, is desirable, some intermediary who can intercede on your behalf. In this case patronage takes "the form of sponsorship, in which the patron provides connections (hence the Spanish *enchufe*—plug-in) with the institutional order. In such circumstances, his stock-in-trade consists less of the relatively independent allocation of goods and services than of the use of influence" (Wolf 1966b:18).

To sum up, thinking in a world of clients and patrons runs as follows: "Clearly I am less powerful than my patrons, as they are less powerful and wealthy than theirs. Clearly my town is less powerful and wealthy than the cities and government. And certainly Mexico is less powerful and wealthy than the United States. How then can I at the bottom of this dung heap possibly change my relationship within it without help from above?"

We have so far examined perceptions of two types of relationships. On the one hand there is the relationship of peasants vis-à-vis nonpeasants; on the other there is the perception of how peasants relate among themselves. Theoretically, the first type of relationship is best seen in terms of social classes. These classes coincide with the two subsections of Mexican agriculture. Thus we have an impoverished rural population that might be designated in statistical surveys as small private land holders, members of agricultural collectives *(ejidos)*, sharecroppers, renters, or wage laborers. Indeed, many individuals occupy several of these categories. As a class they contrast with large land holders who operate according to different rules and constraints.[17] Because of superior land holdings, capital and credit resources, education, technology, and supply of cheap labor, large land holders have tremendous advantage in competing with peasants and agricultural workers. Peasants realize that they have much less wealth and power than the large land owners, who are in reality an extension of the urban bourgeoisie by virtue of financial and political connections. This analysis of class relations thus takes us back to the opposition between countryside and city. The main question is, Why, if the rural poor are superior in numbers, do they not exert political power to improve their situation? Why do they not form collective organizations and engage in more self-interest collective activities generally? This is an extremely important question with great implications for the formation of class consciousness and for development in peasant communities. The most immediate answer is, I believe, that they do not recognize themselves as a political entity. In other words, within any given individual there is a very poorly developed sense of class membership.

Here we have gotten back to world view after this necessary detour through the economics and sociology of Mexican agriculture. An understanding of these relationships is essential for understanding the peasant ideology that they shape and which to a great extent serves to perpetuate these relationships. Although these relationships are primarily responsible for shaping the world view, an understanding of this world view and its role in perpetuating the very same day-to-day society that generates it is necessary in any attempt to successfully organize the latent political power of the agrarian peasantry and proletariat.

Not only does the peasant not have a well-developed, well-thought-out sense of class membership, but to the contrary he has images of himself and the other members of his class that are inimical to such notions of solidarity. Again, I should emphasize that these images and attitudes are nurtured by the short-range view of existence that predominates in one's thinking as he or she struggles through life one day at a time. The macro conditions which structure these day-to-day contexts have their origins deep in history and far away in urban centers of power. These are outside the awareness of the rural peasant. As Stavenhagen (1976:47) says, "the forms of exploitation to which the small land holders are subjected are subtle and indirect and appear to them as 'impersonal forces of the market'." By contrast it was much easier for the *peón* of the great haciendas to understand who exploited him (ibid.).

We can now summarize the main images and assumptions about Self, Other, and Relationship which inhibit the formation of class consciousness. First of all, one sees oneself as pitted against neighbors in a constant struggle to maintain one's own fair share of fortune in an economy of scarcity. Each individual can easily generalize his own sense of deprivation and frustration to his neighbors who share his predicament. He perceives them as he perceives himself: ready to take advantage of any personal weakness in others or any slack in the system. Consequently he is constantly on the defensive, constantly competing so as not to fall behind others.

This individualism and view of competition as a natural quality of social relationships are contrary to the trust and cooperation necessary for collective action. Insofar as one does seek to form relationships, they are one-to-one relationships with other individuals. Moreover, in looking to other people with whom to form economic and social ties, the vertical texture of social structure turns one's view away from one's equals. If you are near the bottom, this means that you mainly seek alliances upward with people whose interests are antithetical to those of your class. In the total society these pyramidal relationships are overlapping. Although there is great distance from the bottom to the top, it is difficult to perceive any clearcut horizontal planes of cleavage. This difficulty blurs class distinctions. Rather than seeing themselves as collectively in opposition to those above them, peasants see themselves in competition with each other for the scarce resources which those above them control. Patrons and their favors are seen as another form of Limited Good. This attitude makes peasants all the more exploitable. For example, as wage laborers it makes them "good" workers because they compete among themselves at working for low wages and rate busting. These atomistic tendencies are favorable to employers who stand to lose when workers organize. For workers as agriculturalists it inhibits the formation of peasant cooperative organizations. For citizens of small towns it undermines the solidarity and trust necessary for defending their common interests and initiating community development projects. This is an old problem. Gibson (1964:289) notes that in the Colonial period, "Under pressures of a markedly disruptive character, Indian society was rarely unanimous in its conception of self-interest."

Time

The world-view theory presented in this book suggests that images of time will be strongly shaped by images of Self, Other, and Relationship. We can begin to look at these logico-structural connections by stating that Mexican peasants are predominantly present oriented. This present orientation results mainly from constantly dealing with the day-to-day exigencies of survival. Attention is riveted on the here and now. The literature on peasants contains much discussion about how they lack a future orientation, about how they seek "immediate gratification" and are not inclined to make long-range plans to improve their situation. The most often cited example is a lack of interest in saving. A simpler explanation is that this lack of saving is not evidence of impulsive behavior and lack of concern for the future, but rather that most peasants cannot afford to save. It is difficult, if not illogical, to be in debt at high interest and save at the same time. It is also difficult to save if you are out of food and other necessities. But these comments aside, it is still accurate to characterize most peasants as basically present oriented, as was noted above.

Ixtepejanos, and also I believe the people of Los Cedros, are also strongly oriented toward the past (Kearney 1972:81–88). By this I mean that they would, if it were possible, prefer to return to conditions that they believe existed at earlier times in their area. This orientation to the past is reinforced by the belief that the condition of their lives is generally deteriorating, such that the present is not as bountiful or secure as the previous century and that in general conditions will continue to deteriorate in the future.

> Myth and folklore, and the ruins of old buildings and mines testify that former times were more prosperous, that the soil was more fertile, and the weather milder. Men remark that crops are now less abundant, that one must go farther from town for firewood, and that there is less gentle rain and more frost.
>
> Ixtepejanos believe that, not only in the local environment but also in the world at large, the forces of entropy and destruction are winning. This process will eventually end in *el día de justicia* (the Judgment Day), when the world will end in a fiery cataclysm—the ultimate catastrophe. (Kearney 1972:81)

Since Ixtepejanos realistically realize that a return to former times is impossible and assume that any change in the status quo will probably be for the worse, they attempt to make the best of the present, while it exists. Much of their behavior is thus consistent with a present orientation. This attitude can be stated as a proposition: "Any change in the status quo will most likely be for the worse; in general things are changing for the worse" (Kearney 1972: 45). A corollary of this which has implication for action within the local environment is this, "since things tend toward the worst and since the future is unknowable, opportunities and resources should be exploited to the fullest in the present" (ibid.: 45). This results in numerous economic choices for short-term maximization versus long-term gain. The reasoning here is that, since resources in the local environment are depleting, one must avail oneself of them while the opportunity exists; at some later time there will be less of them and consequently less opportunity to exploit them.

This thinking has obvious implications for the conservation of natural resources. Conservation as a feasible strategy of relating to the material environment is virtually excluded by the images of time represented by the above propositions. Nor are such attitudes unrealistic from the vantage point of any single adult in the community; within his own experience he has no doubt observed the diminution of such local natural resources as soil and groundcover. The important point for the long-term dynamics of the system is that as individuals act to exploit diminishing resources while they are available, they in fact aggravate this trend and alter the environment in such a way that the perception of it as one of diminishing goods is reinforced. The circular relationship between environment, world view, and behavior thus continues in a positive feedback relationship.[18]

In describing Mexican peasants as present oriented, how do we account for the fact that they prepare fields months in advance of sowing, that they stockpile materials over a period of several years for house construction, and do any number of other such things which require considerable foresight? The answer is given by Bourdieu (1963) in discussing the images of time of Algerian peasants which, because of similar life conditions, are similar to those of Mexican peasants. Bourdieu distinguishes between the "forthcoming" and the "future." The forthcoming refers to situations and actions seen in the present and continuing, as it were, beyond one's field of vision. In this "preperceptive anticipation" the "future" is not a necessary postulate; instead, this forthcoming is but an aspect, a potential of the perceived present.

> So it is that grain is comprehended not only with its colour, form, and other directly perceived properties, but also with qualities potentially inherent in it, such as "meant to be eaten," etc. These potentialities are apprehended by a perceptive consciousness in the same way as are the hidden faces of a cube. . . . The "forthcoming" is perceived in the same manner as the actual present to which it is tied by an organic unity. (Bourdieu 1963:61)

This distinction between the forthcoming and the future is, I think, reflected in language. In Spanish, as spoken in rural Mexico, there are two ways to indicate the future. One is to use a conjugated present-tense form of the verb ir (to go) plus an infinitive specifying the particular action or whatever, for example, voy a comer (I'm going to eat). Although I am not at this moment actually eating, there is the implication that food is prepared and at hand, and that my eating it is imminent and assured. Similarly, "Let's eat now," implying that the food is on the table, is vamos a comer. For less certain events, less certain because they are either problematical or lie in a more remote future, the future tense of the relevant verb is used instead of the ir + infinitive form. Thus, Dice que comeremos bien el año próximo translates literally into English as "He says we will eat well next year," but the Spanish phrase connotes a degree of uncertainty or skepticism.[19]

This uncertainty or skepticism is often underscored by such phrases as si Dios quiere, Dios mediante, and ojalá, which refer to the outcome of some human plans being dependent on the will of God and largely beyond human control. Foster (1967:117) notes that in Tzintzuntzan, "People rarely speak in the future tense without qualifying proposed or hoped-for action with Si Dios me da licencia, if God gives me permission." The future tense is also used to indicate uncertainty, suspicion, or anxiety about things or events in the present. This usage seems to rest on the assumption that the future is inherently uncertain (Kearney 1972:88). By the same token, to emphasize the certainty of something in the future, the present tense may be used: Lo hago (I will definitely do it).

In traditional communities such as Los Cedros and Ixtepeji, time is not a commodity as it is in urban industrial society where "time is money." Peasants do not "lose," "save," "spend," "waste," "make," or "give" time. It is probably safe to assume that such speech forms arose with the appearance of wage labor, where workers "sell" their time, working by the clock. In peasant Mexico one does not work according to a schedule; you work until the task is finished. In the last several generations most of rural Mexico has been to a great extent proletarianized. In the case of Los Cedros, most men work off and on as migrant agricultural laborers and are paid on a piece-work basis rather than an hourly basis. This being paid by units of production rather than by units of work time does not dispose one to think of time in quantitative terms and as a commodity.

Although Mexican peasants are oriented to the present this does not mean that they do not strongly desire to better their life's situation; they obviously do. Indeed, they are constantly comparing local conditions with those in the cities and the United States. As an outsider in Los Cedros and Ixtepeji I am frequently queried about these differences. The point is that they realize that such desires are unrealistic, and that, based on past experience, change, if change does occur, is likely as not to be for the worse rather than the better.

These images of Time, Self, and society predispose peasants to be not receptive to utopian or progressive ideologies. This is seen in the form of religion—Mexican Catholicism—which is prevalent in the countryside. In its early forms and in some varieties of contemporary Protestantism, Christianity is future oriented. It promises salvation. It also at different times and places has been embraced collectively by one or another "chosen people." But these are insignificant themes in Catholicism; they are virtually nonexistent in Mexican folk Catholicism. Mexican peasants are too realistically pessimistic to put much faith in a promise of an afterlife of leisure, milk, and honey. Religion in village Mexico instead focuses on much more immediate problems having to do with health and personal security in general.

Village Catholicism is inextricably intermixed with folk medicine. Religious practices are predominantly magical and are performed to prevent and cure illness. There is little concern here with salvation or the fate of the soul. There is no mystical tradition, no concern with ecstasy. Just as one will worry about next year's problems when the time comes—there is enough to worry about now—so will the problem of what will become of one after death have to be dealt with when the time comes. Mexican peasants are more worried about how God might punish or favor them in the here and now, rather than in some vague undefined future time and place. The function of the Church, as the peasant sees it, is not to help him gain God's favor in the future, but to help him avoid His wrath and punishment now. We will return to religion in the section on projective systems. But here it is to be noted that conversion to Protestant sects is frequently associated with a concerted collective effort at improving economic conditions. These different attitudes about the future are structurally consistent with the millennarian, i.e., forward looking, perspective of evangelical Protestant sects which actively proselytize in Mexico and Central America.[20] In contrast, Catholicism is more consistent with a static view of reality. Not only in Latin America, but throughout the Christian world, Catholicism is most prevalent in the more underdeveloped regions.

Causality

Thinking about processes and the way things in the world affect one another is influenced by images of Self, Other, Relationship, and Time. The Self—which is a main source of the other categories—is seen as relatively impotent to affect conditions in the Other, which acts capriciously on the passive Self. This attitude is not at all like the uniformitarianism of natural science, which sees the world as governed by invariable laws that impart a regularity to reality. Such a view is consistent with the security and regularity of the bourgeois society in which the pioneers of modern science lived. In natural science, knowledge of these laws gives the power to manipulate the world. Such reasoning is poorly developed in Los Cedros and Ixtepeji, and knowledge of natural science is accordingly not highly valued. In any event the necessary education for the acquisition of such attitudes is unavailable. Instead, as in most of the nonmodern world, large areas of material reality are attributed animate qualities which are expressed in an elaborate set of beliefs about personal spirits, saints, God, and magic. Although God is in ultimate control of the universe, He does not have any particular design, nor does He manage it systematically. In Tzintzuntzan, Foster (1967:117) says, God's actions are seen as "capricious and unpredictable, quixotic and surprising." There things happen not because of natural laws, but because of the will of God or some other authority.

> A child dies: it was part of God's plan. The highway comes to town: General Lázaro Cárdenas willed it. Since chance and accident are the mainsprings of the universe, systematic expectations and consistent behavior are seen as valueless. Western-style foresight is a positive value only within a predictable system. (ibid.)

Since these attitudes about a god and about the natural world are uncritical and unrealistic we will defer further discussion of them to the section on projective systems.

One other aspect of causal thinking needs to be discussed, however, and it is a prevalent view of human motivation. One result of living at or near the bottom of the social hierarchy is a high level of frustration and resentment. But these negative feelings are for the most part not directed at appropriate targets, that is, those higher up in the society. For one thing, the higher-ups are more powerful. For another, they are apt to be one's patrons. And furthermore, those at the bottom tend to identify to some degree with those at the top and would like to be like them. As we have discussed earlier, the poor see other have-nots, their neighbors, as their competitors who are striving for the same scarce resources. Since they are also at hand and also relatively powerless, they serve as targets for venting one's frustration and aggression.

Intensive competition, individualism, and poverty are as if designed to provoke invidious comparison. Mexican peasants rightly perceive that envy is a major, possibly even the main, emotion coloring interpersonal relations, making people behave the way they do. The psychology of envy springs directly from the economics and sociology of scarcity. Another person's good fortune is seen as inimical to my best interests. Not only do comparisons of this sort remind me of my poverty, but they are also seen as contributing to it. I get mad and wish that other person his come-uppance. Because it is so easy to arouse envy in others, one is extremely wary of displaying good fortune. If good luck should come to him, the prudent man conceals it if at all possible. If it cannot be concealed, then the next best thing is to mitigate its power to arouse envy in others. There are a number of customary ways of doing this symbolically and otherwise: one may share one's good fortune by spreading some of it around and verbally down play its significance.[21]

The main reason one is so wary of arousing envy in others is that it may provoke them to take out this hostile feeling on the person causing the envy. It is assumed that the most likely way the envious do this is by using witchcraft. Witchcraft is believed to be widespread and effective. Envy is also believed to stimulate the nefarious effects of the evil eye (see below). Perceptions about the propensity for and prevalence of envy in the peasant community are realistic. It is in fact a central force affecting interpersonal relations. But assumptions about the mechanisms (not the efficacy) of witchcraft and the evil eye are, like belief in spirits, unrealistic and thus appropriately discussed in the following section.

PROJECTIVE SYSTEMS

As do all peoples, Mexican peasants have partial and inaccurate information about large areas of existence, especially about phenomena that are distant, invisible, or otherwise not readily understandable. In such situations humans have a strong propensity to fill in the gaps with fantasy and thus provide themselves with complete explanations. They do this unconsciously and collectively over many generations. And the pseudo knowledge so created becomes the myths, proverbs, religion, in a word, the folklore of the society. These folk concepts are not randomly created, but are shaped first and foremost by the social relations of the society and to a lesser extent by the physical environment. The structure of these symbolic systems mirrors social structure, is a projection of it. These images of real society are unwittingly projected out onto the unknown, where they are assumed to be real, rather like confusing the image of a motion picture with the screen. In terms of the world-view model (Figure 7), the contents of the projective system are thought to be actual things in the "real" world. In a word, they are reified. Awareness of their symbolic nature is absent. Projective systems tend to be most elaborate and fill large areas of life where there is little formal education. The great destroyer of magical thought, religious cosmology, folklore, and other superstitions is the questioning, empirically minded scientific world view, which regards knowledge as hypotheses acceptable only until they are disproved. Wherever science and education are absent to explain sickness, astronomy, and physics, then myth, religion, and superstition supply false knowledge.

We have already touched upon some aspects of projection above in discussing the psychology of envy. Envy, it is thought, provokes people to attack by witchcraft the person who is the source of the envy. How do they attack? By magical means that allow them to act at a distance. It is believed that witches attack their victims mainly by causing them to be ill, if not killing them. In communities such as Los Cedros and Ixtepeji there is a great deal of illness, and unexpected death is commonplace. At the same time there is little understanding of the effects on health of germs, viruses, sanitation, water purity, and so forth. Witchcraft thinking thus flourishes as a way of explaining events that demand explanation. But the source of these ideas is not so much sickness and misfortune as it is the social and economic psychology of scarcity and envy. The presence of sickness and death thus confirms the presence and efficacy of witches and the prevalence of envy. Witchcraft and envy in turn explain illness and misfortune. By way of this reification the circle of Figure 7 also closes.

Witches are thought to operate by manipulation of invisible forces that enter into the victim to harm or kill him. These folk concepts of immanent forces are similar to the "power" we discussed in the preceding chapter on California Indian world view. This concept is common to all prescientific magical world views. But its patterning is dependent upon the social structure, which in turn owes its degree and type of differentiation to the economic base of the society. For example, the evil eye, mentioned above, is a variation on the concept of power. Certain people, it is believed, when envious, emit from their eyes rays that can harm others. Children are thought to be the main victims. The envy is aroused by the sight of a beautiful, healthy child—a desirable possession—and the rays enter into it, making it ill, causing grief to the parents. Now, while both the evil eye and witchcraft flourish in peasant Mexico, witchcraft alone occurs in more-or-less egalitarian societies, such as those of aboriginal California, that lack clearly defined social classes. In such societies in both the Old and New Worlds the evil eye is absent. Why this particular patterning and distribution of the power concept? The best answer (see below) is that the evil eye is rooted in the sociology of scarcity, structured as it is by the personalism of client-patron relationships, which give a vertical grain to Mexican peasant society and which is absent in Indian California.

Garrison and Arensberg (1976) argue convincingly that the evil eye is a symbolic recreation of very real threats to the peasant: the perennial openness to seizure of his possessions by others, or loss of them due to natural disaster. The peasant (and other social types with evil-eye beliefs) "is in continual jeopardy of having possessions seized or destroyed. The threat comes not only from the empowered prebendary, bureaucrat, inspector, tax collector, gendarme, or marauder, but also from the stranger, neighbor, or unfortunate that might 'eye' the possession" (ibid.: 293). This argument of Garrison and Arensberg is well supported by a cross-cultural correlational study by Roberts (1976) which shows that the evil eye is limited to complex stratified societies in which personal patronage, *personalismo,* is the backbone of social structure. Consequently, the absence of the evil eye in peasant China and the Orient in general is accounted for by the absence of a personalistic feudalism and its functional replacement by relatively stable state bureaucracy. In the Asiatic mode of production both patronage and the evil eye are absent (cf. Garrison and Arensberg 1976:290n, 297). But in Europe, "the evil eye beliefs seem to shade from least important to most important on the same gradient of time since the destruction of feudalism" (ibid.: 299). And "in Mexico and elsewhere until the land reforms of the twentieth century peasants were dependent upon the allocation of lands from *hacendados,* so that their situation resembled that of peasants in feudal Europe . . ." (ibid.: 301).

The defense against the evil eye symbolically replicates one of the main ways a peasant protects his property: resort to patrons. The main protection against the evil eye is some sort of amulet or talisman, often worn in plain sight. This practice contrasts markedly with witchcraft and its dyadic relationship between witch and victim. The structure of the evil eye is triadic. The evil-eye charm seems to owe its existence to the inherent power differences in the society. "The sign of protection raised says, in effect, 'Beware, I am protected, and I or my power, my patron, saint . . . God, will get you if you harm me' " (ibid: 294).

The most important variant of harmful invisible forces is various "airs" that drift around the environment and cause illness and death. Witches can also send these airs into someone to harm him. This concept of airs is a projection of a general image of the world as pervaded with ubiquitous, insidious dangers that are difficult if not impossible to escape (Kearney: 1972:46–54). Belief in spirits, especially spirits of the dead, is also well developed, and they are a variation of bad airs. They too are invisible most of the time—hallucination of them is common—and move about in the atmosphere causing trouble to the living. Their motivation for these attacks is envy, envy of the living who are still fortunate enough to be alive and in possession of their bodies. The folk psychology of humans is thus generalized to explain the motives of spirits. These beliefs also express the notion that in general the fate of the soul after death is an even less desirable existence than that of the living. This attitude is thus an aspect of the image of time whereby the future is seen as generally less promising than the present.

These folk concepts—airs, spirits, evil eye—are paranoid projections in that they are imaginary dangers. But like all cultural and symbolic creations they have a basis in social and material reality. The world of peasants is a precarious existence fraught with danger. Unfortunately these realistic perceptions tend to generate false concepts which are then reified. The world is seen as even more dangerous than it really is.[22]

Religious beliefs among Mexican peasants are an extension of these beliefs about witchcraft, spirits, and the evil eye. But before examining the projective aspects of Mexican peasant religion a basic observation is in order. As with California Indians, Mexican magic and religion are primarily concerned with day-to-day conditions in the real world—curing illness, love, protecting family and other possessions. We can generalize here and say that insofar as people feel they lack control over their destinies, they tend to rely on magical and spiritual solutions to their problems. In other words, those who lack real power, whether it be technological, economic, or political, are most inclined to seek magical power. It is not surprising then that in places such as Los Cedros and Ixtepeji religion and superstition in general are an elaborate part of the projective system.

We can gain insight into Mexican peasant religion by contrasting it with religion in aboriginal California discussed in Chapter 6. There the concept of power, as a projection, is an unconsciously created metaphor of basic assumptions about the world and people's relationship to it. Power was conceived as regular and consistent in its functioning, and this indicates that the Californians regarded their environment—social and material—as fairly stable and potentially understandable. This is consistent with the picture of social, economic, and general cultural stability that we have for aboriginal California from the archaeological and ethnohistorical records. In peasant Mexico God is a counterpart of power as it exists in California, but with expected differences. In Mexico God is regarded as an "all-powerful" force, *Dios Todopoderoso*. But whereas California Indian power is predictable, understandable, and egalitarian—humans can learn how to handle it—the Mexican God is an unknowable being who arbitrarily and autocratically monopolizes magical power, and in doing so controls the destinies of humans. This image of God is consistent with a harsh, unpredictable environment of general insecurity. Accordingly, prayers, as a form of communication *to* Him (rather than *with* Him) are in the form of requests and proposed contractual relationships. One approaches God on one's knees, with hat in hand, much as one approaches a tyrannical father, feudal lord, or other *patrón*.

Mexican Catholicism, while officially monotheistic, is actually polytheistic in that the spiritual world is populated with a multitude of saints, angels, ghosts, the Devil, and God. These gaseous beings are ranked according to their power and especially their nearness to God. These hierarchical relations in the spiritual world are thus a replication and extension of the human social order. At the top of the hierarchy is the ultimate patron, God the Father. Between the highest power and the lowly peasant stretch innumerable intermediaries, starting with human ones in the form of priests ("fathers"). The priestly hierarchy culminates with the Pope (Sp. *Papa*), a word which also is akin to *father*. One rarely approaches God directly; he is too exalted and distant. Instead one consults one of his lieutenants, that is, a priest or a saint. The theological concept of intercession of saints grew out of European feudal society with its own human hierarchy of lord-vassal relationships. As a system of patronage it makes good sense to Mexican peasants. Just as one often needs human "levers" to get to important patrons in the real world, so it is expedient to rely on spirit intermediaries. Seeking divine favor is not a question of moral living—there are good social reasons for doing that—but of giving saints what they want. For the most part they are interested in respect, deference, and fiestas given in their honor. Nothing makes a saint happier than to have money spent for its glory. And a happy saint is a good *patrón*.

The sociology of the Mexican Catholic spirit world is every bit as feudal as the hacienda: *peones* at the bottom, God—the *señor*, the *patrón*—at the top. How different this imaginary fanciful world is from the spirit sociology in aboriginal California. There, especially in the socially less complex, more egalitarian societies, everyone had direct access to "power." Ownership of land and resources was communal and group decisions were made by consensus, not fiat. Just as there were no appreciable concentrations of wealth and political power in the hands of the few, so there was no concept of distant absolute spiritual power.

PEASANT RATIONALITY

There is considerable debate among anthropologists, economists, and sociologists about whether or not peasants think and behave rationally. This is of great interest because the degree to which peasants rationally calculate economic decisions has implications for economic and social development in countries with large peasant populations. We now take up this issue and in doing so tie together most of the foregoing material in this chapter.[23]

Much of the literature on the nature of peasant thought tends to argue for an essentially "irrational," "backward," "tradition-bound conservatism." Such interpretations seem to have resulted mainly from failing to understand the basic conditions under which peasants must typically operate. The most important of these is, as described above, economic scarcity, which when extreme results in starvation. Lack of academic insight into these conditions has no doubt been largely due to lack of personal experience with rural poverty on a day-to-day basis. In recent years there has, however, been a noticeable shift in the literature on this issue, and peasants are now accorded a much greater degree of rationality than formerly. Are they completely rational? Of course not, for possibly no one is completely rational. But it is fairly easy to make a case that in economic matters peasant thinking is essentially rational. As we saw in the preceding section on projection there are, however, other areas of life—religion and magic— where symbolic thought seems to follow an essentially irrational course insofar as it is based on assumptions that do not square with principles of modern science.

Part of the reason theorists have been led to assume that peasants are economically irrational is that on the face of it a lot of peasant behavior appears so. For example, we have seen how Mexican peasants often buy corn when prices are high and sell when they are low. But they do this not because of a bad business sense, but because of no alternatives. They are in fact almost obsessively concerned with prices. In the town of Mitla, not far from Ixtepeji and Los Cedros, Parsons observes,

> price is of supreme interest to young and old, women and men, the poor and well-to-do. . . . We are talking of the earthquake—"May God pardon us." murmurs Felicitas, and in the same breath, "How much did you pay for your sandals?" To a somewhat more sophisticated friend I have been relating the

story of a fatal motorcycle accident in my family. "What do motorcycles cost in the United States?" I refer to cremation as a substitute for burial. "How much does it cost to be cremated?" There is nothing I wear or use, nothing I refer to, of which the cost is not asked by every new acquaintance. ↓ . . Juan García saw a bullfight on his trip to the Isthmus, a very different sort of show from the bull riding of Mitla, but instead of telling about the horses, the capes, the sword, or the slaughter he mentions that the bullfighters are paid. No, the Mitleyeno is price-minded. Money enters into the evaluation of things and of experience to a degree I have never found equaled in any other society, including the most plutocratic circles. (Parsons 1936:12–13)

Much has also been written about how peasants spend money on things which seem only to buy them prestige, rather than investing in capital improvement. But as Veblen (1912) showed, capitalists are just as prone to spend money on prestige: expensive houses and clothes, jewelry, and whatnot. One of the main forms this takes in places like Ixtepeji and Los Cedros is the sponsorship of fiestas, usually in the honor of some saint. Considerable amounts of savings are dissipated and debts incurred in this way every year. But for the most part these are capital resources that are in excess of household subsistence needs. Still, given the standard of living of all inhabitants, at first glance this seems like a foolish squandering. In what ways can such behavior be rational?[24]

We must start to answer this question by first noting that this "custom," that is, the fiesta tradition, is given by history to any particular would-be sponsor. This system was established in Colonial times, not by peasants, but by the Church, and was and is strongly supported by merchants who gain from the sale of the liquor, food, fireworks, decorations, candles, and other commodities consumed in the fiestas (see Diener 1978). Historically this institution has been both a blessing and a curse. It has resulted in the transfer of wealth out of local communities, but the fiesta complex has also been one of the few ways that the peasant town could symbolically affirm its identity as a group vis-à-vis the outside world. Anthropologists have also pointed out that it often inhibits internal economic differentiation within the community. For it is usually those who can most afford to sponsor a fiesta who do so. This leveling action discourages a widening of wealth differences and promotes the sharing of poverty.

Nevertheless, taken as a whole, this custom does squander a tremendous amount of wealth each year, wealth that could be better spent on improving conditions. Thus, in terms of group action this practice can be seen as irrational, as not in the best interests of peasants as a community or as a class. But it is individuals, not groups, who make decisions. Hence to understand the persistence of this practice and assess its rationality we must look at it from the perspective of a potential sponsor.

First of all we can note that in Los Cedros there are no opportunities for productive investment in amounts most residents have at their command. This point has been made earlier in our discussion of economic intensification. The question, then, that we must ask about someone who volunteers to sponsor a fiesta is, What does he stand to gain from doing so? There is first the enjoyment of the fiesta itself, but more likely than not he will be working too hard at coordinating it to enjoy it as a participant. Instead, what he seems to gain immediately is the approbation of his guests. For sponsorship of a fiesta is one of the few instances in which wealth can be displayed without provoking envy. This is because the sponsor displays his wealth to divest himself of it. And in doing so he affirms his membership in the community as a "good" citizen. This is in a way an investment, for the social good will so generated may be cashed in at a later date when he might come upon hard times. In addition to such voluntary fiesta sponsorship there is also at times a coercive aspect. Not only are subtle pressures placed on particular individuals to assume fiesta obligations, but sponsors are sometimes "named" by town authorities. Failure to comply with these "honors" provokes censure. Here, again, social forces must be taken into account in understanding individual behavior that seems to go against self-interest.

The other area on which discussion of peasant rationality centers is agricultural management. The main issue here is whether or not peasants think and behave like capitalist farmers: do they make the same sorts of cost accounting calculations? And if they do not, are they or are they not nevertheless still rational? Since we have already established that we are dealing with two different modes of production—peasant and capitalist—we expect that different economic conditions and strategies, and consequently different ideologies and thinking in general will be associated with them.

A good place to enter this theoretical thicket is the controversial work of A. V. Chayanov (1966), who was a Soviet agricultural economist until his arrest in 1930.[25] Chayanov described what he called "peasant economy" and argued that it should be added to Marx's social types of primitive communism, slavery, feudalism, capitalism, and socialism. In particular he contrasted it with capitalist agriculture. For Chayanov, the distinguishing feature separating the two was that peasant agriculturists do not hire wage labor and that they produce primarily for their own consumption rather than for a commodity market. Also, since the peasant household must supply its own labor, the "dis-utility" of work (drudgery) enters into their thinking in a way that it does not for capitalists who pay others to do their manual labor. Because of these considerations, Chayanov argues, peasants calculate and make economic decisions differently from capitalists, who are concerned with juggling wages, prices, capital, rent and interest so as to obtain the highest profit.

But there is, according to Chayanov, an even more basic difference between peasants and capitalists. Whereas the capitalist maneuvers to seek profit, the peasant, because of his precarious situation, is most concerned to maximize family security. His first objective is to obtain a standard of living that assures survival. " '[T]he position of the rural population is that of a man standing permanently up to his neck in water, so that even a ripple is sufficient to drown him,' R. H. Tawney wrote in a description of China in 1931; but his graphic simile could as easily be applied to much of the peasantry throughout the Third World" (Scott 1975:505). Under such conditions marginal-utility theory does not apply as it does in capitalist agriculture. For so long as the physical security of the family is in question because of the specter of famine, the peasant will work harder and harder for less return. This is what I earlier referred to as economic intensification and which Chayanov refers to as "self-exploitation." Peasants will thus stay on a poor piece of land and work it seven days a week when a capitalist farmer would have abandoned it and moved on. The peasant stays and works harder for less because of lack of capital or because coercive landlords or the state prevent him from moving. A peasant faced with the prospect of hunger may also "be willing to pay more for land or to offer higher rents than capitalist investment criteria would indicate. A land-poor peasant with a large family and few labor outlets is rationally willing to pay huge prices for land or to agree to 'hunger rent' . . . so long as the additional land will make even a small net addition to the family larder. In fact, the less land a family has, the *more* it will be willing to pay for an additional piece. . ." (ibid.: 507). Thus whereas the capitalist farmer makes decisions mainly in terms of expected rate of profit, the peasant seeks to insure security, and in doing so balances subsistence needs against a subjective distaste for manual labor.

With these considerations in mind we can return to the question of ceremonial expenses. In a place like Los Cedros, a man who has accumulated capital is faced with a decision of how to use it. A likely choice for a capitalist farmer is to buy more land and/or hire more labor, or make some capital improvement to increase production. But in Los Cedros purchasable land is extremely expensive because it is scarce and because after a certain point labor would have to be hired. Moreover, since one of the features of peasant agriculture is the absence of wage labor, to increase land holdings would increase the amount of work (self-exploitation), which would need to be balanced against increased security. Here a conflict comes into the calculations: a family's size and its composition as a work unit versus its consumption needs. Given these constraints, it often makes as much sense to spend the money on a fiesta, which has the positively perceived features noted above. Should the individual decide to hire labor and seek profit, then he is by definition beginning to operate according to nonpeasant principles.

Peasants are often characterized as "conservative" and resistant to economic development programs, as though this were some basic personality or cultural trait that is largely responsible for keeping them backward and in poverty. But more often than not peasant resistance—say to accept new agricultural practices—is found to be the rational choice when a cost-benefit analysis is done. Probably the most frequent barrier to the acceptance of new techniques is simply lack of available capital to finance them initially and to maintain them. For example, hybrid corn and other improved varieties are—under ideal conditions—far more productive than the native corns grown in Los Cedros, Ixtepeji, and hundreds of other similar villages throughout Mexico. But hybrid seed must be newly purchased every year, rather than being saved from the previous harvest. Also, in order to produce abundantly the improved varieties must be heavily fertilized and irrigated; this attention also causes weeds to flourish, requiring yet additional expenses to clear them. Without these extra inputs the improved varieties yield less than the native varieties. A decision of a destitute peasant not to plant hybrid corn is thus probably based on sound economic realities and reasoning rather than on some quirk of his personality. There are many examples of this sort.

Analyses of underdevelopment that invoke personality and cultural traits are common in the social sciences and amount to blaming the poor —whether individuals or nations—for their poverty. The analysts fail to take into account the larger structural relationships between the poor and those with power and wealth, and the mechanisms whereby wealth flows from the poor to the powerful and wealthy. They do not recognize that economic development must involve a reversal, or at least an equalization of this flow of wealth. Changing these larger structural and external relations reconstitutes the immediate environment that shapes world view. World view and action can then change accordingly. A better future will be seen as a possibility.

More important in economic development than the acceptance or rejection of new technology is the reordering of economic and political relations. Since these relations are in part formed and perpetuated by images of Self, Other, Relationship, and Causality, world view here becomes crucial.

Chapter 8

CONCLUSIONS, CRITICISMS, AND SUGGESTIONS

The theory of world view that has been discussed in the preceding chapters of necessity has its own basic assumptions, given to it by the interplay of biography and history. These assumptions are expressed in the various theoretical and political positions and arguments that have guided the world-view analyses that have been offered. As a theory of world view that attempts to be reflexive — to examine itself — this book would be incomplete without further attempt to reveal these assumptions, as was begun in Chapter 1. Now, however, we are in a position to turn the world-view model back onto itself and use some of its own apparatus to examine other assumptions in it. The original three problems posed at the beginning of Chapter 3 provide a way of organizing this critique. They are: (1) What universal categories are necessary for the cross-cultural comparison of world views? (2) How are the contents of these universals determined and organized? and (3) What is the relationship between the contents of the universals of a world view and sociocultural behavior?

With respect to the universals, two issues persist: whether or not they are the most appropriate categories for describing, analyzing, and comparing world views, and whether or not they are truly universal. It is possible that these questions cannot be resolved absolutely. This indefiniteness results from an unavoidable relativism inherent in the selection of the world-view universals. Any attempt at world-view study can utilize only categories that are historically available to it at the time of analysis. At different periods, different choices are possible. The universals that I have proposed here are certainly artifacts of the Western intellectual tradition. There is in this tradition a long history of analysis of these categories and a rich language for carrying out this discussion. A further appeal of the universals presented in Chapter 3 is that they are more or less consistent with the categories of genetic psychology which, with its interactionist approach, is consistent with the general epistemological assumptions of historical materialism. But again, this does not allow us to escape the dangers of relativism, for the degree to which these categories exist in the thought and languages of other world views is still problematical to some degree. This is immediately apparent when we attempt translation from Western European languages into some non-Indo-European languages. If words for such concepts as Self, Other, and Time are not present, it is then possible that these concepts are absent. But in dealing with this problem I have argued that such categories must of necessity be present.

To further illustrate this problem of whether or not the universals are valid, we may look at the treatment of Space and Time universals, and related assumptions made about Causality. Space and Time in the world-view model are treated for the most part in what we might call a pre-Einsteinian manner. That is to say, they are assumed to be two distinct categories of thought. As such, they lend themselves readily to an analysis of, say, Newton's images of space and time, since he also explicitly distinguishes them and made statements about their nature, such as that they are absolute and independent. But the linguistic, let alone the empirical nature of this so-called "space" and "time" are challenged by contemporary physics, which asserts their interdependence. According to Einstein's special theory of relativity, the universe is best described as a four-dimensional continuum in which events are located by three coordinates of space and one of time. In this four-dimensional universe of space-time, as described by Minkowski's symbolic geometry, space and time are interdependent such that each can only be described in terms of the other. Clearly, a world-view theory which was more informed by this image of space-time might posit a set of universals other than the ones I have. In other words, I am willing to speculate that my list of universals is as much a reflection of my own pre-Einsteinian physics as it is of human views in general. Such is the nature of intellectual relativity, and such is the history of human thought. It is with this attitude that I have tentatively offered the world-view universals. They were selected more out of a practical necessity to have some usable categories than out of any sense that they are incontrovertibly the only valid ones.

The solutions offered for the second problem which this world-view theory has addressed—the forces shaping the contents of world views—are obviously dependent on the validity of the universals previously identified. Therefore, the same relativity is built into this aspect of the model. In addition to this, there is another type of relativity that results from the historically given styles of analysis that I have utilized in exploring the ways in which universals fit together and interact. I am referring here to the "internal causes" of Chapter 4, which are distinct from the more influential "external causes." The main method used is suggested by the term "logico-structural integration." There is no need to review the justification presented in Chapter 2 for this hyphenated monster. Instead I should like to note that this concept, rather than being a definitive statement, is more suggestive of future research.

The discussion of logico-structural integration has largely been by way of examples. I have not laid out a complete list of universal features of such integration. Such an undertaking must await a thorough investigation of human logic and cognitive structures in general from a cross-cultural perspective, with the goal of discovering a culture-free method of analysis. It would seem that this task could best be carried out by collaboration between anthropologists and philosophers. The result would be an empirical philosophy in which the traditional issues of logic are liberated by the anthropologists from the confines of Western thought and tested in cross-cultural settings. Since no such well-developed program exists, I have attempted to indicate certain types of logical and structural relationships that can be tentatively assumed to be universal.

Ground has been broken in this direction by cross-cultural application and testing of principles of genetic psychology, which has a strong component of formal logic as interjected by Piaget. Several other existing theoretical orientations also appear to have potential here. Among these are the investigations of "deep structures" carried out by Lakoff and other Chomskian linguists working on the frontier between linguistics and ethnography known as semantics. There is also the Collingwood tradition of presupposition, discussed at some length in Chapter 2, and Tyler (1969b:16) notes the potential for propositional analysis. Each of these different methods, in ways that are cross-culturally applicable, study what I have called images and assumptions, and how they articulate. But for the most part they have been limited to micro analyses of the nooks and crannies of complete world views. It is now necessary to take their insights and their methods and apply these to larger issues such as the world-view universals.

The arguments concerning the third problem this world-view theory raises are the most controversial. They deal with the relation between the contents of a world view, social behavior, and the environment taken broadly. A basic premise of this book is that there is a dialectic relationship between ideas (images and assumptions) and such things as institutions, social classes, technology, and the environment in general. This theoretical orientation and the way it has been elaborated rest on a number of more basic concepts and values that must be revealed if they are to be understood within its historic and social context.

Throughout the preceding pages the argument has been carried forward that both human world view in general and the world view of specific societies are historically relative. The argument here has been that human consciousness as it develops historically is progressive. This argument is undeniable in the case of the increased understanding of the physical universe. And I have argued that there is a similar forward movement in philosophy and the social sciences. But there is difference between the circumstances in which we examine physical phenomena and those in which we attempt to delineate social forms and processes. Physical forms and processes are invariant and therefore absolute. As such they provide unmoveable reference points with reality. True, our images and assumptions of material phenomena are dependent on the general world view in which they exist. But there is still the invariant consistency of matter, which constantly over the long run tends to bring images and assumptions into alignment with physical reality. This is why today most educated people are certain that the earth *does* go around the sun.

But when we leave physics and go to anthropology, we find that our subject matter no longer has such a firm, absolute basis in reality. In the social sciences the counterpart of matter-energy as the subject of physics is society. But society, unlike matter, is different in different places and historic periods. Thus, the dialectic between images about the physical world and matter itself is different from the dialectic between images of ourselves and society and the society itself. One of the main objectives of this book has been to explore the ways in which ideas about Self, Other, Relationship, etc., are formed within specific social systems and in turn become the cultural cement that maintain these social systems (see the analyses of Bali, California Indians, Mexican peasants).

A major assumption here has been that the nature of this dialectic between society and images of Self and between society and the other world-view universals is different in class-based versus classless societies. The distinctive feature of class societies is internal asymmetry —in a word, inequality —between classes. This inequality insures that there will be differences in goals within the overall society, and therefore inherent conflict. The conflict may be latent and unnoticed, much like the static balance between the forces that hold up a roof and those that push down; or the conflict may be obvious, as it is when a building crumbles. A theme running through this book is that the analysis of world view takes place within a context of opposing ideological frameworks, one that is inevitable in a class society.

This situation thus creates the basis for yet another dialectic, which is carried on at right angles, as it were, to the dialectic between human consciousness in *general* and social reality. This other dialectic arises from the conflicting goals of the upper and lower classes within any complex society. And this is the conflict between the conservatives forces of the status quo and the progressive forces of change.

Historically, world-view theory and other academic specialties have come from and have been propagated by the more privileged classes. In this regard, earlier sections of this book have argued, contemporary social theorists structurally occupy a position and discharge a stabilizing function within society analogous to that of the priesthood of ancient civilizations and feudal societies, as well as in monarchies and more secular parliamentary states with established churches.

The argument in this book has been that in periods of relative stability and continuity, like that within the contemporary secular United States, anthropology and the other institutionalized social sciences fulfill the same functional role as does theology in a religious society. It is for this reason that no genuine incisive social theory can emerge from this context which does not first critique its origins and examine its political affinities. In a word, it must be reflexive. This is what I have attempted in this theory of world view.

This theory of world view emphasizes empirical research. But here the similarity with positivist social-science theory ends. For as was stated in Chapter 1, there is no attempt in this theory to be "value free" since—as I have argued—this is impossible. Instead, this book engages in a kind of mental work that constantly attempts to link itself with progressive social practice. The assumption here is that theory and practice are the necessary sides of the same coin. The ideas—the result of the mental work—must accurately analyze historic conditions so that they can point the way forward. At the same time, the application of ideas provides a test of validity. This self-corrective interactionist or dialectic relationship between theory and practice is the way the physical sciences unabashedly operate. That the established social sciences make a fetish out of value-free research seems to come from the realization that objective and practical social knowledge, when imparted to the vast majority, is inherently subversive. To prevent this subversion, most social-science research is diverted into the study of intellectual curiosities and trivialities. From the perspective of world-view theory, this activity serves not to make history but instead to freeze it in the status quo.

Above we discussed the main theoretical issues having to do with world-view theory in general. But the need for more empirical studies is of equal priority. Many projects suggest themselves. The most urgent is work on the world view of different classes and societies. This work must aid oppressed people to understand the mentality of oppression and alienation, and the ways in which class relations and the world in general are mystified. Inequitable and unjust situations, where the few dominate the many, are inherently unstable. More often than not they are perpetuated by false consciousness and reified phantoms that symbolically assume the appearances of "social contracts," "divine will," "property laws," and "human nature." "The tradition of all the dead generations weighs like a nightmare on the brain of the living," as Marx put it, and it is the task of world-view study to rouse people from such troubled slumber.

Also urgent is the study of the effect of mass culture on world view as it displaces traditional popular culture at an increasing rate. Mass culture, propagated by the media and advertising, is pre-eminently ideological in nature, and as such is the means whereby commercial corporate interests extend their cultural hegemony in society as a whole. At present this realm has been virtually unexplored in anthropology. And at the same time it is imperative that we further examine the world views of classless societies so as to better understand how to build social and economic democracy where it has never existed and to constructively critique societies which, with differing degrees of success, are moving toward a more democratic future. There is much work to be done here, and in these pages I have offered some examples for such projects and how one might go about them.

Notes

INTRODUCTION

1. I am indebted to E. K. Hunt for this quotation.

2. Regarding the relevance of historical materialism to tribal societies see Terray (1972) and Godelier (1978).

Chapter 1

1. Harris's analyses do not always live up to his theoretical program. His explanations of India's sacred-cow complex and the Islamic pig prohibition have attracted more attention. Harris's failure to satisfactorily solve these "puzzles" is due to an over reliance on facile functional-ecological explanations and a misunderstanding of the social and economic history of these institutions (see Diener, Nonini, and Robkin 1980:7–8).

2. It is useful to distinguish between these social origins of idealism and the psychological predispositions discussed in connection with the Causality universal in Chapter 3.

3. The literature on materialism and idealism is immense; the following sources provide an introduction to their respective ideological implications: Frederick Engels, *Ludwig Feuerbach and the End of Classical German Philosophy, Anti-Dühring*; Karl Marx and Frederick Engels, *The German Ideology*; V. I. Lenin, *Materialism and Empirio-Criticism*; Max Horkheimer, "Materialism and Metaphysics," in his *Critical Theory*. For an illuminating

and provocative essay on the historically evolving nature of the concept of ideology see Lichtheim (1967); for a critique of the functionalist anthropological studies of ideology see Asad (1979).

4. "Eric Wolf has suggested that during the 1930s and 1940s anthropologists contributed to the obfuscation of political economy by describing cultures as organic entities that were 'all ideology and morality, and neither power nor economy. [These] liberal babes in the darling woods . . . spoke of patterns, themes, world view, ethos, and values, but not of power' " (Harris 1979:228, quoting Eric Wolf).

5. Much of this and the following discussion of Spengler is drawn from Barnouw (1963:29–36).

6. There is ample evidence that Boas from the beginning of his ethnological studies was concerned to uncover "the unconscious origin of ethnic phenomena"; see Boas (1911), Stocking (1968:133–160), and Harris (1968: 261–273). "Many discussants of Boas have utilized statements in his writings to show that his stress . . . was historical, and doubtless it was during earlier decades of his long career. Some of his most famous students asserted that he stood at all times for employment of the method of mapping culture traits as a principal means of offering a sound basis for short-perspective historical deductions. But in 1927 Boas said to me that he then thought ultimate statements, ideological foundation stones, about the world's nonliterate peoples had to be in psychological, not historical or descriptive ethnographical, terms. He was saying, in effect, that his earlier insistence upon a diffusionist and historicist position had been only a way station to psychological formulations and that the latter were fundamental" (Jacobs 1964:10).

7. "We can mark off periods within the course of history, in which an intelligible unity embracing everything from the conditions of life to the highest ideas is formed, reaches its climax, and dissolves again. Every such period has an internal structure in common with all other periods, and this structure determines the interconnection of parts, the unfolding and modification of tendencies. . . . The structure of a given age proves to be . . . a coherent association of subordinate connections and movements within the great complex of forces that make up the period. Out of very diverse and changeable elements a complicated whole is formed" (Dilthey, quoted from Horkheimer 1972:50).

8. For further discussion and illustration of ethnosemantics see Spradley (1972), Tyler (1969b).

9. See also Agar (1975); Fjellman (1976); and Geohegan (1973).

10. Concerning the relationship between world view and ethnosemantics see Keesing (1979:34), who foresees "that ethnographies of cultural knowledge and linguistic grammars will increasingly emerge as complementary sides of a single enterprise."

11. Redfield first wrote at some length about world view in *The Folk Culture of Yucatan* (1941). He later presented his ideas more fully developed in two slightly different versions. The first of these is a paper titled "The Primitive World View" (1952). The second is Chapter 4, "Primitive World View and Civilization," in his book *The Primitive World and Its Transformations* (1953).

Chapter 2

1. Another encouragement for theoretically linking world view to perception is the possibility of eventually applying to the world-view analyses and their contents formal logical methods of analysis similar to those that have been used in the psychology of sensation-perception (see for example Miller and Johnson-Laird 1976). It is in part with this in mind that I have developed the logical part of logico-structural integration as discussed above and in Chapter 5.

2. This diagram is adapted from Neisser (1976:112), who uses a similar one to discuss perceptual cycles. The main modification made on Neisser's diagram is the addition of the world-view level, which is also represented by Figure 7 in Chapter 4 of this book.

3. This same basic position is taken by Miller and Johnson-Laird (1976:29): "Sensations are not psychic atoms in perceptual compounds; they are abstracted from percepts by a highly skilled act of attention."

4. For a review of literature dealing with cultural, environmental, experimental, and psychological influences on visual perceptions see Cole and Scribner (1974:61-97).

5. In general anthropological usage no such distinction is made between images/assumptions and propositions. "Proposition," "postulate," "basic assumption," etc. are used indiscriminately in reference to both the presumed native system and the hypothetical modeling of it. I prefer to employ this distinction in terminology so as to clearly distinguish these two conceptual levels.

6. This redefinition of metaphysics occurs mainly in Collingwood (1940), which is addressed primarily to Ayer and logical positivists in general. It is

to be noted that Collingwood's redefinition of "metaphysics" is quite different from the traditional meaning of the term as used in Chapter 1. For studies of Collingwood see Rubinoff (1970), Donagan (1962), Ketner (1972), and Mink (1969).

7. Collingwood's idealism in this regard is exemplified in his observation that it was not the external attacks by barbarians (much less the internal socioeconomic dynamics that made these attacks successful—a type of explanation he is apparently unaware of) that destroyed ancient civilization, but ". . . its own failure to keep alive its own fundamental convictions" (1940:225). Rubinoff (1970:7), on the same point in Collingwood: ". . . a change in the moral, political, and economic theories generally accepted by society will result in a change in the very structure of that society itself, while a change in one's own personal theories will result in change in one's relation to that society. In either case, the end result will be change in the way we act." Presumably this can be taken to mean, for example, that classical economic theory, epitomized say in the work of Adam Smith, was the cause of capitalism, rather than a reflection and eulogy of its pre-existing presence.

8. Perhaps the intriguing aspect of Collingwood's argument that presuppositions are linked together as questions and answers is the suggestion it offers for world-view methodology. In the "Science of Absolute Presuppositions" (1940:34–48) he gives examples of "experiments," such as the imaginary dialogue quoted above, which serve to lay bare the presuppositions inherent in someone's thought, so that they may be scientifically described. This method is similar to the technique of frame elicitation used by some ethnosemanticists, but differs from it by probing relationships among world-view assumptions rather than classificatory relationships among things (nouns), and by exploring tacit knowledge instead of attempting to elicit terms (which of course may be taxonomically ordered by implicit rules). For further discussion of the relevance of Collingwood's "questioning" to world-view methods see Ketner (1972:28–49, 79–83).

9. It is Ketner's (1972) dissertation that led me to Collingwood after I had developed the model and terminology of world view presented here.

10. See Kuhn (1970) for a theory of how this second type of inconsistency is the major means whereby scientific models that are more consistent with observed "facts" replace those that are less consistent.

11. A view such as this also rejects the relativism and skepticism in Thomas Kuhn's (1970) theory of how the history of science unfolds, which, although having a dialectic motor, in effect denies criteria for judging the validity of competing paradigms.

12. Beals and Siegel (1966:78–80) develop a similar concept in terms of "ideological strain," and give as an example inconsistencies in the Indian concepts of dharma and karma. In the same vein Collingwood talks about how absolute presuppositions undergo changes because of "strains" in a "constellation" of them. He says that the metaphysician, as he defines him, ". . . will expect the various presuppositions he is studying to be consupponible only under pressure, the constellations being subject to certain strains and kept together by dint of a certain compromise or mutual toleration having behind it a motive like that which causes parties to unite in the face of an enemy. This is why the conception of metaphysics as a 'deductive' science is not only an error but a pernicious error, one with which a reformed metaphysics will have no truce. The ambition of 'deductive' metaphysics is to present a constellation of absolute presuppositions as a strainless structure like a body of propositions in mathematics. This is all right in mathematics because mathematical propositions are not historical propositions. But it is all wrong in metaphysics. A reformed metaphysics will conceive any given constellation of absolute presuppositions as having in its structure not the simplicity and calm that characterize the subject-matter of mathematics but the intricacy and restlessness that characterize the subject-matter, say, of legal or constitutional history." (Collingwood, quoted from Ketner (1972:67.)

13. Quotation marks are used here to indicate point of view. From what I have just said, it is obvious that to a devotee one of these special "statues" or "paintings" of the Virgin is not a mere representation but rather the embodiment of the actual principle.

14. This apparent inconsistency is an instance of the theological problem of "the one and the many." In a study of Dinka religion, Godfrey Leinhardt notes another instance of it, and comments that, the "unity and multiplicity of Divinity causes no difficulty in the context of Dinka language and life, but it is impossible entirely to avoid the logical and semantic problems which arise when Dinka statements bearing upon it are translated, together, into English" (Leinhardt, quoted in Gellner 1970:25). For a discussion of conditions under which such premises could become intelligible to the members of a given society, see MacIntyre (1970:72). Also see the section on Classification in Chapter 6 of this book for a discussion of this generic style of thought.

15. For a review of cross-cultural research on syllogistic reasoning see Cole and Scribner (1974:160–168).

16. Ward Goodenough makes the same point. "The extent to which propositions about the manipulation of propositions differ among different

societies has not as yet been ascertained. The author's own experience with
so-called primitive people suggests that in most respects the differences are
slight. Once he had learned the local language and could use it with some
facility, and once he had learned what were the propositions people accepted as axiomatic, then their procedures for manipulating these propositions
to arrive at new ones and the points at which they caught one another out in
arguments seemed entirely reasonable to him" (Goodenough 1963:151).
Cole and Scribner (1974:170) arrive at the same conclusion after reviewing
the relevant cross-cultural psychological literature.

17. The principle of identity is the basis of Piaget's concept of the *conservation* of objects' volume, number, and amount as they undergo changes in
appearance, and in this guise has been most extensively studied cross-
culturally (see Cole and Scribner 1974:146–156).

18. I have found that Collingwood also makes what amounts to a parallel
distinction between logical and structural integration; the terms he uses are
"logicism" and "historicism." He develops this distinction in his criticism of
traditional logic and positivism's limitations in analyzing and understanding historic contexts and systems of thought. Rubinoff comments on this:
"The logic of 'logicism' is the abstract logic of classification and division, or
the logic of genus and species. The new logic of 'historicism,' however
(which Collingwood attributes mainly to the efforts of Hegel and nineteenth-century historical idealism . . .), is undoubtedly the basis of what
Collingwood himself later describes as the dialectical logic of the overlap of
classes *(An Essay on Philosophical Method)* and the logic of question and
answer *(The Autobiography). Ruskin's Philosophy,* then, provides clear
and unequivocal evidence that what in the *Autobiography* is called the logic
of question and answer is in fact a development of the dialectical logic of
Hegel.

"The old logic, according to Collingwood, lays it down that of two
contradictory propositions one must be false and the other true. To contra-
dict yourself, on this view, is a sign of mental confusion. According to the
new view, however, it is recognized that there are two sides to every
question, and that there is right on both sides: '. . . from this, the inference
is drawn that truth is many sided and that self-contradiction may easily be a
mark not of weakness but of strength—not of confusion, but of a wide and
comprehensive view which embraces much more truth than the one-sided
consistency of the logicians.' " (Rubinoff 1970:226, quoting Collingwood.)

Chapter 3

1. This idea is similarly developed in an essay by Hallowell entitled "The

Self and Its Behavioral Environment," in which he points out that Self-identification and culturally constituted notions of the nature of the Self are essential to the operation of all human societies and that a functional corollary is the cognitive orientation of the Self to a world of objects other than Self (in Hallowell 1955).

2. Planarians—flatworms—are delightful little aquatic creatures of the phylum Platyhelminthes and are, compared to humans, quite simple organisms. I shall occasionally refer to these flatworms in order to demonstrate characteristics of world view in general. Understanding them, we will be in a better position to examine the special features of human world view.

3. The Relationship universal is somewhat comparable to Kluckhohn and Strodtbeck's (1961) "man-nature orientation," and is not to be confused with their "relational orientation."

4. For a discussion of the historic relationship between individualism and capitalism see Hunt (1975:34–39; 1979:23–28), and Tawney's discussion of "The Growth of Individualism" in his *Religion and the Rise of Capitalism* (1947:149–163). For a contrary view see Macfarlane (1978).

5. For a further criticism of Durkheim's theory of classification, see Needham (1963).

6. It can be argued that awareness of location is not necessarily present in plants and other sessile or nonmotile life forms, but with the possible exception of viruses and prions all organisms demonstrate internal transport of materials and trophisms. Thus while the throughput of matter and energy by cells can be explained in terms of osmosis, or the leaning of geraniums toward the sun by variations in cell turgidity on different sides of its stalk, in another sense, these "behaviors" are complex interactions that involve "knowledge" of locations.

7. We are not here concerned with the perceptions of children, since it is quite apparent that they differ markedly from those of adults, and it is difficult enough to study those of adults. The development of adult cognition out of children's, of course, offers many valuable clues, some of which are discussed below.

8. Another argument for the universality of Time as a cognitive category in human thought follows from the presence of the category of Classification. Classification is based on the notion of identity of things and concepts. The perception of identity itself involves duration—a continuance of substance or properties—and therefore temporality.

9. See Dundes (1969) for analysis of such future-oriented figures of speech in American English.

10. One notable instance of actual cyclical time imagery in a traditional society is strongly suggested by Mayan cosmology and verbal expressions that make extensive use of circular and revolving phenomena (see León-Portilla 1973).

11. Re the history of images of linear time in Western civilization, see Toulmin and Goodfield (1965), and Collingwood (1946).

12. Note here how English-language usage reflects a linear image of time in that time, like space, has length that may be "long" or "short."

Chapter 4

1. An interesting example of this course of development occurs in the progression of Freud's thinking. In the early phases of his psychoanalytic model he attempted to speak strictly in terms of analogs of physical events and systems (e.g., the so-called hydraulic model with its libidinal energy, etc.). In the first edition of *The Interpretations of Dreams* Freud barely discusses symbolism as a means of "dream work" whereby forbidden, taboo desires (images) may evade the dream censor. Mainly through the work of Wilhelm Stekel he came to realize its importance.

"Freud's original and indeed lifelong Grand Design was to construct a science of mind which would be analogous to the physical sciences, which used concepts such as force and energy, which was strictly determinist, and in which all explanations were in terms of [mechanical] causation. But here in symbolism he encountered phenomena which required explanations in terms of meaning, not of cause, and in which convincing explanations could be arrived at by 'a method which must be rejected as scientifically untrustworthy' and by persons who possessed not a training in the rigors of the scientific method but a 'peculiar gift for the direct understanding' of symbolic equations." (Rycroft 1974:13)

2. For further discussion of reification beyond Marx's preliminary insights, see Lukács (1971), for whom it was "the central structural problem of capitalist society in all its aspects" (p. 94). Lukács' analysis is discussed in Arato and Breines, Chapter 8, "Theory of Reification" (1979). To my knowledge the only extensive application of reification and the inextricably related concept of commodity fetishism to a non-Western society is Taussig's (1980) excellent study of the image of the devil among peasants undergoing the process of proletarianization in Colombia.

3. Chapter 3 of *The Winds of Ixtepeji* (Kearney 1972) presents a summary of the town's history and documents a number of such events that have altered local conditions and in doing so have affected contemporary world view.

Chapter 5

1. Geertz does not mention it, but here it seems we also have an instance of structural replication of the birth-order naming system; both are fourfold and cyclical.

2. Geertz depicts this structural principle as a single six-element cycle in which the generations are arranged: "own," "parent," "grandparent," "*kumpi*," "grandchild," and "child." This six-element cycle is not, however, as efficient at collapsing generations as the two three-element ones, which are therefore a better depiction of this means of negating diachrony.

3. For critical debate concerning Geertz's analysis of Balinese temporal concepts see Bloch (1977, 1979), Bourdillon (1978), and Appadurai (1981).

Chapter 6

1. Concerning the applicability of historical materialism to classless societies see Terray (1972).

2. See Cannon (1942), Lex (1974), and Eastwell (1982) for a discussion of the physiological and psychological processes involved in magical death.

Chapter 7

1. Although the next pages examine the formation and functioning of world view in hundreds of villages in Mexico, it should be noted that much of what we are discussing here applies also to peasant communities in much of Latin America, Asia, Indonesia, Africa, and parts of Europe. Indeed, peasants make up about 65 percent of the world's population; approximately one-fourth of them are in China. However, there have been such basic changes in social and economic relations in the Chinese countryside since the consolidation of the Chinese Revolution in 1949 that most of this discussion does not apply to contemporary China. The like is also true of Cuba, Vietnam, and the European Soviet Bloc countries. For a good introduction to peasant society and economics see Wolf (1966a).

2. With respect to banking, in the period from 1942 to 1960 the net total of earnings minus loans was 2,491.2 million pesos, which were taken out of agriculture and transferred to other sectors of the national economy. In the same period there was an overall tendency for agricultural prices to rise more slowly than the general price index. This kind of lag results in a decline in the buying power of the agricultural sector vis-à-vis other sectors and in effect is a transfer of capital out of the agricultural. From 1942 to 1960 this transfer amounted to 3,584 million pesos. The other area of agricultural finance for which there are aggregate data is the fiscal practices

of the federal government. From 1942 to 1960 the government spent 2,977 million pesos more on direct agricultural development (in 1970 prices) than it received from agriculture in the form of taxes on agricultural exports. Thus, although government spending on agriculture represents a positive flow of wealth, this sum was more than offset by the wealth transferred from agriculture by banking and price differences. These more than 3,000 million pesos constitute 2.3 percent of the agricultural value produced during this 19-year period. For the most part these figures are aggregated from statistics of larger producers who have access to bank credit and who benefit most directly from government expenditures and subsidies. During this 19-year period 85 percent of the government funds spent on agricultural development went for large dams and irrigation projects, of which agribusiness firms and large land holders were the main beneficiaries. These data are taken from Solís (1967). See Stavenhagen (1978:32–33) for discussion of other mechanisms which transfer wealth from peasants to capitalists.

3. See Bartra (1975a), Esteva (1976), and Kearney (1980) for further discussion of this dual nature of Mexican agriculture, which is only an "apparent dualism" since the two types are functionally integrated so that wealth is transferred from the dependent peasant sector to the commercial.

4. Presently, one of the main ways in which agribusiness is penetrating into peasant holdings is the legal and illegal leasing of *ejido* (collective) lands. In such cases *ejidatarios* often become seasonal wage laborers for outside concerns on lands the *ejidatarios* ostensibly control.

5. For further discussion of the negative impact of the Green Revolution on the Mexican peasantry see Hewitt de Alcántara (1976).

6. The presence of more full-time farm workers and part-time peasant-workers than jobs also keeps wages down. In 1970, "Underemployment affected 45 percent of the country's economically active population, equal to 23 percent of total unemployment, to which should be added 4 percent of open joblessness [sic] recorded in the 1970 Census. Of these unemployed, 61 percent belonged to the farm sector. . . . Of the total farm labor force in 1970, 36.1 percent eked out a bare living from exploitation of their parcels and were forced to seek temporary work as laborers or in other activities. Another 57.6 percent, made up of landless peasants or those obtaining a minimum income from the exploitation of their parcels, constituted a vast population mass inserted in the farm sector, but really marginal to it. 'This mass,' it has been maintained, 'constitutes a labor force reserve for commercial agriculture,' which, however, is incapable of providing it with jobs. . . . As regards temporary or permanent employment as day laborers, not only was less than minimum rural wage paid, but among certain groups, as for example sugar cane cutters, working conditions were inhuman." (Esteva 1976:7–8; see also Dirección General de Estadística 1972).

7. I have emphasized elsewhere these sorts of relationships between local environment, social structure, and world view (Kearney 1972).

8. Since about 1972 illegal wage-labor migrants from Los Cedros to the United States have, by local standards, been making reasonably good money, although with much hardship and insecurity. At best this is a precarious resource, the long-term future of which is uncertain. For the present, the money migrants have brought back to Los Cedros and other similar communities appears to have accentuated wealth differences and caused a sharp rise in land and house prices (Stuart and Kearney 1981).

9. Foster presents the Image of Limited Good as an ideal model. It is possible to find many trivial counterexamples both in Tzintzuntzan and other Mexican villages. These exceptions do not, however, negate the basic value of the model. Nor does the logic of the model imply that Limited Good thinking is unchangeable. To the contrary, improving economic conditions should bring lessening of Limited Good thinking and associated behavior. This seems to have been the case in Tzintzuntzan in recent years, owing mainly to expansion of its pottery market, and for this reason all reference to it is in the ethnographic present, that is, to the time during which Foster developed the model.

10. There has been considerable misunderstanding among anthropologists about the basic theoretical premises of the Image of Limited Good. Many of its critics have accused it of being in effect a sort of naive cultural idealism. This failure to understand the primacy of economic conditions in the model can result only from a failure to read Foster's work carefully.

11. No exact data on population growth are available, but it is apparent that the birth rate is much higher than the death rate. In 1978 the median age was 15, and approximately 26 percent of the population was 5 years old or younger (Stuart and Kearney 1981:4). These figures are about the same for the rest of rural Mexico.

12. For example, for such economic and other reasons 100 out of 330 school-age children in Los Cedros were not enrolled at the beginning of the new term in January 1979.

13. In 1978 a survey of 50 Los Cedros households revealed that 41 of them had one or more members who had migrated out of the community in search of work during the preceding year. Of these 50, 47 contained members who had been migrants during the prior three years, and only 3 households had no members who had ever worked as migratory laborers (Stuart and Kearney 1981).

14. "In 1973, two million families, making up 50% of the rural population and 20% of the total, had incomes below 10,000 pesos per year. At that

time, it was considered necessary for a family living in the countryside to have an income of at least 12,000 pesos per year to meet minimum subsistence needs. Over the course of the 25 years from 1950 to 1975, 40% of the population at the poorest end suffered a 38% drop in real income. 12 million inhabitants in the rural zones are seen as living in conditions of extreme poverty" *Comercio Exterior de México* 1979:243–244).

15. This system operates on the basis of *personalismo,* which is but an aspect of the individualism discussed above. Having roots in Spanish feudal society, *personalismo* was a fundamental aspect of Mexican Colonial administration. Historically and today these relationships tend to be multifunctional; a "good" *patrón* is one who takes care of a wide range of his clients' needs: work, credit, protection, etc. See Foster (1963), Grindle (1977: 30–40), and Wolf (1966b).

16. The presidency dominates the legislature: all bills proposed by the executive are approved, and if not unanimously then with only a small percentage of opposition votes (Gonzales Casanova 1970:19, 201).

17. There is much debate about the class nature of the various kinds of peasants, defined as such in terms of mode of production, and their similarities and differences with agricultural workers. The position taken here is that their general degree of impoverishment and their position on the margin of the national society and economy give Mexican peasants in general close economic, social, and cultural affinities with rural wage laborers. Furthermore, as Rello (1976), Bennholdt-Thomsen (1976), and Paré (1977) argue, "the lower strata of the peasantry, despite the fact that they may be employed as agricultural workers and day laborers, continue to cultivate the land, maintain the ideology of peasants, and struggle for maintaining a piece of land which is their own" (Harris 1978:4–5). Bartra (1974, 1975b), to the contrary, argues for a much greater degree of proletarianization of Mexican peasants. But as Warman (1972) points out, although most agricultural workers do not *own* land directly, the majority have access to the land of relatives or else occasionally rent land, and are therefore quite unlike complete proletarians. Esteva also similarly claims that rural workers "retain their qualities of peasants, in virtue of their ties with the peasant form of existence of their rural communities" (quoted from Harris 1978:8).

18. "The most immediately obvious contradiction into which increasing poverty forces subsistence agriculture is the destruction of productive natural resources. As poverty increases, more intensive use of available resources is necessary and the land is mined. Lower yields imply growing poverty which, in turn, forces more mining of land. The ecology is gradually destroyed in the subsistence sector and underdevelopment progresses" (de Janvry and Garramón 1977:211–212). "In other words, *the rate of discount for time increases with poverty* as immediate survival becomes the

prime preoccupation. Higher incomes today become increasingly more valuable than higher incomes tomorrow. The economic value of land conservation decreases and the rationality of mining the land increases" (ibid.: 216, n. 2, emphasis added).

19. When speaking Spanish as a second language there is a tendency to use predominantly *ir + infinitive* rather than the future tense because doing so eliminates having to learn the future tense forms. It is my impression that, for this reason, the use of *ir + infinitive* versus the future tense is more common in Indian communities where the main language is not Spanish, such as Los Cedros, than elsewhere in Mexico.

20. See Nash (1960) for a Guatemalan case of conversion to Protestant sects and what might be referred to as "progressive" social change. Similar changes are also now taking place in Los Cedros and Ixtepeji: see Kearney (1972:106–109).

21. See Foster (1965b) and Kearney (1972:70–80) for analysis and examples of the central role of envy in personal relations in peasant Mexico. See Foster (1972) and Schoeck (1966) for discussions of the role of envy in interpersonal relations in general.

22. I have elsewhere (Kearney 1976) argued for this generalized paranoid aspect of the evil eye. Garrison and Arensberg (1976) have sidestepped my hypothesis by insisting on a strict definition of paranoia as necessarily involving Freudian defense mechanisms. However, Freud himself (1938) came to recognize the prevalence of such generalized projection.

23. For a general introduction to the problem of assessing rationality cross-culturally see the collection of articles in Wilson (1970) which are reviewed by Kearney (1975:260–266). For a discussion of rationality and irrationality in economics from an anthropological perspective see Godelier (1972) and Cancian (1972:189–199).

24. For a review of competing anthropological theories of the fiesta complex in Mesoamerica see Greenberg (1981).

25. There are several recent papers criticizing Chayanov from a Marxist perspective (Harrison 1975, 1977, 1979; Patnaik 1979; Ennew et al. 1977), while Durrenberger and Tannenbaum (1979) defend him. Chayanov's critics point out his reliance on subjective neoclassic economic concepts in modeling production decisions of individual peasants. Also, Chayanov is little concerned with how the peasant mode of production articulates with the greater society, or with the class nature of the peasantry. I concur with these criticisms, but at the same time recognize that Chayanov's model of peasant economy does provide useful insights into economic values and individual behavior.

References Cited

Agar, M.
  1975 "Selecting a Dealer." *American Ethnologist* 2:47–60.
Angulo, Jaime de
  1928 "La Psychologie religieuse des Achumawi." *Anthropos* 23:141–146 (English translation by Annette Boushey, ms. Special Collections Library, University of California, Santa Cruz).
  1973 *Indians in Overalls.* San Francisco: Turtle Island Foundation. Reprinted from *Hudson Review,* Autumn, 1950.
  1975 "The Achumawi Life-force." *Journal of California Anthropology* 2:60–63. (A portion of Angulo 1928, above)
Appadurai, Arjun
  1981 "The Past as a Scarce Resource." *Man* 16:201–219.
Arato, Andrew
  1972 "Lukács' Theory of Reification." *Telos* 11:25–66.
Arato, Andrew, and Paul Breines
  1979 *The Young Lukács and the Origins of Western Marxism.* New York: Seabury Press.
Aronowitz, Stanley
  1972 Introduction to *Critical Theory: Selected Essays by Max Horkheimer,* transl. M. J. O'Connell and others. New York: Herder and Herder.
Asad, Talal
  1979 "Anthropology and the Analysis of Ideology." *Man* 14:607–627.
Barnouw, Victor
  1963 *Culture and Personality,* first edition. Homewood, Ill.: Dorsey Press.
  1973 *Culture and Personality,* revised edition. Homewood, Ill.: Dorsey Press.
  1979 *Culture and Personality,* second edition. Homewood, Ill.: Dorsey Press.

Bartra, Roger
   1974   *Estructura agraria y classes sociales en México.* México, D.F.: Ediciones Era.
   1975a "Peasants and Political Power in Mexico: A Theoretical Approach." *Latin American Perspectives* 2:2:125–145.
   1975b "Sobre la articulación de modos de producción en América latina." *Historia y Sociedad* 5:5–19.
Beals, Alan R., and Bernard J. Siegel
   1966   *Divisiveness and Social Conflict.* Stanford: Stanford University Press.
Bean, Lowell J.
   1972   *Mukat's People: The Cahuilla Indians of Southern California.* Berkeley: University of California Press.
   1975   "Power and Its Applications in Native California." *Journal of California Anthropology* 2:25–33.
Beard, Charles A.
   1932   Introduction to *The Idea of Progress: An Inquiry into Its Growth and Origin,* by J. B. Bury. New York: Macmillan.
Bell, Wendell
   1974   "Social Science: The Future as a Missing Variable," in *Learning for Tomorrow: The Role of the Future in Education,* A. Toffler, ed. New York: Random House.
Benedict, Ruth
   1922   "The Vision in Plains Culture." *American Anthropologist* 24:1–23.
   1934   *Patterns of Culture.* Boston: Houghton Mifflin.
Bennholdt-Thomsen, Veronika
   1976   "Los campesinos en las relaciones de producción del capitalismo periférico." *Historia y Sociedad* 10:29–38.
Berger, John
   1978   "Towards Understanding Peasant Experience." *Race and Class* 19:345–359.
Blackburn, Thomas
   1975   *December's Child: A Book of Chumash Oral Narratives.* Berkeley: University of California Press.
Bloch, Maurice
   1977   "The Past and the Present in the Present." *Man* 12:278–292.
   1979   "Knowing the World or Hiding It." *Man* 14:165–167.
Boas, Franz
   1911   *The Mind of Primitive Man.* New York: Macmillan.
Boulding, Kenneth
   1956   *The Image: Knowledge in Life and Society.* Ann Arbor: University of Michigan Press.
Bourdieu, Pierre
   1963   "The Attitude of the Algerian Peasant toward Time," in *Mediterranean Countrymen: Essays in the Social Anthropology of the Mediterranean,* J. Pitt-Rivers, ed. Paris: Mouton.

Bourdillon, M. F. C.
  1978 "Knowing the World or Hiding It: A Response to Maurice Bloch," [1977]. *Man* 13:591–599.
Bury, John B.
  1932 *The Idea of Progress: An Inquiry into Its Growth and Origin.* New York: Macmillan.
Cancian, Frank
  1972 *Change and Uncertainty in a Peasant Economy: The Maya Corn Farmers of Zinacantan.* Stanford: Stanford University Press.
Cannon, Walter B.
  1942 "Voodoo Death." *American Anthropologist* 44:169–181.
Chayanov, A. V.
  1966 *A. V. Chayanov on the Theory of Peasant Economy,* D. Thorner and B. Kerblay, *et al.,* eds. Homewood, Ill.: Irwin.
Cohen, Morris R., and Ernest Nagel
  1962 *An Introduction to Logic.* New York: Harcourt. (First published 1934)
Cole, Michael, and Sylvia Scribner
  1974 *Culture and Thought: A Psychological Introduction.* New York: Wiley.
Collingwood, R. G.
  1940 *An Essay on Metaphysics.* London: Oxford University Press.
  1946 *The Idea of History.* London: Oxford University Press.
Comercio Exterior de México
  (Monthly publication of the Banco de Comercio Exterior, S.A., México, D.F.)
D'Amico, Robert
  1972 Review of *Epistémologie des sciences de l'homme,* by Jean Piaget. *Telos* 13:156–160.
Dasen, P. R.
  1974 "Cross-cultural Piagetian Research: A Summary," in *Culture and Cognition: Readings in Cross-cultural Psychology.* J. W. Berry and P. R. Dasen, eds. London: Methuen.
De Grazia, Sebastian
  1971 "Time and Work," in *The Future of Time: Man's Temporal Environment.* Henri Yaker, *et al.,* eds. Garden City, N.Y.: Anchor.
de Janvry, Alain, and Carlos Garramón
  1977 "The Dynamics of Rural Poverty in Latin America." *Journal of Peasant Studies* 4:206–216.
Diener, Paul
  1978 "The Tears of St. Anthony: Ritual and Revolution in Eastern Guatemala." *Latin American Perspectives* 5:3:92–116.
Diener, Paul, Donald Nonini, and Eugene E. Robkin
  1980 "Ecology and Evolution in Cultural Anthropology." *Man* 15:1–31.
Dilthey, Wilhelm
  1957 *Philosophy of Existence: Introduction to Weltanschauungslehre,* transl. W. Kluback and M. Weinbaum (from *Gesammelte Schriften,* vol. 8). New York: Bookman Associates. (First published 1931)

1961   *Pattern and Meaning in History,* H. P. Rickman, ed. (from *Gesammelte Schriften,* vol. 7). New York: Harper. (First published 1905–1910)

Dirección General de Estadística

1972   *IX censo general de población, 1970, resumén general.* México, D.F.

Donagan, Alan

1962   *The Later Philosophy of R. G. Collingwood.* London: Oxford University Press.

Douglas, Mary

1966   *Purity and Danger.* New York: Praeger.

Downs, Roger M., and David Stea, eds.

1973   *Image and Environment: Cognitive Mapping and Spatial Behavior.* Chicago: Aldine.

DuBois, Cora

1935   *Wintu Ethnography. University of California Publications in American Archaeology and Ethnology,* vol. 36, no. 1.

Dundes, Alan

1969   "Thinking Ahead: A Folkloristic Reflection on the Future Orientation in American Worldview." *Anthropological Quarterly* 42:53–72.

Durkheim, Emile

1965   *The Elementary Forms of the Religious Life.* New York: Free Press. (First published 1912)

Durkheim, Emile, and Marcel Mauss

1963   *Primitive Classification.* Chicago: University of Chicago Press. (First published 1903)

Durrenberger, E. Paul, and Nicola Tannenbaum

1979   "A Reassessment of Chayanov and His Recent Critics." *Peasant Studies* 8:48–63.

Dykstra, Vergil H.

1960   "Philosophers and Presuppositions." *Mind* 69:63–68.

Eastwell, Harry D.

1982   "Voodoo Death and the Mechanism for Dispatch of the Dying in East Arnhem, Australia." *American Anthropologist* 84:5–18.

Eliade, Mircea

1954   *The Myth of the Eternal Return.* Princeton: Princeton University Press.

1964   *Shamanism: Archaic Techniques of Ecstasy.* Princeton: Princeton University Press.

Engels, Frederick

1939   *Anti-Dühring: Herr Eugen Dühring's Revolution in Science.* New York: International Publishers. (First published 1878)

1970a   *Ludwig Feuerbach and the End of Classical German Philosophy.* Reprinted in *Karl Marx and Frederick Engels: Selected Works,* vol. 3, pp. 337–376. Moscow: Progress Publishers. (First published 1886)

1970b   Letter to J. Bloch. Reprinted in *Karl Marx and Frederick Engels: Selected Works,* vol. 3, pp. 487–489. Moscow: Progress Publishers. (First published 1895)

Ennew, Judith, Paul Hirst, and Keith Tribe
  1977 " 'Peasantry' as an Economic Category." *Journal of Peasant Studies* 4:295–322.
Esteva, Gustavo
  1976 "Agriculture in Mexico from 1950 to 1975: The Failure of a False Analogy." *Comercio Exterior de México* 22:1:3–14.
Evans-Pritchard, E. E.
  1937 *Witchcraft, Oracles and Magic among the Azande.* Oxford: Oxford University Press.
  1939 "Nuer Time-reckoning." *Africa* 12:109–126.
  1940 *The Nuer.* Oxford: Oxford University Press.
Femia, Joseph V.
  1981 *Gramsci's Political Thought: Hegemony, Consciousness and Revolutionary Process.* Oxford: Clarendon.
Feuer, Lewis S.
  1975 *Ideology and the Ideologists.* New York: Harper and Row.
Fjellman, S.
  1976 "Natural and Unnatural Decision-making: A Critique of Decision Theory." *Ethos* 4:73–94.
Flavell, John
  1963 *The Developmental Psychology of Jean Piaget.* New York: Van Nostrand Reinhold.
Foster, George M.
  1963 "The Dyadic Contract in Tzintzuntzan, II: Patron-client Relationship." *American Anthropologist* 65:1280–1294.
  1965a "Peasant Society and the Image of Limited Good." *American Anthropologist* 67:293–315.
  1965b "Cultural Responses to Expressions of Envy in Tzintzuntzan." *Southwestern Journal of Anthropology* 21:24–35.
  1967 *Tzintzuntzan: Mexican Peasants in a Changing World.* Boston: Little, Brown (Revised 1979)
  1972 "The Anatomy of Envy: A Study in Symbolic Behavior." *Current Anthropology* 13:165–202.
Freud, Sigmund
  1938 "Totem and Taboo," in *Basic Writings of Sigmund Freud.* New York: Modern Library. (First published 1918)
Garrison, Vivian, and Conrad Arensberg
  1976 "The Evil Eye: Envy or Risk of Seizure? Paranoia or Patronal Dependency?" in *The Evil Eye,* C. Maloney, ed. New York: Columbia University Press.
Gayton, A. H.
  1930 *Yokuts-Mono Chiefs and Shamans. University of California Publications in American Archaeology and Ethnology,* vol. 24, no. 8.
Geertz, Clifford
  1973 "Person, Time, and Conduct in Bali," in *Interpretations of Cultures.* New York: Basic Books.

Gellner, Ernest
   1970   "Concepts and Society," in *Rationality*, B. Wilson, ed. New York: Harper Torchbooks.
Geohegan, William
   1973   *Natural Information Processing Rules.* Monographs of the Language-Behavior Research Laboratory, No. 3. University of California, Berkeley.
Gibson, Charles
   1964   *The Aztecs under Spanish Rule: A History of the Indians of the Valley of Mexico, 1519–1810.* Stanford: Stanford University Press.
Gladwin, H., and C. Gladwin
   1971   "Estimating Market Conditions and Profit Expectations of Fish Sellers at Cape Coast, Ghana," in *Studies in Economic Anthropology*, George Dalton, ed. Washington, D.C.: American Anthropological Association.
Godelier, Maurice
   1972   *Rationality and Irrationality in Economics.* New York: Monthly Review Press.
   1978   "Infrastructure, Societies, and History." *Current Anthropology* 19:763–771; 1979, 20:108–111.
Gombrich, E. H.
   1969   *Art and Illusion: A Study in the Psychology of Pictorial Representation.* Princeton: Princeton University Press.
Gonzales Casanova, Pablo
   1970   *Democracy in Mexico.* London: Oxford University Press.
Goodenough, Ward
   1963   *Cooperation in Change.* New York: Russell Sage Foundation.
Gramsci, Antonio
   1971   *Selections from the Prison Notebooks of Antonio Gramsci*, edited and translated by Quintin Hoare and Geoffrey Nowell Smith. London: Lawrence and Wishart.
Greenberg, James B.
   1981   *Santiago's Sword: Chatino Peasant Religion and Economics.* Berkeley: University of California Press.
Grindle, Marilee
   1977   *Bureaucrats, Politicians, and Peasants: A Case Study in Public Policy.* Berkeley: University of California Press.
Gutiérrez, Gustavo
   1973   *A Theology of Liberation: History, Politics and Salvation.* Translated and edited by Sister Caridad Inda and John Eagleson. Maryknoll, N.Y.: Orbis.
Hall, Edward T.
   1959   *The Silent Language.* Garden City, N.Y.: Doubleday.
Hallowell, A. Irving
   1955   *Culture and Experience.* Philadelphia: University of Pennsylvania Press.
   1964   "Ojibwa Ontology, Behavior, and World View," in *Primitive Views of the World*, Stanley Diamond, ed. New York: Columbia University Press.

Hallpike, C. R.
  1976 "Is there a Primitive Mentality?" *Man* 11:253–270.
Harris, Marvin
  1968 *The Rise of Anthropological Theory: A History of Theories of Culture.* New York: Thomas Y. Crowell.
  1979 *Cultural Materialism: The Struggle for a Science of Culture.* New York: Random House.
Harris, Richard
  1978 "Marxism and the Agrarian Question in Latin America." *Latin American Perspectives* 5:4:2–26.
Harrison, Mark
  1975 "Chayanov and the Economics of the Russian Peasantry." *Journal of Peasant Studies* 2:389–417.
  1977 "The Peasant Mode of Production in the Work of A. V. Chayanov." *Journal of Peasant Studies* 4:323–336.
  1979 "Chayanov and the Marxists." *Journal of Peasant Studies* 7:86–100.
Hewitt de Alcántara, Cynthia
  1973 "The 'Green Revolution' as History: The Mexican Experience." *Development and Change* 5:2:25–44.
Hill, W. W.
  1944 "The Navajo Indians and the Ghost Dance of 1890." *American Anthropologist* 46:523–527.
Hoebel, E. Adamson
  1954 *The Law of Primitive Man.* Cambridge: Harvard University Press.
  1960 *The Cheyennes: Indians of the Great Plains.* New York: Holt.
Horkheimer, Max
  1972 *Critical Theory: Selected Essays,* transl. M. J. O'Connell, *et al.* New York: Herder and Herder.
Hsu, Francis L. K.
  1981 *Americans and Chinese: Passage to Differences,* third edition. Honolulu: University Press of Hawaii.
Hunt, E. K.
  1975 *Property and Prophets: The Evolution of Economic Institutions and Ideologies,* second edition. New York: Harper and Row.
  1979 *History of Economic Thought: A Critical Perspective.* Belmont, Calif.: Wadsworth.
Jacobs, Melville
  1964 *Pattern in Cultural Anthropology.* Homewood, Ill.: Dorsey Press.
Kazantzakis, Nikos
  1965 *Report to Greco,* transl. P. A. Bien. New York: Simon and Schuster.
Kearney, Michael
  1972 *Winds of Ixtepeji: World View and Society in a Zapotec Town.* New York: Holt.
  1975 "World View Theory and Study." *Annual Review of Anthropology* 4:247–270.

1976 "A World View Explanation of the Evil Eye," in *The Evil Eye*, C. Maloney, ed. New York: Columbia University Press.

1977 "Oral Performance by Mexican Spiritualists in Possession Trance." *Journal of Latin American Lore* 3:309–328.

1978a "Spiritualist Healing in Mexico," in *Culture and Curing: Anthropological Perspectives on Traditional Medical Beliefs and Practices*, Peter Morely and Roy Wallis, eds. Pittsburgh: University of Pittsburgh Press.

1978b "*Espiritualismo* as an Alternative Medical Tradition in the Border Area," in *Modern Medicine and Medical Anthropology in the United States-Mexico Border Population*, Boris Velimirovic, ed. Washington, D.C.: Pan-American Health Organization.

1980 "Agribusiness and the Demise or the Rise of the Peasantry." *Latin American Perspectives* 7:4:115–124.

Keesing, Roger
1979 "Linguistic Knowledge and Cultural Knowledge: Some Doubts and Speculations." *American Anthropologist* 81:14–36.

Ketner, Kenneth L.
1972 *An Essay on the Nature of World Views*. Ph.D. dissertation, Department of Philosophy, University of California, Santa Barbara.

Kluckhohn, Florence, and Fred Strodtbeck
1961 *Variations in Value Orientations*. Evanston, Ill.: Row, Peterson.

Kroeber, Alfred
1925 *Handbook of the Indians of California*. Washington, D.C.: Bureau of Ethnology Bulletin 78.

1948 *Anthropology: Race, Language, Culture, Psychology, Prehistory*. New York: Harcourt.

1957 *Style and Civilization*. Ithaca: Cornell University Press.

1963 *An Anthropologist Looks at History*. Berkeley: University of California Press.

Kuhn, Thomas S.
1957 *The Copernican Revolution*. Cambridge: Harvard University Press.

1970 *The Structure of Scientific Revolutions*, second edition. Chicago: University of Chicago Press.

Leach, E. R.
1966 *Rethinking Anthropology*. New York: Humanities.

Leacock, Eleanor
1972 Introduction to *The Origin of the Family, Private Property, and the State*, by Frederick Engels. New York: International Publishers.

1978 "Women's Status in Egalitarian Society: Implications for Social Evolution." *Current Anthropology* 19:247–275.

Lee, Dorothy
1944a "Categories of the Generic and the Particular in Wintu." *American Anthropologist* 46:362–369.

1944b "Linguistic Reflection of Wintu Thought." *International Journal of American Linguistics* 10:181–197.

1950   "Notes on the Conception of Self among the Wintu Indians." *Journal of Abnormal and Social Psychology* 45:538–543.

Lenin, V. I.
1927   *Materialism and Empirio-Criticism: Critical Comments on a Reactionary Philosophy.* New York: International Publishers. (First published 1909)

León-Portilla, Miguel
1973   *Time and Reality in the Thought of the Maya,* transl. C. L. Boiles and F. Horcasitas. Boston, Beacon Press.

Lex, Barbara W.
1974   "Voodoo Death: New Thoughts on an Old Explanation." *American Anthropologist* 76:818–823.

Lichtheim, George
1967   *The Concept of Ideology and Other Essays.* New York: Random House.

Lowery-Palmer, Alma
1980   *Yoruba World View and Patient Compliance.* Ph.D. Dissertation, Department of Anthropology, University of California, Riverside.

Lukács, Gyorgy
1971   *History and Class Consciousness: Studies in Marxist Dialectics,* transl. R. Livingstone. Cambridge: M.I.T. Press. (First published 1923)

Macfarlane, Alan
1978   *The Origins of English Individualism: The Family, Property and Social Transition.* Oxford: Blackwell.

MacIntyre, Alasdair
1970   "Is Understanding Religion Compatible with Believing?" in *Rationality,* B. Wilson, ed. New York: Harper Torchbooks.

McNeill, William H.
1976   *Plagues and People.* New York: Doubleday.

Malinowski, Bronislaw
1922   *Argonauts of the Western Pacific.* London: Routledge and Kegan Paul.

Mannheim, Karl
1936   *Ideology and Utopia,* transl. L. Wirth and E. Shils. New York: Harcourt.

Marx, Karl
1967   *Capital: A Critique of Political Economy.* Volume I, *The Process of Capitalist Production.* New York: International Publishers. (First published 1867)

1969a   *The Eighteenth Brumaire of Louis Bonaparte.* Reprinted in *Karl Marx and Frederick Engels: Selected Works,* vol. 1, pp. 398–487. Moscow: Progress Publishers. (First published 1852)

1969b   Preface to *A Contribution to the Critique of Political Economy.* Reprinted in *Karl Marx and Frederick Engels: Selected Works,* vol. 1, pp. 502–506. Moscow: Progress Publishers. (First published 1859)

1975   *Contribution to the Critique of Hegel's Philosophy of Law.* Reprinted in *Karl Marx, Frederick Engels: Collected Works,* vol. 3, pp. 3–129. New York: International Publishers. (First published 1844)

1976   "Results of the Immediate Process of Production." Appendix to *Capital,* vol. 1. New York: Vintage. (Written 1863 to 1866; first published 1933)

Marx, Karl, and Frederick Engels
  1975 *The Holy Family, or Critique of Critical Criticism.* Reprinted in *Karl Marx, Frederick Engels: Collected Works,* vol. 4, pp. 5–211. New York: International Publishers. (First published 1844)
  1976 *The German Ideology,* vol. 1. Reprinted in *Karl Marx, Frederick Engels: Collected Works,* vol. 5., pp. 19–452. New York: International Publishers. (First published 1845–1846)
Mathews, Linda
  1980 "China: Where History Is Never Dead." *Los Angeles Times,* Sept. 7.
Mauss, Marcel, and H. Beuchat
  1906 "Essai sur les variations saisonniéres des sociétés eskimos: étude de morphologie sociale." *L'Année sociologique* 9:39–132.
Mbiti, John S.
  1970 *African Relations and Philosophy.* New York: Doubleday.
Mead, Margaret
  1949 "Ruth Fulton Benedict 1887–1948." *American Anthropologist* 51:457–468.
Miller, George A., and Phillip N. Johnson–Laird
  1976 *Language and Perception.* Cambridge: Harvard University Press.
Mink, Louis O.
  1969 *Mind, History, and Dialectic: The Philosophy of R. C. Collingwood.* Bloomington: Indiana University Press.
Miranda, José
  1969 *Marx and the Bible: A Critique of the Philosophy of Oppression,* transl. John Eagleson. Maryknoll, N.Y.: Orbis.
Mumford, Lewis
  1963 *Technics and Civilization.* New York: Harcourt. (First published 1934)
Nash, June
  1960 "Protestantism in an Indian Village in the Western Highlands of Guatemala." *Alpha Kappa Delta* 30:1:49–53.
Needham, Rodney
  1963 Introduction to *Primitive Classification,* by Emile Durkheim and Marcel Mauss. Chicago: University of Chicago Press.
  1972 *Belief, Language, and Experience.* Oxford: Blackwell.
Neisser, Ulric
  1976 *Cognition and Reality: Principles and Implications of Cognitive Psychology.* San Francisco: W. H. Freeman.
Opler, Morris E.
  1945 "Themes as Dynamic Forces in Culture." *American Journal of Sociology* 51:198–206.
  1968 "The Themal Approach to Cultural Anthropology and Its Applications to North Indian Data." *Southwestern Journal of Anthropology* 24:215–227.
Paré, Luisa
  1977 *El proletariado agrícola en México: ¿campesinos sin tierra o proletarios agrícolas?* México, D.F.: Siglo XXI.

Parsons, Elsie Clews
   1936   *Mitla, Town of Souls.* Chicago: University of Chicago Press.
Patnaik, Utsa
   1979   "Neo-populism and Marxism: The Chayanovian View of the Agrarian Question and Its Fundamental Fallacy." *Journal of Peasant Studies* 6:375–420.
Piaget, Jean
   1969   *The Child's Conception of Physical Causality.* Totowa, N.J.: Littlefield, Adams. (First published 1930)
   1971   *Biology and Knowledge: An Essay on the Relations between Organic Regulations and Cognitive Processes,* transl. B. Walsh. Chicago: University of Chicago Press.
Quinn, Naomi
   1975   "Decision Models of Social Structure." *American Ethnologist* 2:19–46.
   1976   "A Natural System Used in Mfantse Litigation Settlement." *American Ethnologist* 3:331–352.
Randall, Robert
   1977   *Change and Variation in Samal Fishing: Making Plans to Make a Living in the South Philippines.* Ph.D. dissertation, Department of Anthropology, University of California, Berkeley.
Redfield, Robert
   1941   *The Folk Culture of Yucatan.* Chicago: University of Chicago Press.
   1952   "The Primitive World View." *American Philosophical Society, Proceedings* 96:30–36.
   1953   *The Primitive World and Its Transformations.* Ithaca: Cornell University Press.
Rello, Fernando
   1976   "Modo de producción y clases sociales." *Cuadernos Políticos* 8:100–105.
Reyes Osorio, Sergio, *et al.*
   1974   *Estructura agraria y desarrollo agrícola en México.* México, D.F.: Fondo de Cultura Económico.
Riegel, Klaus F., and George C. Rosenwald, eds.
   1975   *Structure and Transformation.* New York: Wiley.
Riesman, David, *et al.*
   1970   *The Lonely Crowd: A Study of the Changing American Character,* new edition. New Haven: Yale University Press. (First published 1950)
Roberts, John M.
   1976   "Belief in the Evil Eye in World Perspective," in *The Evil Eye,* C. Maloney, ed. New York: Columbia University Press.
Robinson, Joan
   1970   *Freedom and Necessity: An Introduction to the Study of Society.* New York: Pantheon Books.
Rothstein, Frances
         "The Class Basis of Patron-Client Relations." *Latin American Perspectives* 21:2:25–35.
Rubinoff, Lionel
   1970   *Collingwood and the Reform of Metaphysics: A Study in the Philosophy of Mind.* Toronto: University of Toronto Press.

Russell, Bertrand
  1945 *A History of Western Philosophy.* New York: Simon and Schuster.
  1981 "On the Notion of Cause," in *Mysticism and Logic, and Other Essays,*
        2nd edition. New York: Barnes and Noble. (First published 1917)
Rycroft, Charles
  1974 "Is Freudian Symbolism a Myth?" *New York Review of Books,* January
        10, pp. 13–16.
Sahlins, Marshall
  1976 *Culture and Practical Reason.* Chicago: University of Chicago Press.
Sapir, Edward
  1949 "Culture, Genuine and Spurious," in *Selected Writings of Edward Sapir,*
        David Mandelbaum, ed. Berkeley: University of California Press. (First
        published 1924).
Saussure, Ferdinand de
  1966 *Course in General Linguistics,* ed. C. Bally and A. Sechehaye, transl.
        and intro. W. Baskin. New York: McGraw-Hill. (First published 1915)
Schoeck, Helmut
  1966 *Envy: A Theory of Social Behavior,* transl. M. Glenny and B. Ross. New
        York: Harcourt [1969].
Scott, James C.
  1975 "Exploitation in Rural Class Relations: A Victim's Perspective."
        Comparative Politics 7:489–532.
Simpson, George Gaylord
  1964 *This View of Life: The World of an Evolutionist.* New York: Harcourt.
Solís, Leopoldo
  1967 "Hacia un análisis general a largo plazo del desarrollo económico de
        México." *Demografía y Economía* 1:40–91.
Spengler, Oswald
  1926–28 *The Decline of the West,* transl. C. F. Atkinson. New York: Knopf.
Spradley, James P., ed.
  1972 *Culture and Cognition: Rules, Maps, and Plans.* San Francisco:
        Chandler.
Stavenhagen, Rodolfo
  1976 "Aspectos sociales de la estructura agraria in México," in *Neolati-
        fundismo y explotación de Emiliano Zapata a Anderson Clayton y Co.,*
        R. Stavenhagen, ed. México, D.F.: Editorial Nuestro Tiempo.
  1978 "Capitalism and the Peasantry in Mexico." *Latin American Perspectives*
        5:3:27–37.
Stocking, George W., Jr.
  1968 *Race, Culture, and Evolution: Essays in the History of Anthropology.*
        New York: Free Press.
  1974 "Introduction: The Basic Assumptions of Boasian Anthropology," in *The
        Shaping of American Anthropology, 1883–1911: A Franz Boas Reader,*
        G. W. Stocking, Jr., ed. New York: Basic Books.
Stuart, James, and Michael Kearney
  1981 *Causes and Effects of Agricultural Labor Migration from the Mixteca of
        Oaxaca to California.* Working Papers in U.S.-Mexican Studies, 28.
        Program in U.S.-Mexican Studies, University of California, San Diego.

Taussig, Michael T.
 1980 *The Devil and Commodity Fetishism in South America.* Chapel Hill:
       University of North Carolina Press.
Tawney, R. H.
 1947 *Religion and the Rise of Capitalism.* New York: Mentor Books. (First
       published 1926)
Terray, Emmanuel
 1972 *Marxism and "Primitive" Societies,* transl. M. Klopper. New York:
       Monthly Review Press.
Thompson, E. P.
 1967 "Time, Work-discipline and Industrial Capitalism." *Past and Present*
       38:56–97.
Toulmin, Stephen, and June Goodfield
 1965 *The Discovery of Time.* New York: Harper and Row.
Traugott, Elizabeth Closs
 1975 "Spatial Expressions of Tense and Temporal Sequencing: A Contribu-
       tion to the Study of Semantic Fields." *Semiotica* 15:207–230.
 1975 "Spatial Expressions of Tense and Temporal Sequencing: A Contribution
       to the Study of Semantic Fields." *Semiotica* 15:207–230.
Turnbull, Colin
 1961 *The Forest People.* New York: Simon and Schuster.
Tyler, Stephen A., ed.
 1969a *Cognitive Anthropology.* New York: Holt.
 1969b Introduction to *Cognitive Anthropology,* S. A. Tyler, ed. New York:
        Holt.
Veblen, Thorstein
 1912 *The Theory of the Leisure Class.* New York: Macmillan.
Volosinov, V. N.
 1973 *Marxism and the Philosophy of Language,* transl. L. Matejka and I. R.
       Titunik. New York: Seminar Press.
Vygotsky, L. S.
 1962 *Thought and Language,* ed. and transl. E. Hanfmann and G. Vakar.
       Cambridge: M.I.T. Press.
 1978 *Mind in Society: The Development of Higher Psychological Processes,*
       Michael Cole, *et al.,* eds. Cambridge: Harvard University Press.
Wallace, Anthony F. C.
 1968 "Cognitive Theory," in *International Encyclopedia of the Social Sciences*
       2:536–540.
 1970 *Culture and Personality,* second edition. New York: Random House.
Wallerstein, Immanuel
 1974 *The Modern World-System.* New York: Academic Press.
Warman, Arturo
 1972 *Los campesinos: hijos predilectos del régimen.* México, D.F.: Editorial
       Nuestro Tiempo.
Waterman, T. T.
 1920 *Yurok Geography. University of California Publications in American
       Archaeology and Ethnology,* vol. 16, no. 5.

Williams, Raymond
  1977 *Marxism and Literature.* Oxford: Oxford University Press.
Wilson, Bryan, ed.
  1970 *Rationality.* New York: Harper and Row.
Wissler, Clark
  1917 *The American Indian: An Introduction to the Anthropology of the New World.* New York: D. C. McMurtie.
Wogaman, Philip J.
  1977 *The Great Economic Debate: An Ethical Analysis.* Philadelphia: Westminster.
Wolf, Eric R.
  1966a *Peasants.* Englewood Cliffs, N.J.: Prentice-Hall.
  1966b "Kinship, Friendship, and Patron-client Relations in Complex Societies," in *The Social Anthropology of Complex Societies,* M. Banton, ed. New York: Praeger.
Young, James Clay
  1981 *Medical Choice in a Mexican Village.* New Brunswick, N.J.: Rutgers University Press.

Index

Achumawi, 158
Action, 44–45
Agar, M., 214
Agriculture: in Mexico, 221–223; peasant v. capitalist, 177–182
Alienation, 77
Altruism, 77–78
Angulo, Jaime de, 156, 158
Animism, in Causality, 87
Anthropology: Boas tradition, 25–36; Redfield tradition, 37–40; idealism in, 11, 23–40; social role, 211
Appadurai, Arjun, 221
Arato, Andrew, 220
Arensberg, Conrad, 199, 225
Aristarchus, 129
Aristotle, 47, 66, 90, 124–130
Aronowitz, Stanley, 19–20
Arificialism, in Causality, 87
Asad, Talal, 214
Assumptions, 10, 41–42, 47–51, 215; orders of, 48 50, 51
Astrology, 86
Ayer, A. J., 49, 215–216
Aztecs, 173

Bali, 135–145
Band societies, 6
Barnouw, Victor, 24, 25, 30, 63, 151, 214
Bartra, Roger, 178, 222, 224
Base, 12, 16
Bastian, Adolf, 67
Beals, Alan R., 217
Bean, Lowell J., 149, 157, 160, 163–164
Beard, Charles A., 101–102
Belief, 51
Benedict, Ruth, 28–31
Bennholdt-Thomsen, Veronika, 224
Bentham, Jeremy, 14
Berger, John, 172
Beuchat, H., 111
Bible, world view of, 130–134
Blackburn, Thomas, 160, 164
Bloch, Maurice, 221
Boas, Franz, 25–37, 214
Body, Self and, 69–70
Boole, George, 60
Boulding, Kenneth, 52

Bourdieu, Pierre, 194
Bourdillon, M. F. C., 211
Breines, Paul, 220
Bruno, Giordano, 133
Burckhardt, Jacob, 24
Bury, John B., 101–102, 132

Calendars, 141–142
California Indians, 7; world view, 147–169
Cannon, Walter B., 221
Carnegie Institution, 37
Categories: of thought and knowledge, 3; in world view, 80–84
Catholicism, Mexican, 195–196
Causality, 3, 48, 84–89; Aristotelian, 125–128; in California Indian world view, 148–149; integration of, 106; in Mexican peasant world view, 196–197; Yoruba assumptions of, 75
Ceremony, in Bali world view, 143–145
Change, 89–92; outside sources of, 110, 119–120, 172–173
Chayanov, A. V., 204–205, 225
Chicago, University of, 37
Children: Self image, 73; Causality notions, 86–87
Chinese, Time and, 97
Chinese Revolution, 221
Christianity, world view and, 131–134
Chumash, 164
Class-based societies, world view and, 210
Class conflict, 6
Classification, 3, 78, 84, 219; in California Indian world view, 155–158; integration of, 106; origins of, 78–80
Classless societies, 6–7, 210, 212; Relationship in, 76–77
Climax, Absence of, 143–145
Clock orientation, of time, 103–104
Cognitive maps, 45, 46
Cole, Michael, 215, 217, 218
Collingwood, R. G., 49–51, 56–58, 84, 215–218, 220
Colombia, 220
Columbia University, 26, 37
Comercio Exterior de México, 182, 224
Communication, universals and, 66
Competition, between peasants, 190–192
Concepts: basic, 41–64; formation of, 110
Congregaciones, 174
Conservatism, of idealism, 17–23

Constancy, 89–92
Copernicus, 54
Cosmology, Aristotelian, 124–130
Creation, 131–134; in California Indian world view, 155, 160
Cultural anthropology, idealism, 11
Cultural idealism, 1–2, 10–40; explanation, 15–16
Culture, 25–40; idealism and, 22–23; nature of, 5–6; personality and, 28–30
Culture areas, 26–27
Cycles, perpetual, 45
Cyclical time, 220

D'Amico, Robert, 87
Darwin, Charles, 22
Darwinism, 110; social, 21–22
Dasen, P. R., 87
De Grazia, Sebastian, 104
de Janvry, Alain, 224
Democracy, classless societies and, 212
Depersonalization, 70
Depth, of time, 102
Descartes, René, 11, 131
Determinants, historic, 7
Devil, 156, 220; in Mexico, 201
Dialectics, 14–15
Diener, Paul, 203, 213
Differences, in world view, 109–119
Dilthey, Wilhelm, 28, 66, 214
Diminishing Good, Image of, 185
Dinka religion, 217
Dirección General de Estadística, 222
Directions, 93–94; in Wintu world view, 162–163
Domains, in world view, 71–72
Donagan, Alan, 216
Douglas, Mary, 62
Dream helpers, 149, 161
Dreaming, in California Indian world view, 159
DuBois, Cora, 154, 162
Dundes, Alan, 219
Durkheim, Emile, 79–80, 84–85, 165, 219
Durrenberger, E. Paul, 225
Dykstra, Vergil H., 62

Earth, in Aristotle's cosmology, 127–128
Eastwell, Harry D., 221
Ecological relationship, 74–75
Einstein, Albert, space-time, 101, 208
Ejidos, 172, 190, 222
Eliade, Mircea, 99, 159, 164
Empirical studies, of world view, 212
Empiricism, 3, 10–12, 211–212
Encomienda, 174
Engels, Frederick, 12, 13–15, 25, 35, 89, 213
Ennew, Judith, 225
Environment, 44–45; Mexican peasant, 181–183; world view and, 110–114, 209–210
Envy, 197–201
Epistemology, 10–16
Eskimo, 111
Esteva, Gustavo, 180, 222, 224
Ether, 125
Ethnosemantics, 209; world view and, 31–36

Evans-Pritchard, E. E., 87, 104–106
Evil eye, 86, 197–201
External causes, of world view differences, 110–114, 209
External forces, in world view, 123
External inconsistency, in world view, 54–58

Fairbank, John, 97
Farrand, Livingston, 27
Feedback, 6
Femia, Joseph V., 17
Feuer, Lewis S., 22
Fiestas, 203–206
Finalistic assumption, 87
Fjellman, S., 214
Flavell, John, 85
Fontenelle, Bernard, 132
Force, Causality and, 87
Foster, George M., 30, 31, 184–185, 194, 196, 223–225
Franklin, Benjamin, 104
Freud, Sigmund, 29, 70–71, 89, 220
Future orientation, 95–96

Galileo, 54, 124, 133
Garramon, Carlos, 224
Garrison, Vivian, 199, 225
Gayton, A. H., 165–166
Geertz, Clifford, 135–145, 221
Gellner, Ernest, 217
Geocentrism, 127–130
Geohegan, William, 214
Gestalten, 28, 47
Ghost Dance, 55, 160
Ghosts, 88–89, 118
Gibson, Charles, 45, 174, 175, 192
Gladwin, C., 35
Gladwin, H., 35
God/Gods, 118, 156; Aristotle's idea of, 126; inconsistent concepts of, 59; in Mexican peasant world view, 196, 201–202; Redfield, 39; in scientific world view, 131–134
Godleier, Maurice, 13, 213, 225
Gombrich, E. H., 81
Gonzales Casanova, Pablo, 224
Goodenough, Ward, 217–218
Goodfield, June, 220
Gramsci, Antonio, 17
Great Spirit, 156
Green Revolution, 179, 222
Greenberg, James B., 225
Grindle, Marilee, 224
Gutiérrez, Gustavo, 21

Hacienda, 175–176
Hall, Edward T., 105
Hallowell, A. Irving, 42, 82–84, 93–94, 218–219
Hallpike, C. R., 87
Harris, Marvin, 14–15, 33, 205, 214
Harris, Richard, 224
Harrison, Mark, 225
Healing, among California Indians, 165–168
Hebrews, time image, 100

Hegel, G. W. F., 217
Hegelianism, 14–15
Heliocentrism, 130, 132
Heraclides, 129
Herodotus, 25
Hewitt de Alcántara, Cynthia, 222
Hill, W. W., 55
Hirst, Paul, 225
Historical materialism, 1–2, 10–40, 213; explanation, 12–15
Historicism, 218
History, 5–6
Hoebel, E. Adamson, 30
Horkheimer, Max, 19, 45–46, 213–214
Hsu, Francis L. K., 30
Human, Redfield, 39
Human nature, 77–78
Hunt, E. K., 213, 219

I and me, Mead's 38–39
Idalism, 213; approaches to world view, 23–40; epistemology of, 10–12; political economy of, 16–23; psychological sources of, 88–89
Idealist fallacy, 114
Ideas, 5
Ideology, 7; world view and, 2
Images, 42, 47–51, 215; of Limited Good, 31, 184, 185, 192, 223; in world view, 10
Individual, in Wintu society, 152
Individualism, 75–78, 151; peasant, 188–189, 191
Inequalities, Redfield, 38
Interactionism, 3
Internal causes, 209; of world view differences, 114–117
Internal consistency, in world view, 53–54
Internal dynamics, in world view, 123
Internal inconsistency, in world view, 58–64
Ixtepeji/Ixtepejanos, 59, 64, 203, 206, 225; Causality in, 96, 198; time image in, 105; time orientation, 193; world view, 182

Jacobs, Melville, 214
Johnson-Laird, Phillip M., 215

Kant, Immanuel, 90
Kazantzakis, Nikos, 132–133
Kearney, Michael, 1, 30, 35, 48, 64, 70, 95, 158, 182, 189, 193, 194, 200, 213, 220, 222–223, 225
Keesing, Roger, 215
Ketner, Kenneth L., 51, 66, 216–217
Kinship, Time and, 139
Kinship terms, 221; in Bali, 137–138
Kluckhohn, Florence, 95–97, 102, 219
Knowledge, 44–45; acquisition of, 35; categories of, 3, 42; sociology of, 21; source of, 19
Kroeber, Alfred, 27, 31, 63, 149, 159, 161–163, 167
Kuhn, Thomas S., 129, 216
Kumpi, 137–138, 221

Lakoff, G., 209
Land: in California Indian world view, 161–162; in Mexican peasant world view, 171–172, 176–180, 205

Languages, 31–35; Space in, 91; Time in, 91, 94, 99–100; time orientation and, 194; universals and, 208; Wintu world view and, 158
Latin America, 21
Latin Americans, Time and, 96
Leach, E. R., 98–99
Leacock, Eleanor, 76
Lee, Dorothy, 150–153, 155, 162
Leinhardt, Godfrey, 217
Lenin, V. I., 15, 213
León-Portilla, Miguel, 220
Lex, Barbara W., 221
Lichtheim, George, 214
Limited Good, Image of, 31, 184–185, 192, 223
Linear time, 99–106, 220; as urban datum, 113
Linguistics, 33–35
Living conditions, world view and, 171
Location, 89–92, 219; world view differences and, 110–112
Locke, John, 11
Logicism, 218
Logico-structural integration, 3–4, 31, 52–64, 209; of universals, 106–107
Logico-structural relationships, in world views, 123–145
Los Cedros, 185–190, 193, 195, 196, 198, 203, 206, 222, 225; Causality in, 196; time orientation in, 193; world view in, 182
Lowery-Palmer, Alma, 74–75
Lukács, Gyorgy, 118, 220

Macfarlane, Alan, 219
MacIntyre, Alasdair, 59, 217
McLennan, John F., 26
McNeill, William H., 172
Malinowski, Bronislaw, 18, 37
Mannheim, Karl, 63
Mao Zedong, 97
Market economy, Relationship in, 77
Marsh, Sadie, Wintu informant, 151
Marvell, Andrew, 100
Marx, Karl, 1, 5, 12–16, 26, 35, 76, 77, 118–119, 212, 213, 220
Marxism, on religion, 18
Materialism: cultural, 14–15; historical, 1–2, 10–40, 213; idealism vs., 1–6; political economy of, 16–23
Materialist fallacy, 114
Mathews, Linda, 99
Matter, Space and, 125
Mauss, Marcel, 79, 111
Mbiti, John S., 74
Me and I, Mead's 38–39
Mead, George Herbert, 38
Mead, Margaret, 28–29
Meaning, in mental phenomena, 115–116
Metaphysical propositions, 56
Metaphysics, 215–217
Mexican peasants, 7, 221; cultural behavior, 31; world view, 171–206
Mexican Revolution of 1910, 176, 177
Mexico, 221; agriculture in, 221–223; history, 171, 173–181
Millenium, 100

Miller, George A., 215
Mind, 11
Mink, Louis O., 216
Minkowski, Hermann, 208
Miracles, 157
Miranda, José, 21
Mitla, 202–203
Mixtec, 182
Mohave, 149, 159
Mono, 165
Morgan, Lewis Henry, 26
Mormons, Time and, 97
Motion, Aristotle theory of, 126–129
Mumford, Lewis, 103
Mystics, Self sense, 70–71

Names, in Bali, 136–141
Nash, June, 225
Natural/Supernatural, 81–82, 157
Nature, Redfield, 39
Navaho, Time and, 96–97
Needham, Rodney, 51, 219
Neisser, Ulric, 45, 215
Newton, Isaac, 101, 128
Nonini, Donald, 213
Nuer, time perception, 105–106, 112

Ojibwa, world view, 82–84
Opler, Morris E., 30, 62
Oscillating time, 98–99; 112–113; in California Indian world view, 160
Other, 3, 38–39, 62–63; in California Indian world view, 150–152; integration of, 106; in Mexican peasant world view, 184–187; Self relationship, 153–155; in world view, 68–72

Pain, 72–73
Paré, Luisa, 224
Parsons, Elsie Clews, 202–203
Participation, Causality and, 87
Passage of time, 102–103
Past orientation, 97
Patnaik, Utsa, 225
Patron-client relationship, 189–191
Patrons, saints as, 200
Peasants, 221; as a class, 7, 204, 224; Mexican, 7, 31, 171–206, 221; rationality, 202–206; wage labor, 180–183, 185–187, 222–223; world view, 171–206
Perception, 5–6, 219; world view and, 42–47, 120–121
Pericles, 25
Personalismo, 224
Personality, culture and, 28–30
Persons, Ojibwa, 82–83
Philosophy, politics and, 18–19
Piaget, Jean, xii, 34–35, 43, 71, 84–91, 127, 209, 218
Planarians, 68–69, 72, 91, 219
Planets, motion of, 129
Plato, 11
Pleasure, 72–73
Political economy, 16–23
Positivism, in politics, 19–20

Poverty: peasant agriculture and, 224–225; world view and, 193–197
Power, 201; in California Indian world view, 145–168; Causality and, 87; misuse of, 166–167; social control and, 164–168
"Prelogical mentality," 60
Present orientation, 96–97
Presuppositions, 48–51; absolute and relative, 56–57, 216
Principia, 51
Process, 89–92
Production: forces of, 12–13; relations of, 12–13
Profane, 156–157
Progressivism, materialism and, 20–21
Projection, in world view differences, 117–119
Projective systems, in Mexico, 197–202
Property, individualism and, 76
Prophets, 21
Propositions, 42, 47–51, 215
Protestantism: in Guatemala, 225; Mexican peasants and, 195–196
Psychic unity of mankind, 67
Public titles, in Bali, 140
Pygmies, world view, 92–93

Quinn, Naomi, 35

Randall, Robert, 35
Range, of time, 102
Rationalism, 10–12
Rationalists, 3
Real/Unreal, 81–82
Reality, world view and, 43
Redfield, Robert, 66, 73, 107, 215
Reification, 220; in world view differences, 117–119
Relationship, 3, 72–78, 219; ecological, 74–75; integration of, 106; in the Mexican peasant world view, 187–192
Relativity, in world view universals, 208–209
Religion, 81–82, 88–89, 118, 119; in California Indian world view, 156; Dinka, 217; Marxism on, 18; Mexican peasant, 200–201; politics and, 18–19; protest movements, 21; in village Mexico, 195–196
Rello, Fernando, 224
Revolution, 21
Reyes Osorio, Sergio, 180
Riegel, Klaus F., 34
Riesman, David, 63
Roberts, John M., 199
Robinson, Joan, 2
Robkin, Eugene E., 213
Rosenwald, George C., 34
Rothstein, Frances, 224
Rubinoff, Lionel, 49, 216, 218
Russell, Bertrand, 84, 126
Rycroft, Charles, 220

Sacred, 156–157
Sahlins, Marshall, 6
Salteaux, world view, 93–94
Santos, inconsistent view, 59–60
Sapir, Edward, 27–28

Saussure, Ferdinand de, 34
Schemata, 45
Schoeck, Helmut, 225
Scholastics, 11
Schutz, Alfred, 135, 141
Science, 81–82; Self in, 133; world view of, 130–134
Scott, James C., 205
Scribner, Sylvia, 215, 217, 218
Seasonal changes, world view differences and, 111–112
Self, 3, 38–39, 62–63; awareness of, 68; in Bali, 135–141; in California Indian world view, 150–152; of English speakers, 153–154; image of, 76; integration of, 106; Mead's, 38–39; in Mexican peasant world view, 187–192; Other relationship, 153–155; Redfield, 38; soul and, 70, 152; in U.S. culture, 150–151; Wintu, 153–154; in world views, 68–72, 132–133
Sensation, 43
Shamans, California Indian, 149, 157, 159, 165–168
Sickness, among California Indians, 165–167
Siegel, Bernard, 217
Simpson, George Gaylord, 10
Smith, Adam, 216
Social behavior, world view and, 209–210
Social control, power and, 164–168
Social Darwinism, 21–22
Social sciences: advances in, 210; world view and, 211
Society: creation of, 5; world view and, 134–145
Solís, Leopoldo, 222
Soul, Self and, 70, 152
Space, 3, 48; in California Indian world view, 161–164; integration of, 106; matter and, 125; perception of, 92–94; in world view model, 208
Spaniards, in Mexico, 173–176
Spanish language, future tense in, 225
Spengler, Oswald, 24–25, 28, 151, 214
Spirits, 88–89
Spradley, James P., 46, 214
State, idealism im, 18–19
Status titles, in Bali, 139–140
Stavenhagen, Rodolfo, 176, 180, 191, 272
Stekel, Wilhelm, 220
Stocking, George W., Jr., 26, 67, 213
Strodtbeck, Fred, 95–97, 102, 219
Structure, of the universals, 3
Struggle for existence, 76
Stuart, James, 35, 182, 213
Stylistic integration, 63
Supernatural, 81–82, 157
Superstructure, 12; cultural idealism in, 16
Surroundings, Self and, 68–69

Tannenbaum, Nicola, 225
Task orientation, of time, 103–104
Taussig, Michael T., 220
Tawney, R. H., 219
Teknonyms, in Bali, 138
Terray, Emmanuel, 213, 221
Theology of liberation, 21
Thompson, E. P., 103
Thought, categories of, 3, 42

Thucydides, 25
Time, 3, 48, 219; in Bali world view, 141–142; in California Indian world view, 158–161; clock orientation, 103–104; depth of, 102; imagery, 220; images of, 95, 98–106; integration of, 106; kinship and, 139; in Mexican peasant world view, 192–196; passage of, 102–103; perception of, 94–106; range of, 102; task orientation of, 103–104, units of, 104; in world view, 89–106, 208
Titles, in Bali, 139–140
Tribal societies, 6–7, 213
Toulmin, Stephen, 220
Traugott, Elizabeth Closs, 100
Tribe, Keith, 225
Truth: types of, 61; world view and, 55–58
Turnbull, Colin, 92–93
Tyler, Stephen A., 32, 48, 89, 209, 214
Tylor, E. B., 26, 67
Tzintzuntzan, 184, 194, 223

Understanding, need for, 66–67
Uniformitarianism, 131–132
United States, Mexican labor in, 183, 223
Universals, 3, 42, 44, 65–106, 207; content of, 3; integration of, 106–107; language and, 208; Redfield view, 37–40; social systems and, 210; validity of, 207–209
Universe, Self and Other in, 71
Ussher, James 132

Vacuums, abhorred, 125
Validity, in world view, 56–57
Value-free notion, 2, 19
Veblen, Thorstein, 203
Villages, peasant, 181–183
Volosinov, V. N., 35
Vygotsky, Lev S., 34–35

Wallace, Anthony F. C., 52–53, 55, 60
Warman, Arturo, 224
Waterman, T. T., 162
Williams, Raymond, 17
Wilson, Bryan, 225
Windigo, 83
Wintu, 150–153; direction in world view, 162–163
Wissler, Clark, 26–27
Witchcraft, 81–82; in Mexico, 197–201
Wogaman, Philip J., 76
Wolf, Eric R., 180, 188, 190, 214, 221, 224
World view, 1 et passim; as a basic concept, 41–47; California Indian, 147–169; cross-cultural model, 109–121; differences in, 109–119; environment and, 209–210; logico-structural aspects, 123–145; Mexican peasant, 171–206; model, 119–121; social behavior and, 209–210; Yoruba, 74–75

Yokuts, 165
Yoruba, world view, 74–75
Young, James Clay, 35
Yurok, 161, 162, 163

Zapotec, 182
Zeitgeist, 28